Bullet Point Bible Notes

A Verse-by-verse Synopsis of Scripture

Kenneth W. Lowry, L.B.T., D.P.M., D.MIN.

© Copyright 2021 by Kenneth Lowry All rights reserved.

No part of this publication may be reproduced or transmitted in any form or by any means, electronic or mechanical, including photocopying and recording, or by any information storage and retrieval system, except in the case of brief quotations for use in articles and reviews, without written permission from the author.

The views expressed in this book are the author's and do not necessarily reflect those of the publisher.

7710-T Cherry Park Dr, Ste 224
Houston, TX 77095
(713) 766-4271

Cover design by Teresa Granberry, www.HarvestCreek.net
Printed in the United States of America

ISBN:

The Benefit to the Reader of Bullet Point Bible Notes

"The benefit to the reader of this Bullet Point Bible Notes is incalculable because Pastor Kenneth Lowry pulls out the nuggets of truth that can be easily digested in each paragraph."

Pastor Dennis Key
Previous director of Lakewood Bible Institute, Houston, Texas

"I have known Kenneth Lowry for almost 30 years and this book is a perfect summary and picture of his life of Bible studies."

Dr. George Lowery
Founder of New Spirit Ministries

"As I read through these bullet points, I thought about how powerful the Word of God is and how His Word isn't confined to a single form."

Bro. Gustavo Serrano
Youth Pastor at Vida Covenant Church

"You are the son that Acts 2:17-18 spoke about. Thank you, Jesus, for your continued anointing upon Kenneth Lowry."

Sis. Elizabeth Nemecheck, Author
Longtime Friend and Supporter

ACKNOWLEDGMENTS

I thank Pastor Manuel Montez, Jr. and Miss Sandra Montez for compiling this book from handwritten notes.

Also, I am deeply grateful to Youth Pastor Gustavo Serrano for his many hours of proofreading.

Thanks to my friend and Professor Dr. Frank Longino of Liberty Theological Seminary in Houston, Texas, for his oversight in my theological studies.

Thanks to Dr. Steve Lowry for his helpful suggestions. Thanks to Dennis Harlan and Arturo Chavez for the hours we spent together reading and outlining the Bible.

I watched my dad, George Lowry, read and meditate on the Scripture each morning before going to work. His meditations influenced me greatly.

I thank my wife, Deany, for her encouragement over these 21 years in finalizing this manuscript.

Sincerely,

Kenneth W Lowry

Kenneth W. Lowry

These two young men, Dennis Harlan and Arturo Chavez spent more than two years studying with Kenneth Lowry to produce this Bullet Point Bible Notes book.

INTRODUCTION

Dear Bible Student,

As a student at Hardin-Simmons University, my professor suggested I study psychology and speech in preparation for the ministry… but I only desired to study the Bible.

When I was at Southwestern Baptist Theological Seminary, my professors taught me Greek, Hebrew, and biblical background studies… but I only wanted the Bible.

When I worked on my doctorates at Liberty Theological Seminary, I studied church history, biblical and systematic theology… but I only wanted the Bible.

This verse-by-verse study of Scripture came directly from meditation and study of the Bible. My sincere hope is that you will develop a synopsis of the Bible for yourself. To summarize every paragraph of the Bible in just a phrase or two, you will need to pray, read, meditate, and write. Eventually, you will have your own verse-by-verse synopsis of the Bible.

Our Lord God bless you as you meditate on the Scripture.

Kenneth W. Lowry

CONTENTS

ACKNOWLEDGMENTS v
INTRODUCTION vii

The Old Testament

GENESIS 2
EXODUS 14
LEVITICUS 28
NUMBERS 38
DEUTERONOMY 50
JOSHUA 62
JUDGES 69
RUTH 77
1 SAMUEL 78
2 SAMUEL 86
1 KINGS 94
2 KINGS 104
1 CHRONICLES 112
2 CHRONICLES 118
EZRA 128
NEHEMIAH 131
ESTHER 135

JOB	137
PSALMS	145
PROVERBS	173
ECCLESIASTES	179
SONG OF SOLOMON	181
ISAIAH	183
JEREMIAH	196
LAMENTATIONS	210
EZEKIEL	213
DANIEL	225
HOSEA	229
JOEL	232
AMOS	234
OBADIAH	237
JONAH	238
MICAH	239
NAHUM	241
HABAKKUK	242
ZEPHANIAH	243
HAGGAI	245
ZECHARIAH	246
MALACHI	249

The New Testament

MATTHEW	252
MARK	263
LUKE	270
JOHN	281
ACTS	289
ROMANS	300
1 CORINTHIANS	306
2 CORINTHIANS	312
GALATIANS	316
EPHESIANS	318
PHILIPPIANS	320
COLOSSIANS	322
1 THESSALONIANS	324
2 THESSALONIANS	326
1 TIMOTHY	327
2 TIMOTHY	329
TITUS	331
PHILEMON	332
HEBREWS	333
JAMES	338
1 PETER	340
2 PETER	342
1 JOHN	343
2 JOHN	345
3 JOHN	345

JUDE 346

REVELATION 347

BOOKS COMPARED WITH THE KING JAMES VERSION 356

The Old Testament

GENESIS

Chapter 1	**Creation**
vv. 1-2	God created by a long process or within moments?
vv. 3-4	God created light on 1st day; day in heaven is as 1,000 years. See Moses in Psalm 90:6; Peter in II Peter 3:8 and John in Revelation 1:10.
vv. 5-6	Firmament on first day
v. 8	Land appeared on second day.
vv. 9-12	Vegetables and fruit on third day
vv. 13-15	Moon, sun and stars on fourth day
vv. 16-20	Two of everything that swims and flies,
vv. 21-23	Fish and fowl on fifth day
vv. 24-27	Beast, cattle and man created on sixth day.
Chapter 2	**Garden of Eden**
vv. 1-3	Sabbath was sanctified for rest from labor.
vv. 4-6	Mist appeared before rain came.
vv. 7-9	God made man come alive by His Spirit.
vv. 10-14	Four rivers divided from main river in Eden throughout Ethiopia
vv. 15-16	Adam (man) created to enjoy work.
v. 17	Commanded not to eat of tree of knowledge of good and evil.
vv. 18-19	Adam is promised a helpmate.
v. 20	Adam named the animal kingdom.
vv. 21-23	Adam was given a wife.
v. 24	Prophecy of Matthew 19:5 and Ephesians 5:31
Chapter 3	**Fall of Mankind**
vv. 1-2	Serpents originally walked on legs and were intelligent.

v. 3	Woman added to words " neither shall you touch it".
v. 4	Satan lies to Eve saying, "You'll not immediately die".
vv. 5-7	Lies continue and Eve eats forbidden fruit.
vv. 8-11	Lord God walks in Garden.
vv. 12-19	Curses on serpent, Satan, woman and Adam.
v. 20	Woman is named Eve, mother of all living.
v. 21	First sacrifice for sin
vv. 22-24	Mankind cast out of Paradise (Eden).
Chapter 4	**Cain and Abel**
vv. 1-2	Twins are born.
vv. 3-4	Twins bring offerings to God.
vv. 5-7	Cain's offering is not accepted.
vv. 8-12	Cain's killing of Abel and his punishment
vv. 13-15	Many people on the earth by now
vv. 16	Cain lost fellowship with God.
vv. 17-24	Progression of Cain's sin is plurality of marriage and murder.
vv. 25-26	Seth is a new beginning of people calling upon the Lord.
Chapter 5	**Descendants of Adam through Seth**
vv. 1-2	Adam was male and female in beginning.
vv. 3-5	Adam lived 930 years and had many sons and daughters.
vv. 6-8	Seth lived 912 years.
vv. 9-11	Enos lived 905 years.
vv. 12-14	Cain lived 910 years.
vv. 15-17	Mahalalel lived 895 years.
vv. 18-20	Jared lived 962 years.
vv. 21-24	Enoch lived on earth only 365 years; God took him because he walked with God.
vv. 25-27	Methuselah lived 969 years.
v. 28-31	Lamech lived 777 years.
v. 32	Noah lived 500 years before flood and begot Shem, Ham and Japheth.

Chapter 6	**Noah Builds Ark.**
vv. 1-2	Sons of God marry daughters of men.
vv. 3-4	Giants marry normal women.
vv. 5-7	Earth became very wicked and God was grieved.
vv. 8-10	Noah finds favor with God because he walked with Him.
vv. 11-13	God ready to destroy earth and mankind by water
vv. 14-18	Preparation of ark
vv. 19-22	Animals enter ark.
Chapter 7	**The Flood**
vv. 1-4	God's judgment covers earth.
vv. 5-10	Animals come to Noah's ark in twos before flood.
vv. 11-16	When Noah was 600 years old the Lord closed ark.
vv. 17-24	Rained forty days and nights covering all life on earth and prevailing 150 days.
Chapter 8	**Waters Recede.**
vv. 1-5	Tops of mountains are visible.
vv. 6-12	Noah sent a raven once and a dove three times.
vv. 13-14	Earth becomes dry.
vv. 15-19	Mankind and creatures leave ark.
vv. 20-22	Noah's offering accepted by the Lord; ground never again to be cursed.
Chapter 9	**Rainbow is God's Covenant with Noah.**
vv. 1-7	Capital punishment is mentioned 1,000 years before the Ten Commandments.
vv. 8-17	Never will the earth be destroyed again by water.
vv. 18-19	Noah's children repopulate the earth.
vv. 20-29	Canaan, cursed due to Ham's mockery of Noah and serves Shem and Japheth.
Chapter 10	**Descendants of Noah's Sons**
vv. 1-5	Sons of Japheth (middle son)
vv. 6-14	Sons of Ham (youngest son)
vv. 15-20	Sons of Canaan mentioned

vv. 21-32	Sons of Shem (oldest son)
Chapter 11	**Tower of Babel**
vv. 1-9	The Lord causes people to scatter, changing their languages.
vv. 10-26	Generations of Shem
vv. 27-32	Generations of Terah (Abraham's grandfather) from family of Eber (Hebrews)
Chapter 12	**Call of Abram**
vv. 1-5	Leaving Haran and going to Canaan
vv. 6-9	Promise of God to give Canaan to Abram (fulfilled by War of 1947)
vv. 10-13	Abram tells Sarai to act as his sister to save his life.
vv. 14-20	God rescues Sarai from Pharaoh.
Chapter 13	**Abram and Lot**
vv. 1-4	Abram leaves Egypt and calls on the Lord in Bethel (House of the Lord).
vv. 5-13	Lesson in humility: Abram gave first choice of land to Lot.
vv. 14-18	God gave land of Canaan to Abram and his descendants forever.
Chapter 14	**Four Kings Defeat Five Smaller Kings.**
vv. 1-12	Four greater kings subdue five lesser kings and capture Lot who lived in Sodom.
vv. 13-16	Abram rescues Lot and his possessions.
vv. 17-24	Melchizedek blesses Abram and receives tenth of his possessions.
Chapter 15	**Prophecy of Israel's Bondage**
vv. 1-21	Israel to receive land between the Nile and Euphrates Rivers
Chapter 16	**Sarai and Hagar**
vv. 1-6	Sarai blames Abram for submitting to her in "siring" Hagar's child.
vv. 7-16	Hagar returns to serve Sarai; angel of Lord promises Ishmael many sons.

Chapter 17	**Circumcision, Sign of Covenant**
vv. 1-8	The Lord promises Abraham that he will be father of many nations.
vv. 9-14	Circumcision is everlasting covenant between the Lord and Abraham.
vv. 15-22	God tells Abraham Sarah will bear a son next year and be named Isaac (Laughter).
vv. 23-27	Abraham is obedient by circumcising himself, Ishmael and all his men.
Chapter 18	**Three Angels Visit Abraham and Promise Him and Sarah a Son.**
vv. 1-8	Abraham met the Lord and prepared feast for him and angels (Oriental hospitality).
vv. 9-15	The Lord rebukes Sarah for doubting; nothing is too hard for the Lord.
vv. 16-22	Two angels go to Sodom and Gomorrah to check seriousness of their sins.
vv. 23-33	Abraham intercedes for Lot and family due to judgment on Sodom and Gomorrah.
Chapter 19	**Doom of Sodom**
vv. 1-3	Lot invites two guests (angels) to spend night in his house knowing that homosexuals would molest them if they remained outside.
vv. 4-11	Lot tries to protect guests, but they protect him from homosexuals.
vv. 12-14	Lot tries to rescue his family but his sons-in-law mock him.
vv. 15-28	God destroys Sodom and Gomorrah; Lot and two daughters survive.
vv. 29	The Lord answers Abraham's prayer by rescuing Lot and daughters.
vv. 30-38	Incest by Lot's daughters brings Moabites and Ammonites, becoming thorns to Israel.

Chapter 20	**Abraham's Treachery with Abimelech**
vv. 1-18	God rescues Abraham and Sarah from Abimelech who later prospers them.
Chapter 21	**Covenant at Beersheba between Abraham and Abimelech**
vv. 1-8	Isaac born to Sarah and Abraham
vv. 9-21	Hagar and Ishmael driven away by Sarah and Isaac
vv. 22-32	Abraham covenants with Abimelech not to harm each other.
vv. 33-34	Abraham calls on name of the Lord at Beersheba.
Chapter 22	**Abraham's Offering of Isaac**
vv. 1-14	God provides ram for offering, not Isaac. Place called Jehovah- Jireh.
vv. 15-19	Many nations will come through Abraham's seed as promised by the Lord.
vv. 20-24	God's blessings on Nahor, Abraham's brother
Chapter 23	**Death and Burial of Sarah**
vv. 1-2	Abraham mourns for loss of Sarah.
vv. 3-20	Abraham purchases Machpelah in Hebron for Sarah's burial.
Chapter 24	**Rebekah Chosen for Isaac**
vv. 1-9	Abraham sends servant Eleazar, to Haran (Mesopotamia) to get wife for Isaac.
vv. 10-14	Eleazar prays the Lord to send Isaac's future wife to draw water for his camels.
vv. 15-28	God answers Eliezer's prayer.
vv. 29-60	Rebekah prepares to leave with Eleazar to meet her future husband.
vv. 61-67	Isaac marries Rebekah.
Chapter 25	**Abraham Remarries and Later Dies at 175 Years of Age.**
vv. 1-11	Abraham marries Keturah and has five sons; Abraham, buried at Machpelah.
vv. 12-18	Ishmael has 12 sons and dies at 137 years of age.
vv. 19-34	Twins born to Isaac at 60 years of age. Later Jacob gets Esau's birthright.

Chapter 26		**Due to Famine Isaac Moves to Gerar.**
vv. 1-5		Isaac obeys God's commands as did Abraham.
vv. 6-16		God prospers Isaac and Philistines ask him to leave their land.
vv. 17-25		Isaac moves to Beersheba and there God blesses him.
vv. 26-33		Isaac and Abimelech make covenant; God blesses Isaac with well at Beersheba.
vv. 34-35		Isaac and Rebekah grieve over Esau's marriage to Judith, a local Hittite girl.
Chapter 27		**Jacob Obtains Isaac's Blessing by Deception.**
vv. 1-5		Isaac asks Esau for meal of venison; Rebekah overhears request.
vv. 6-17		Rebekah uses Jacob and food to deceive Isaac for Esau's birthright.
vv. 18-29		Isaac gives Jacob elder son's birthright blessing.
vv. 30-40		Esau loses blessing of Isaac and weeps loudly. Isaac gives Esau lesser blessing.
vv. 41-46		Rebekah tells Isaac to send Jacob away so Esau won't kill Jacob.
Chapter 28		**Jacob Sent to Padan-aram (Where Uncle Laban Lives in Haran).**
vv. 1-5		Isaac blesses Jacob and sends him to Laban's home in Syria.
vv. 6-9		Esau marries to please parents by obtaining wife from Ishmael's people.
vv. 10-15		Jacob sees angels on a ladder; God tells him of His protection and blessings.
vv. 16-22		Jacob vows to give a tithe when God returns him safely to Bethel.
Chapter 29		**Jacob Meets Rachel**
vv. 1-8		Jacob talks with sheepherders.
vv. 9-14		Jacob rolls stone away, waters Rachel's sheep and meets Laban.
vv. 15-20		Jacob works seven years for Laban to marry Rachel.

vv. 21-30		Jacob is deceived by Laban and works seven years for second wife, Rachel.
vv. 31-35		God blesses Leah by giving her four sons by Jacob.
Chapter 30		**Jacob's Children**
vv. 1-13		Leah and her servant have six sons and Rachel's maid has two sons, all by Jacob.
vv. 14-21		Leah has two more sons and daughter by Jacob.
vv. 22-24		Rachel bears Joseph; Jacob's first son by her.
vv. 25-36		Jacob and Laban agree on Jacob's wages.
vv. 37-43		Jacob's flocks increase over Laban's.
Chapter 31		**Jacob Secretly Departs for Canaan.**
vv. 1-16		Laban's attitude toward Jacob changes when Jacob decides to leave.
vv. 17-24		Jacob flees; Laban pursues; God gives Laban a dream to be careful with Jacob.
vv. 25-35		Laban catches Jacob and searches in vain for his idols.
vv. 36-42		Jacob rebukes Laban for wrongs he did.
vv. 43-55		Jacob and Laban make covenant. Laban blesses his children and grandchildren.
Chapter 32		**Jacob's Fear in Meeting Esau**
vv. 1-5		Jacob returns to Edom to find Esau.
vv. 6-8		Jacob prepares to meet Esau and his 400-armed men.
vv. 9-12		Jacob prays to God for safety.
vv. 13-23		Jacob sends gifts to appease Esau to protect his family.
vv. 24-32		Jacob struggles with God; is renamed "Israel"; he prevailed with God and men.
Chapter 33		**Jacob and Esau Reconciled**
vv. 1-15		Jacob finds favor with Esau and gives him gifts.
vv. 16-17		Jacob settles in Succoth and Esau in Seir.
vv. 18-20		Jacob settles in Shalom, a city of Shechem.
Chapter 34		**Dinah's Defilement Avenged by Treachery**
vv. 1-5		Shechem rapes Dinah and wants to marry her.

vv. 6-24	Hamor, Shechem and all men are circumcised to be accepted by Jacob's sons.
vv. 25-30	Simeon and Levi kill men in Hamor and Shechem's village. Jacob's sons loot city.
Chapter 35	**God Blesses Jacob at Bethel.**
vv. 1-5	God protects Jacob as he goes to Bethel.
vv. 6-9	Jacob builds another altar to God in Bethel.
vv. 10-15	God reconfirms His blessing on Israel.
vv. 16-20	Rachel dies giving birth to Benjamin.
vv. 21-26	Reuben defiles Bilhah, losing his elder son's birthright.
vv. 27-29	Esau and Jacob bury Isaac when he was 180 years old.
Chapter 36	**Descendants of Esau**
vv. 1-8	Esau and family live in Mt. Seir (Edom) giving more room for livestock.
vv. 9-14	Families of Esau
vv. 15-19	Chiefs (dukes) of Esau's sons
vv. 20-30	Chiefs (dukes) of Esau's sons continued
vv. 31-39	Kings who ruled in Edom prior to kings of Israel
vv. 40-43	Repeat of names of chiefs of Esau (Edom)
Chapter 37	**Joseph's Dreams**
vv. 1-4	Joseph is favored by Jacob over other sons; brothers resented Joseph.
vv. 5-11	Joseph dreams father and brothers will bow to him.
vv. 12-17	Joseph sent to report on welfare of brothers and flocks.
vv. 18-22	Reuben keeps brothers from killing Joseph.
vv. 23-28	Joseph sold to Ishmaelites by brothers for 20 pieces of silver
vv. 29-30	Reuben didn't know brothers had sold Joseph.
vv. 31-36	Jacob mourns for Joseph whom he thinks is dead.
Chapter 38	**Judah and Tamar**
vv. 1-11	Judah marries and has three sons; the Lord kills first two for wickedness.
vv. 12-23	Judah has physical relations with Tamar, his daughter-in-law.

vv. 24-30	Tamar's twins, Pharez and Zarah are born.

Chapter 39 — Joseph's Success in Egypt

vv. 1-6	Joseph finds favor with Potiphar who knows God is with Joseph.
vv. 7-23	Joseph, falsely accused and cast into prison, finds favor with God.

Chapter 40 — Joseph Interprets Dreams.

vv. 1-4	Joseph cares for e Pharaoh's baker and butler who are in prison.
vv. 5-19	Joseph interprets dreams of butler and baker for good and bad.
vv. 20-23	Baker is hung and butler is restored.

Chapter 41 — Pharaoh's Dreams

vv. 1-8	Dream of seven fat and seven lean cows and seven fat and seven lean ears of corn
vv. 9-13	Butler tells Pharaoh of Joseph's ability to interpret dreams.
vv. 14-24	Pharaoh tells Joseph his dream.
vv. 25-36	Joseph tells Pharaoh what to do in fat and lean years so Egypt will prosper.
vv. 37-52	Joseph elevated to number two man in Egypt; he marries and has twins.
vv. 53-57	All come to Joseph for food. (Symbolic of coming to Jesus for spiritual life).

Chapter 42 — Joseph's Brothers Come to Egypt for Grain.

vv. 1-2	Jacob sends his sons to Egypt to buy corn.
vv. 3-20	Joseph tests brothers to see if they have changed during 14 years.
vv. 21-24	Joseph puts Simeon in jail continuing to test his 10 brothers.
vv. 25-28	Jacob refuses to let Benjamin go with brothers to Egypt for grain and free Simeon.

Chapter 43 — Joseph's Brothers Return to Egypt with Benjamin.

vv. 1-14	Jacob grieves as sons return to Egypt with Benjamin to buy grain.

vv. 15-34	Joseph eats with Benjamin and brothers. (Again, the brothers bow before Joseph).
Chapter 44	**Joseph's Final Test of His Brothers**
vv. 1-17	Joseph's cup is found in Benjamin's saddlebag and Benjamin is to be Joseph's slave.
vv. 18-34	Judah pleads to be Joseph's slave in place of Benjamin.
Chapter 45	**Joseph Reconciles with Brothers.**
vv. 1-15	Joseph reveals himself to his brothers.
vv. 16-28	Jacob realizes Joseph is alive!
Chapter 46	**Jacob and Family Move to Egypt.**
vv. 1-7	God tells Jacob not to fear; He will make a mighty nation of Israel in Egypt.
vv. 8-27	Genealogy of Jacob's 70 children
vv. 28-34	Israel (Jacob) is reunited as shepherds with Joseph in Goshen.
Chapter 47	**Jacob's Family Settles in Goshen.**
vv. 1-10	Jacob, at 130 years of age, blesses Pharaoh.
vv. 11-12	Jacob and family settle in Goshen, land of Rameses.
vv. 13-26	Egyptians and other nationalities become sharecroppers under Pharaoh.
vv. 27-31	Joseph promises Jacob he will be buried in Canaan with Abraham and Isaac.
Chapter 48	**Israel Blesses Joseph's Twin Sons, Ephraim and Manasseh.**
vv. 1-14	Israel blesses younger over elder of two sons, Ephraim over Manasseh.
vv. 15-22	Israel blesses Joseph's children with more land in Canaan than other eleven.
Chapter 49	**Israel's Prophecy Concerning His Sons**
vv. 1-2	Israel gathers his sons together.
vv. 3-4	Reuben loses his place as elder son due to adultery with Jacob's concubine.

vv. 5-7	Simeon and Levi killed men of Shechem; due to violence, they lose their position.
vv. 8-12	Judah receives Jacob's blessing. Messiah (Shiloh) will come through Judah.
vv. 13	Zebulun will be haven for ships at sea.
vv. 14-15	Issachar becomes burden bearer.
vv. 16-18	Dan is a judge among his people.
vv. 19	Gad overcomes at the last.
vv. 20	Asher enjoys royal, fat food.
vv. 21	Naphtali gives good counsel (words).
vv. 22-26	Joseph is blessed beyond all his brothers who hated him; now they bow to him.
vv. 27	Benjamin overcomes his enemies and gathers their goods.
vv. 28-33	Conclusion of Jacob's blessings and place for him to be buried with his fathers.
Chapter 50	**Burial of Jacob (Israel)**
vv. 1-6	Joseph takes Jacob to Canaan for burial.
vv. 7-14	Joseph buries Jacob in the cave of Machpelah and returns with his brothers to Egypt.
vv. 15-21	Joseph reassures his brothers of his kindness to them after Jacob's death.
vv. 22-26	Joseph asks Israelites to re-bury him with his fathers when they arrive in Canaan.

EXODUS
Departing from Egypt

Chapter 1	**Israel Multiplies and Now Oppressed by New Pharaoh.**
vv. 1-7	Sons of Jacob and descendants become mighty nation.
vv. 8-14	Egyptians put Israelites into bondage as servants.
vv. 15-22	Pharaoh commands newborn male Israelites drowned in Nile River.
Chapter 2	**Birth of Moses**
vv. 1-4	Moses' mother puts him in basket in Nile for his sister to watch Moses.
vv. 5-10	Moses is rescued and adopted by Pharaoh's daughter.
vv. 11-22	Moses flees to Midian to escape Pharaoh. He marries Zipporah and has son, Gershon.
vv. 23-25	God hears cries of Israelites.
Chapter 3	**God Commissions Moses at Burning Bush.**
vv. 1-6	God speaks to Moses from burning bush.
vv. 7-10	God commissions Moses to lead Israelites out of Egypt.
vv. 11-22	God tells Moses what to call Him when he talks to Israelites.
Chapter 4	**Moses Given Authority and Returns to Egypt.**
vv. 1-5	God turns Moses' rod into serpent and back into a rod to make Moses a believer.
vv. 6-9	God shows Moses two more signs, leprosy and blood.
vv. 10-17	God lets Aaron be Moses' spokesman.
vv. 18-23	God tells Moses to warn Pharaoh his oldest son will die if Israelites don't go free.
vv. 24-26	Zipporah saves Moses' life by circumcising their son.

vv. 27-28	Aaron meets Moses in wilderness and explains what God is going to do.
vv. 29-31	Israelites accept Moses and signs God gave him.
Chapter 5	**Israel's Labors Get Harder as Pharaoh Laughs at Moses.**
vv. 1-9	Moses asks 3-day trip for Israelites; Pharaoh refuses; Israelites work harder.
vv. 10-14	Egyptians beat Israelites for not meeting daily quota of brick-making.
vv. 15-19	Israelite foremen ask Pharaoh for relief but are refused.
vv. 20-23	Israelite foremen complain to Moses who complains to God.
Chapter 6	**God Renews Covenant with Moses.**
vv. 1-8	The Lord tells Moses He will deliver Israelites and give them Canaan.
vv. 9-13	Moses is discouraged because people's murmuring; the Lord encourages him.
vv. 14-27	Lineage of Aaron and Moses
vv. 28-30	Moses explains his speech weaknesses to the Lord.
Chapter 7	**Moses Stretches Out His Hand before Pharaoh.**
vv. 1-7	Eighty-year-old Moses listens to what the Lord is soon to do to Egyptians.
vv. 8-9	The Lord explains miracle of Moses' staff becoming serpent before Pharaoh.
vv. 10-13	Moses' staff becomes serpent and swallows magician's serpents.
vv. 14-18	The Lord explains to Moses He will turn Nile into blood and fish will die.
vv. 19-25	Moses strikes Nile; waters turn to blood; Pharaoh's heart hard. (1st plague).
Chapter 8	**Plagues of Frogs, Lice and Flies**
vv. 1-4	The Lord tells Moses He will soon send frogs throughout Egypt.
vv. 5-7	Aaron's rod as well as magicians' rods cause frogs to cover Egypt. (2nd plague).

vv. 8-15	Moses prays and the Lord kills all frogs except those in Nile.
vv. 16-19	Dust becomes stinging gnats in Egypt. (3rd plague).
vv. 20-24	Egypt has swarm of flies but Goshen does not. (4th plague).
vv. 25-32	Moses prays and flies depart but Pharaoh hardens his heart.
Chapter 9	**Plagues of Boils and Hail Cause Egyptian Livestock to Die.**
vv. 1-7	The Lord kills all Egyptian livestock; Pharaoh hardens his heart. (5th plague).
vv. 8-12	The Lord turns dust into boils; Pharaoh refuses to release Israelites. (6th plague).
vv. 13-21	The Lord warns Pharaoh unsheltered livestock will die due to hailstorm.
vv. 22-26	Hail destroys livestock and vegetation in Egypt. (7th plague).
vv. 27-35	Moses prays; the Lord stops hail; Pharaoh does not repent.
Chapter 10	**Plagues of Locusts and Darkness**
vv. 1-11	The Lord sends locusts upon Egypt; Pharaoh says he will let Israelites leave.
vv. 12-15	Moses stretches rod over Egypt; locusts devour vegetation. (8th plague).
vv. 16-20	The Lord hardens Pharaoh's heart; he refuses Israelite's departure.
vv. 21-23	Thick darkness covers land of Egypt but not Goshen, for three days. (9th plague).
vv. 24-26	Pharaoh agrees to let Israelites leave Egypt but without livestock.
vv. 27-29	The Lord hardens Pharaoh's heart; Pharaoh threatens to kill Moses if he sees him.
Chapter 11	**Death of Firstborn Threatened**
vv. 1-3	Israelites borrow jewelry from Egyptians; Moses becomes esteemed.
vv. 4-10	Moses warns people about last plague, death of their firstborn.

Chapter 12	**Feast of Passover (Lamb) Instituted**
vv. 1-2	First month of Israelites begins with Passover.
vv. 3-14	Moses tells of Passover Lamb, blood over door and sides, protection of 1st born.
vv. 15-20	Institution of Feast of Unleavened Bread
vv. 21-28	Israelites obey Moses' instructions to apply blood of lambs over doorways.
vv. 29-30	Death angel kills 1st born who refused to put blood over doorways. (10th plague).
vv. 31-36	Israelites plunder Egyptians as they depart from Egypt.
vv. 37-39	Israelites (about three million) leave Egypt in haste.
vv. 40-42	After 430 years (to the day) Israelites exit Egypt. (This is a memorial forever).
vv. 43-51	All circumcised males partake of Passover Supper before departing Egypt.
Chapter 13	**Consecration of Firstborn**
vv. 1-2	The Lord claims ownership of all firstborn males of man and livestock in Israel.
vv. 3-10	Feast of Unleavened Bread with Passover is observed forever among Israelites.
vv. 11-13	Firstborn son and livestock are His. Donkey redeemed by lamb, or neck broken.
vv. 14-16	Firstborn son, redeemed by lamb. Passover, remembered by Phylacteries
vv. 17-19	Israelites pass Philistine territory carrying Joseph's bones to Canaan for burial.
vv. 20-22	The Lord leads Israelites by cloud by day and fire by night.
Chapter 14	**Crossing of Red Sea**
vv. 1-4	The Lord shows Israelites where to go, tempting Pharaoh to follow and drown.
vv. 5-9	Pharaoh pursues Israelites with 600 horses and chariots.
vv. 10-12	Israelites complain to Moses as they see Egyptian army approaching.

vv. 13-14	Moses exclaims "… stand still and see the salvation of the Lord."
vv. 15-18	The Lord tells Moses to lift rod and divide Sea.
vv. 19-22	Angel of Lord between Egyptians and Israelites. Lord divides water by wind.
vv. 23-31	Lord destroys Egyptian soldiers, and chariots in Red Sea; He delivers all Israelites. |//

Chapter 15 — Song of Moses

vv. 1-21	Israelites sing song of triumph over Egyptians and nations they must pass.
v. 22	Israelites go into wilderness three days finding no water.
vv. 23-26	The Lord exhorts Israelites to obey, so they will not suffer plagues of Egyptians.
v. 27	Israelites encamp at Elim by 12 water wells and 70 palm trees.

Chapter 16 — God Sends Quails and Manna.

vv. 1-3	Israelites complain to Moses of hunger.
vv. 4-9	Moses exhorts people to gather manna and not murmur against God.
vv. 10-21	The Lord sends quails for evening meals and manna for morning and Sabbath meals.
vv. 22-26	Manna did not stink when stored for Sabbath but did when stored for other days.
vv. 27-31	People who tried to gather on seventh day found no manna (wafers and wild honey).
vv. 32-36	Moses told Aaron put homer of manna in Ark of Covenant, for future decades.

Chapter 17 — Water Miraculously Supplied from Rock

vv. 1-7	Moses is told to strike rock in Horeb to give the Israelites water.
vv. 8-16	The Lord delivers Israel from Amalek as Aaron and Hur support Moses' hands.

Chapter 18	**Jethro Advises Moses to Appoint Judges.**
vv. 1-12	Jethro, brings Zipporah with two sons, to Moses at mountain of God.
vv. 13-26	Jethro counsels Moses to appoint capable men to help him judge Israelites.
v. 27	Jethro returns to Midian.
Chapter 19	**Israel Hears God's Voice on Mt. Sinai.**
vv. 1-6	God tells Moses He will make Israel a kingdom if they obey Him.
vv. 7-9	The Lord appears in thick cloud so people can hear when He speaks to Moses.
vv. 10-13	The Lord warns Moses not to allow man or beast to touch borders of Mt. Sinai.
vv. 14-15	Moses prepares people to sanctify themselves for third day.
vv. 16-25	Moses tells people not to come on mountain lest God break out against them.
Chapter 20	**Giving of Ten Commandments**
vv. 1-17	The Lord gave these 10 commands to Israel:
	v. 3 …no other gods before you
	v. 4 …. no graven images … no bowing to them …
	v. 7 …. .do not take Lord's name in vain.
	v. 8 …. Remember Sabbath day to keep it holy.
	v. 12 … Honor your father and mother …
	v. 13 … You shall not kill.
	v. 14 … You shall not commit adultery.
	v. 15 … You shall not steal.
	v. 16 … You shall not bear false witness against others.
	v. 17 … You shall not covet anything belonging to another.
vv. 18-21	People ask Moses to intercede for them.
vv. 22-26	Idolatry is absolutely forbidden.
Chapter 21	**Laws Concerning Treatment of Servants**
vv. 1-6	After six years, Hebrew servants are freed.

vv. 7-11	Maidservants can be redeemed by someone who pays purchase price.
vv. 12-15	Distinctions of intentional and non-intentional murders; penalty for striking parents.
v. 16	Death to kidnappers of Israelites
v. 17	Death to children who curse parents
vv. 18-19	Repayment for anyone maimed in a quarrel for lost time and injuries
vv. 20-21	Masters who kill their servants are punished.
vv. 22-25	If a man hurts pregnant woman and she loses baby, he shall be punished.
vv. 26-27	Servants injured by masters go free due to injuries.
vv. 28-32	Oxen stoned as penalty for goring people.
vv. 33-34	If pit is uncovered and another's livestock injured, the pit owner makes payment.
vv. 35-36	If ox kills another man's ox, restitution is required.
Chapter 22	**Laws Regarding Human Relationships**
vv. 1-4	Restitution to be made for anyone caught stealing.
v. 5	Restitution to be made for livestock that eats someone else's crops.
v. 6	Restitution is to be made by anyone guilty of burning another's crops.
vv. 7-13	If one keeps goods for friend, and goods damaged, judge decides if he is to pay.
vv. 14-15	Payment to be made for anything borrowed if borrower doesn't take care of it.
vv. 16-17	You marry a seduced girl or pay a virgin's dowry.
v. 18	Witches are to be put to death.
v. 19	People who have intercourse with animals are to die.
v. 20	People are to die who sacrifice to false god.
vv. 21-24	The Lord avenges strangers, widows and orphans.
vv. 25-27	Don't charge usury to poor.
v. 28	Don't curse rulers of your people.

vv. 29-30	God demands first-fruit offerings.
v. 31	Don't eat any meat torn by livestock.
Chapter 23	**Laws, Feasts and Leadership of Lord's Angel**
vv. 1-3	We are to give true reports and not pervert justice.
vv. 4-5	We are to help both friends and enemies.
vv. 6-7	God will not justify wicked people.
v. 8	We are never to take a bribe.
vv. 9-13	Don't oppress strangers; land rests 7th year; poor and animals to eat from land.
vv. 14-19	Keep three feasts yearly: Passover, Pentecost and Feast of Tabernacles.
vv. 20-25	Obey angel and God will protect, bless, prosper and keep you healthy.
vv. 26-33	God to drive out Canaanites; Israelites to get 1,500 square miles of land.
Chapter 24	**Moses and Elders on Mt. Sinai**
vv. 1-2	God calls all elders and priestly families but only Moses shall come near God.
vv. 3-8	Moses reads Book of Covenant to people and makes blood covenant with Israel.
vv. 9-11	Leaders only see lower parts of God.
vv. 12-14	Moses takes Joshua partway up Mt. Sinai, leaving Aaron and Hur with people.
vv. 15-18	Moses waits till 7th day; God speaks to him; Moses stays on mountain 40 days.
Chapter 25	**Ark of Testimony**
vv. 1-9	Lord tells Moses what materials needed" for construction of Tabernacle.
vv. 10-16	Construction of Ark made of shittim wood overlaid with pure gold
vv. 17-22	Construction of Mercy Seat and two cherubim made of pure gold
vv. 23-30	Construction of Table of Showbread to be of shittim wood

vv. 31-40	Construction of Candlestick to be made of pure gold

Chapter 26 — Directions for Tabernacle

vv. 1-6	Instructions for Tabernacle curtains
vv. 7-14	"… Couple the tent together, that it may be one." Curtain instructions given
vv. 15-25	Boards and 40 silver sockets for Tabernacle, explained
vv. 26-30	Bars of shittim wood overlaid with gold, like wooden boards
vv. 31-35	Instructions for veil to be blue, purple and scarlet
vv. 36-37	Hanging for door of tent to be blue, purple, scarlet and fine linen of needlework.

Chapter 27 — Altar of Burnt Offering

vv. 1-8	Altar to be made of shittim wood overlaid with brass as shown on Mt. Sinai.
vv. 9-19	Instructions for court of Tabernacle
vv. 20-21	"Pure olive oil beaten for light …"

Chapter 28 — Garments for Priests

vv. 1-5	Holy garments for Aaron and sons made of gold, blue, purple, scarlet and linen
vv. 6-14	Ephod of gold shall carry names in 12 stones for 12 tribes of Israel.
vv. 15-29	On Aaron's shoulder is breast piece of judgment, holding Urim and Thummim.
v. 30	"Aaron to bear judgment of Israel upon his heart before Lord continually."
vv. 31-35	Ephod has pomegranates with bells; he needs bells if he dies in Holy Place.
vv. 36-38	Aaron wears scriptures on forehead, "Holiness to Lord;" this makes Israel acceptable.
v. 39	Instructions for Aaron's coat, turban, and girdle
vv. 40-43	Aaron's sons have coats and caps to show God's glory and beauty.

Chapter 29 — Service for Ordination of Priests

vv. 1-9	Instructions on ordaining Aaron and his sons

vv. 10-14	Sin offering for priests
vv. 15-18	Burnt offering is a pleasing odor, offering by fire to the Lord.
vv. 19-21	Make priestly garments holy by sprinkling blood from a ram
vv. 22-25	Wave offering is an offering by fire to the Lord.
vv. 26-28	Peace offering is portion priests keep for their food.
vv. 29-30	Holy priestly garments are worn seven days in Tent of Meeting.
vv. 31-34	Only priests can eat holy meat and bread. Leftovers to be burned next morning.
vv. 35-37	Seven days of ordination for priests and altar; touching altar makes anything holy.
vv. 38-46	God meets with His people to remind them He brought them out of Egypt.

Chapter 30 — Altar of Incense

vv. 1-10	Altar of incense is holy to the Lord. Aaron shall make atonement upon it annually.
vv. 11-16	Everyone 20 and over gives half-shekel for atonement so no plague comes on them.
vv. 17-21	Laver of bronze for washing priest's hands and feet lest they die in ministry.
vv. 22-33	Ingredients for holy anointing oil can only be blended and used by priests.
vv. 34-38	Perfume made and used by priests. Faking perfume is to be cut off from Israel.

Chapter 31 — Sabbath as Sign

vv. 1-11	Moses told to use Bezaleel and Oholiab to be God's appointed craftsmen.
vv. 12-17	Sabbath is God's covenant and sign to Israel. God worked 6, rested 7th day.
v. 18	God gives Moses two stone tablets of Testimony written with finger of God.

Chapter 32 — Golden Calf and Breaking of Covenant

vv. 1-6	Moses with God 40 days people get Aaron to make a golden calf to worship.

vv. 7-10	God tells Moses to go down mountain to people; God's wrath to destroy idolaters.
vv. 11-14	Moses intercedes for Israelites and God does not destroy them at this time.
vv. 15-20	Moses breaks stone tablets, melts golden calf, and makes people drink it.
vv. 21-24	Aaron blames people for asking him to make golden calf.
vv. 25-29	Moses commands Levites to destroy revilers and 3000 men slain by sword.
vv. 30-34	Moses again intercedes for Israel upon Mt. Sinai.
v. 35	God plagues rebels because of golden idol.
Chapter 33	**Moses Prays for God's Presence.**
vv. 1-3	God tells Moses go to Promised Land. Angel will drive enemies from land.
vv. 4-11	Moses talks with God "face to face" in Tabernacle of congregation.
vv. 12-16	God tells Moses His presence shall go with Moses to give him rest.
vv. 17 – 23	Moses sees God's back but not His face as God's glory, goodness and mercy pass.
Chapter 34	**Renewal of God's Covenant**
vv. 1-3	God instructs Moses to come alone to top of Mt. Sinai.
vv. 4-9	Moses returns to Mt. Sinai with new tablets for God and intercedes for Israel.
v. 10	God makes covenant with Israel promising to do miracles among them.
vv. 11-16	God warns Israelites not to make covenants with other nations.
v. 17	"No molten idols"
vv. 18-20	Firstborn is God's and observes Feast of Unleavened Bread seven days during Abib.
v. 21	They are to work six days and rest on seventh day.
vv. 22	They shall observe Feast of Weeks.

vv. 23-24	Males shall appear before the Lord three times yearly.
vv. 25-26	Nothing from Feast of Passover to be left till morning. God owns first fruits of land.
vv. 27-28	Moses writes on tablets of covenant the Ten Commandments.
vv. 29-35	Moses' face shines; he wears veil when speaking to people but not to God.

Chapter 35 — Regulations for Sabbath

vv. 1-3	Workers (dishonor) on Sabbath put to death
vv. 4-9	Moses tells people to willingly bring offerings of various substances to the Lord.
vv. 10-19	People are to come with offerings to furnish Tabernacle and clothe priests.
vv. 20-29	Wise-hearted, willing people bring things for Tabernacle and priestly garments.
vv. 30-35	God gives wisdom to Bezaleel and Oholiab to do craftsmanship for Tabernacle.

Chapter 36 — Making of Tabernacle

vv. 1-3	People bring to Bezaleel and Oholiab offerings for construction of Tabernacle.
vv. 4-7	Moses commands people to stop bringing offerings since they have enough.
vv. 8-13	Making clasps and curtains to become one Tabernacle.
vv. 14-18	Curtains made of goats' hair for tent over Tabernacle.
v. 19	Cover for tent made first of rams' skins and covered by badgers' skins.
vv. 20-30	Boards of shittim wood cut to frame Tabernacle.
vv. 31-34	Bars of acacia wood or shittim wood are overlaid with gold.
vv. 35-36	Veil has cherubim and made of fine linen in colors of blue, purple, and scarlet.
vv. 37-38	Hanging for Tabernacle door was blue, purple and scarlet linen.

Chapter 37	**Furnishings of Tabernacle**
vv. 1-5	Ark of covenant made of shittim or acacia wood overlaid with gold
vv. 6-9	Mercy seat was pure gold and at top were two cherubim from one piece of gold
vv. 10-16	Table for showbread was of shittim or acacia wood overlaid with pure gold.
vv. 17-24	Candlesticks made from one piece of pure gold
vv. 25-28	Altar of incense made of shittim or acacia wood overlaid with pure gold
v. 29	Holy anointing oil and pure incense are work of apothecary or perfumer.
Chapter 38	**Court of Tabernacle**
vv. 1-7	Altar of burnt offering made of shittim or acacia wood overlaid with brass
v. 8	Laver was of brass covered with mirrors from women at door of tent of meeting.
vv. 9-20	Hangings and pillars made of linen, brass and silver
vv. 21-23	Cost of Tabernacle was counted by Ithamar, son of Aaron the priest.
vv. 24-31	Gold for Tabernacle, 29 talents and 730 shekels. Silver, 100 talents and 1715 shekels. Brass was 70 talents and 2,400 shekels.
Chapter 39	**Priestly Garments**
vv. 1-2	Ephod, made of gold, blue, purple, scarlet and fine twined linen.
vv. 3-5	Gold, made into wires and worked into linen to hold shoulder-piece and ephod.
vv. 6-7	Onyx stones, called stones of remembrance and set in shoulders of ephod.
vv. 8-21	Blue, purple, and scarlet breastplate had 12 stones with names of 12 tribes of Israel.

vv. 22-26	Blue, purple and scarlet robe of ephod had gold bells with pomegranates at hem.
vv. 27-29	Coats, mitre and girdle were also of blue, purple and scarlet linen.
vv. 30-31	Plate of holy crown was of pure gold with writing on it: "Holiness to the Lord."
v. 32	Conclusion of all work of Tabernacle of tent of congregation
vv. 33-43	When work was completed for furnishings, Moses reviewed it for God's exactness.
Chapter 40	**Consecration of Aaron and His Sons**
vv. 1-16	Furniture, all in place, Aaron and sons, sanctified and anointed for priestly office.
vv. 17-19	Covering of Tabernacle was set up as the Lord had commanded.
vv. 20-21	Ark was set up and brought into Tabernacle.
vv. 22-23	Table and bread were set up in Tabernacle.
vv. 24-25	Candlestick was set up and lit.
vv. 26-27	Golden altar was put in place and sweet incense was burned.
vv. 28-29	Door was hung and altar of burnt sacrifice was used.
vv. 30-33	Laver, with water, Aaron and sons washed hands and feet before serving.
vv. 34-38	Cloud covered Tabernacle by day and fire by night. As cloud moved so did Israelites.

LEVITICUS

Chapter 1	**Law of Burnt Offerings**
vv. 1-2	Offerings from cattle, sheep or goats
vv. 3-9	Instructions given for sacrificial offerings
vv. 10-13	Offerings from sheep and goats are a sweet, acceptable aroma to God.
vv. 14-17	Offering birds is something poor people can give.
Chapter 2	**Law of Cereal Offerings**
vv. 1-4	Grain offering is prepared with flour, oil and frankincense. Leftovers given to priests.
vv. 5-6	Cereal offering is in pieces with oil poured upon it and baked in a pan.
vv. 7-11	Offerings are a sweet aroma to the Lord. Priests can eat remnants of cereal offerings.
vv. 12-13	Cereal offerings are salted out of respect for the Lord's covenant.
vv. 14-16	Grain offerings are a memorial to the Lord.
Chapter 3	**Law of Peace Offerings**
vv. 1-5	Kidneys and fat are burned; meat without blemish is offered to the Lord.
vv. 6-11	The Lord's portion of peace offering is fat and organs.
vv. 12-17	Fat and blood are never to be eaten but sacrificed to the Lord.
Chapter 4	**Law of Sin Offerings**
vv. 1-12	This is a sacrifice of repentance for sin committed unwittingly, not premeditated sin.

vv. 13-21	Young bull offered as sin offering when congregation sins unwittingly.
vv. 22-26	Rulers offer a young, male goat for sin offering if they sin unwittingly.
vv. 27-35	Common people sacrifice a young, female goat or lamb if they sin unwittingly.
Chapter 5	**Law of Guilt Offerings**
vv. 1-6	Anyone sins unknowingly; he shall offer a female lamb or goat for a sin offering.
vv. 7-10	If poor man sins, he offers young pigeon for sin, another pigeon for burnt offering.
vv. 11-13	Man cannot afford pigeon, he brings tenth of ephah of flour for sin burned on altar.
vv. 14-16	One commits breach of faith; sins unwittingly; brings unblemished ram for offering.
Chapter 6	**Instructions to Priests Concerning Offerings**
vv. 1-7	Man takes wrongfully from another, he restores it plus 1/5th of its value.
vv. 8-13	Fire upon altar shall always be burning for peace offerings.
vv. 14-18	Cereal or grain offerings have oil, flour and frankincense; sweet aroma to the Lord.
vv. 19-23	Cereal offerings of priest are holy, and not to be eaten by non-priests.
vv. 24-30	Sin and burnt offering, killed at same place. Priests eat sin offerings in holy place.
Chapter 7	**Peace Offering**
vv. 1-10	Guilt/trespass offering, killed at burnt offering site. Priest shall eat guilt offering.
vv. 11-21	Peace as a thanksgiving offering, accompanies cereal offering, eaten that same day.
vv. 22-27	Whoever eats fat or blood of ox, sheep or goat offered by fire, is cut off from people.
vv. 28-34	Breast offering, shoulder offering of peace offerings given to Aaron and sons to eat.

vv. 35-38	Law of burnt, cereal, sin, trespass and peace offerings
Chapter 8	**Ordination of Priests**
vv. 1-13	Moses anoints Aaron as well as Tabernacle in the presence of all the people.
vv. 14-17	Aaron and sons lay hands on head of bull and kill it to make reconciliation for Israel.
vv. 18-21	Moses brings ram for burnt offering; Aaron and sons lay hands on its head.
vv. 22-30	Moses slays ram of consecration and puts blood on of priests' ear, thumb and toe.
vv. 31-36	Aaron and sons remain seven days and nights at door Tabernacle of congregation.
Chapter 9	**Commencement of Aaron's Priesthood**
vv. 1-4	On 8th day Aaron prepares for sin, burnt, peace and cereal offerings.
vv. 5-7	Moses exhorts Aaron to make atonement for Aaron and people.
vv. 8-14	Aaron and his sons do burnt offerings as Moses tells them.
vv. 15-24	Fire and Glory of God fall on altar; Aaron observes burnt, sin and peace offerings.
Chapter 10	**Restrictions for Priesthood**
vv. 1-7	Nadab and Abihu offer human fire on altar; God sends His fire and destroys them.
vv. 8-11	Moses warns Aaron not to drink wine in tabernacle lest he be destroyed by God.
vv. 12-15	Aaron, Eleazar and Ithamar are to eat cereal offering remnants in holy place.
vv. 16-20	Moses rebukes Eleazar and Ithamar for not eating sin offerings in holy place.
Chapter 11	**Clean and Unclean Animals**
vv. 1-8	God tells Moses Israelites may eat animals that chew cud and have divided hooves.
vv. 9-12	Israelites are not to eat fish without scales and fins.

vv. 13-20	These fowl not to be eaten are listed here.
vv. 21-23	They may eat locust, bald locust, beetle and grasshopper.
vv. 24-28	Carcasses shall be unclean to people.
vv. 29-30	The weasel, mouse, tortoise, ferret, chameleon, lizard, snail and mole are unclean.
vv. 31-41	Admonition not to eat dead things
vv. 42-47	People to be holy for God is holy; therefore, laws for animals, fish, fowl and insects.

Chapter 12 — Purification of Women After Childbirth

vv. 1-4	A woman delivering son, is unclean for 7 days; son is circumcised on 8th day. She purified after 33 days.
v. 5	Woman having girl is unclean for 14 days and purified after 66 days.
vv. 6-7	She shall bring offerings for burnt and sin offering.
v. 8	Priest shall make atonement for her and she shall be clean.

Chapter 13 — Signs and Treatment of Leprosy

vv. 1-3	Man with scab on skin, hair turns white, scab is deeper than skin, it is leprosy.
vv. 4-6	If spot is skin deep, man is quarantined 7 days. If scab has not spread, he is clean.
vv. 7-8	If scab spreads after seeing priest twice, he is pronounced unclean; it is leprosy.
vv. 9-13	If he turns white all over, he is clean; no raw flesh.
vv. 14-15	If he has raw flesh, he has leprosy.
vv. 16-17	If raw flesh turns white and there is no further raw flesh, he is clean.
vv. 18-23	This refers to a boil in which leprosy may break out.
vv. 24-28	This refers to a burn in which leprosy may break out.
vv. 29-37	This is an itching disease similar to ringworm.
vv. 38-39	This is a vesicular skin disease.
vv. 40-44	Falling hair, unless accompanied by other symptoms, is not a sign of leprosy.

vv. 45-46	If leper, person must appear as mourner in torn clothes and go into isolation.
vv. 47-59	Leprous disease in garment refers to mold, mildew or rot.
Chapter 14	**Cleansing of Leprosy**
vv. 1-9	Priest examines leper outside camp; kills bird and sprinkles blood 7 times on him.
vv. 10-20	Sacrifices offered: guilt, wave, sin, burnt and cereal offerings for atonement.
vv. 21-32	Poor offers lamb and 2 pigeons for guilt, sin, burnt offerings with cereal offering.
vv. 33-42	Ritual done for house declared unclean
vv. 43-47	After 7 days if plague is in house, it is dismantled and discarded in "unclean" place.
vv. 48-53	If plague disappears in 7 days, atonement is made by priest and house is clean.
vv. 54-57	Conclusion: itch, swelling, eruption, spot, green or red colorings in walls of house.
Chapter 15	**Bodily Discharges That Are Unclean**
vv. 1-12	Rituals observed if one contacts anyone with a bodily discharge of blood or spittle.
vv. 13-15	Cleansed from discharge, he waits 7 days, washes clothes, bathes in running water.
vv. 16-18	Ritual for emission of a man's semen
vv. 19-24	One touching menstrual woman is unclean until evening. She is unclean for 7 days.
vv. 25-30	Woman with discharge after menstruation is unclean.
v. 31	Unclean people cannot enter Tabernacle lest they die.
vv. 32-33	Conclusion on bodily uncleanness: emissions, discharges of blood, menstrual cycles.
Chapter 16	**Ritual for Day of Atonement**
vv. 1-5	Instructions concerning high priest entering holy place within veil… lest he dies

vv. 6-10	Bull is sin offering for Aaron's family. Lots casts over God's and Satan's goats.
vv. 11-14	Aaron puts incense on fire making cloud over mercy seat, not to see God and die.
vv. 15-19	High priest atones for Tabernacle and altar because of people's sin and uncleanness.
vv. 20-22	Ritual symbolizes transfer of people's sins to goat that carries sins into wilderness.
vv. 23-28	Contact with holiness, like contact with uncleanness, requires ceremonial bath.
vv. 29-34	Day of Atonement is held annually as Sabbath rest on 7th month and 10th day.
Chapter 17	**Only One Place for Sacrifice**
vv. 1-7	People cut off from Israel if slaying sacrifice in fields; it is to be brought to priest.
vv. 8-9	Man giving burnt offering not at door of Tent of Meeting is cut off from his people.
vv. 10-13	God prohibits eating of blood of any creature.
vv. 14-16	Life of every creature is in its blood.
Chapter 18	**Acts of Immorality Forbidden**
vv. 1-5	Israelites are to keep God's statutes and ordinances to live.
vv. 6-18	List of 12 sexual prohibitions: (see 12 curses in Deut. 27:20- 23).
vv. 19-23	Forbidden: adultery, sacrificing children, homosexuality and bestiality.
vv. 24-30	God will move Israelites from Canaan, if immoral as Egyptians and Canaanites.
Chapter 19	**Laws of Holiness and Justice**
vv. 1-4	God tells people to revere parents; keep Sabbaths and no idol worship.
vv. 5-8	Peace offering eaten within two days. If eaten on third day you're cut off from Israel.

vv. 9-10	During harvest, owners are to leave some grain for poor to glean.
v. 11	People are not to steal, deal falsely or lie.
v. 12	People are not to swear or profane God's name.
v. 13	People are to pay hired person's wages daily.
v. 14	People are not to curse deaf or harm blind.
v. 15	In righteousness you shall judge one's neighbor.
v. 16	People are not to slander other Israelites.
v. 17	People are not to hate but reason with each other.
v. 18	Not vengeance, but love for one's neighbor.
v. 19	No mixture in livestock, seeds or garments
vv. 20-22	Trespass offering for man lying with another's woman is offered at Tent of Meeting.
vv. 23-25	Not to eat any fruit in land of Canaan until 4th year; it is uncircumcised.
vv. 26-28	Not to eat blood, witchcraft, cut hair wrongly, cuts in flesh or making tattoos.
v. 29	Not to make daughters become harlots
v. 30	Keep Sabbaths and reverence His sanctuary.
v. 31	Not to seek after mediums (familiar spirits) nor wizards to be defiled by them
v. 32	People are to honor older people.
vv. 33-34	People are to honor strangers.
vv. 35-37	People are to use just measurements.
Chapter 20	**Penalties for Acts of Immorality**
vv. 1-5	Anyone offering child to Molech will be put to death.
vv. 6-8	Israel is to be holy for the Lord is holy; therefore, no mediums or wizards are allowed.
v. 9	Anyone who curses father or mother shall be put to death.
vv. 10-12	Adultery with another man's wife or one's mother or daughter-in-law is to die.
vv. 13-16	Death for homosexuality; marrying a mother and a daughter as a unit and bestiality

vv. 17-21	Sexual relations with sister, menstrual woman, aunt, etc. shall be childless or cut off.
vv. 22-26	Israelites are not to eat unclean animals.
v. 27	Wizards and mediums are to be stoned to death.
Chapter 21	**Holiness of Priests**
vv. 1-9	Priests cannot marry harlot or divorced woman; harlot daughter is to be burned.
vv. 10-15	High priest can't uncover head; tear clothes; touch dead; marry virgin from people.
vv. 16-24	No priest with physical blemish can offer bread or burnt offering to God.
Chapter 22	**Holiness of Priests**
vv. 1-9	Only "clean" priests can eat sacrifices dedicated to the Lord or die.
vv. 10-16	Children and slaves of priest may eat consecrated food, but not an outsider.
vv. 17-25	Only perfect animals are accepted as a votive (vowed) offering.
vv. 26-28	No calf or lamb offered till 8th day. Mother and calf not offered on same day.
vv. 29-30	Thanksgiving offering to be eaten on same day and nothing left till morning.
vv. 31-33	Israelites are to keep God's commandments and never profane His name.
Chapter 23	**Appointed Feasts**
vv. 1-3	All Israelites shall rest on Sabbaths.
vv. 4-8	Passover and Unleavened Bread are observed on 14th and 15th days of first month.
vv. 9-14	First Fruits is day after concluding Sabbath of Feast of Unleavened Bread.
vv. 15-21	Since Festival of Weeks is celebrated at wheat harvest, it is called Pentecost.
v. 22	Landowners shall leave some gleaning for poor.

vv. 23-25	Festival of Trumpets or Jewish New Year falls at beginning of 7th month.
vv. 26-32	Day of Atonement occurs during 7th month; day of rest and affliction of one's soul.
vv. 33-36	Feast of Booths or thanksgiving is held at time of autumn ingathering.
vv. 37-38	These sacrifices are offered at holy convocations (see Numbers, chapters 28 and 29).
vv. 39-43	Israelites shall dwell in booths for 7 days in 7th month as reminder of leaving Egypt.
v. 44	These feasts were made known to Israel by Moses.

Chapter 24 — Various Priestly Laws

vv. 1-4	Lamp outside veil of testimony is to be kept burning continuously.
vv. 5-9	Priests, alone, are to eat showbread.
vv. 10-12	A half-Jew, half-Egyptian blasphemed God's name in a quarrel.
vv. 13-23	Law for blasphemy and murder is death. A boy is stoned for blasphemy.

Chapter 25 — Sabbatical Year and Year of Jubilee

vv. 1-7	Land rests every seventh year; it belongs to God who lets man steward land.
vv. 8-12	The 50th year is Year of Jubilee. Everything goes back to its original owner.
vv. 13-17	People to be fair in business to number of years left before Year of Jubilee.
vv. 18-24	Land belongs to the Lord who lets Israelites use the land as inheritance.
vv. 25-28	At Year of Jubilee, land returns to original owner.
vv. 29-34	Exception made for city and village houses; exception for Levites' prosperity.
vv. 35-38	Israelites are to maintain their poor people.
vv. 39-46	Israelites can be servants, but not slaves as other nations.

vv. 47-55	Israelite can be redeemed from first year till jubilee by himself or his relatives.
Chapter 26	**Penalties for Disobedience**
vv. 1-2	Prohibition against Canaanite idolatry
vv. 3-13	God promises His blessings for obedience.
vv. 14-20	God promises His curses for disobedience.
vv. 21-22	He promises plagues and wild beasts for disobeying Him.
vv. 23-26	More punishments if they continue to disobey
vv. 27-33	Greater punishments if they still disobey
vv. 34-39	Still more punishments for further disobedience
vv. 40-46	God pardons Israelites who repent; He blesses them in captivity in foreign lands.
Chapter 27	**Laws Concerning Dedications**
vv. 1-8	Values of males and females ...
vv. 9-13	Values of animals to be sacrificed ...
vv. 14-15	Values of houses ...
vv. 16-25	Values of lands ...
vv. 26-27	Values of first-born and unclean animals
vv. 28-29	All devoted things are holy to the Lord. Devoted means to be set apart to God.
vv. 30-34	Tenth of the land, herds and flocks belong to the Lord.

NUMBERS
Numbers in Hebrew language means "In Wilderness".

Chapter 1	**Numbering Men 20 and over for Warfare**
vv. 1-16	Older list reflects twelve-tribe league formed in Joshua's time.
vv. 17-19	Moses, as the Lord commanded, numbered people in wilderness of Sinai.
vv. 20-21	Reuben's tribe numbered 46,500 males 20 years and older for warfare.
vv. 22-23	Simeon's tribe numbered 59,300.
vv. 24-25	Gad's men 20 and over numbered 45,650. (Gad was from Leah's handmaid, Zilpah).
vv. 26-27	Judah's men twenty and over numbered 74,600.
vv. 28-29	Issachar's men twenty and over numbered 54,400.
vv. 30-31	Zebulan's men twenty and over numbered 57,400.
vv. 32-33	Ephraim's men twenty and over numbered 40,500. (Joseph's tribe).
vv. 34-35	Manasseh's men twenty and over numbered 32,200. (Joseph's tribe).
vv. 36-37	Benjamin's men twenty and over numbered 35,400.
vv. 38-39	Dan's men twenty and over numbered 62,700. (Dan from Rachel's handmaid, Bilhah).
vv. 40-41	Asher's men twenty and over numbered 41,500. (Asher of Leah's handmaid, Zilpah).
vv. 42-43	Naphtali's men twenty and over numbered 53,400. (Naphtali from handmaid, Bilhah).

vv. 44-46	All males twenty and upwards able to fight numbered 603,550.
vv. 47-54	Levites were not numbered; their ministry was Tabernacle. |//

Chapter 2 — Organization of Camp

vv. 1-2	Tribes were to encamp by their standards facing Tabernacle.
vv. 3-9	Those encamped on east are Judah, Issachar and Zebulon.
vv. 10-16	Those encamped on south are Reuben, Simeon and Gad.
v. 17	Levites encamped in center of tribes around the Tabernacle
vv. 18-24	On west are Ephraim, Manasseh and Benjamin.
vv. 25-31	On north are Dan, Asher and Naphtali.
vv. 32-33	Total numbered 20 upwards for warfare with exception of Levites were 603,550.
v. 34	They were numbered according to what God commanded Moses to tell people.

Chapter 3 — Number and Duties of Levites

vv. 1-4	Aaron's sons exercised chief priestly functions in sanctuary; others assisted.
vv. 5-13	Levites replaced firstborn who belong to the Lord.
vv. 14-20	Names of Levi's sons: Gershon, Kohath, and Merari. Males, of 1 month in census.
vv. 21-26	Gershonites numbered 7,500; their responsibilities were Tabernacle and its covering.
vv. 27-32	Kohathites numbered 8,600; tasks were ark, table, lampstand, altars and vessels.
vv. 33-37	Merarites numbered 6,200; jobs are frames, bars, pillars, bases of Tabernacle.
vv. 38-39	Moses, Aaron and sons in charge of rites in sanctuary. Males 1 month up, 22,000.
vv. 40-43	Israelites from 1 month up was 22,273 (the exact number) of Israelites.
vv. 44-51	The 273 numbered of Levites were redeemed by money given to Aaron and sons.

Chapter 4	**Tasks Assigned to Levites**
vv. 1-3	Kohathites from 30 years upwards were to serve in Tabernacle of congregation.
vv. 4-16	Kohathites not to touch holy thing lest they die; have charge of most holy things.
vv. 17-20	Kohathites cannot see covering of holy things lest they die.
vv. 21-28	Gershonites, supervised by Ithamar are in charge of coverings and door hangings.
vv. 29-33	Merarites from 30-50 in charge of boards, bars, pillars, sockets, pins, cord, etc.
vv. 34-37	Kohathites numbered 2,750 from 30 to 50 years of age.
vv. 38-41	Gershonites numbered 2,630 from 30 to 50 years of age.
vv. 42-45	Merarites numbered 3,200 from 30 to 50 years of age.
vv. 46-49	The total from 30 to 50 years of age was 8,580 males.
Chapter 5	**Law Concerning Jealousy**
vv. 1-4	Lepers put outside camp to keep Tabernacle sanctified
vv. 5-10	Law of trespass offering deals with priest if no kinsman.
vv. 11-15	Cereal offering tests a woman's fidelity.
vv. 16-22	Curse for guilty woman is childlessness.
vv. 23-28	If woman is clean, she shall have children.
vv. 29-31	If she is unclean, she shall bear iniquity.
Chapter 6	**Vow of a Nazarite**
vv. 1-4	Nazarite eats nothing from grapes.
v. 5	Not shave as long as he is a Nazarite.
vv. 6-8	Cannot go near dead family member.
vv. 9-12	If accidentally touches dead person former time of separation is void.
vv. 13-20	After separation completed and Nazarite offered sacrifices, he can drink wine.
vv. 21-27	Benediction," bless you, face shine on you, be gracious, His countenance, peace."

Chapter 7	**Offerings from Tribal Leaders**
vv. 1-11	Leaders provide wagons. Kohathites carefully carry holy things on shoulders.
vv. 12-17	Nahshon, son of Amminadab of Judah brings offerings for first day.
vv. 18-23	Nethaneel, son of Zuar of Issachar brings offerings for second day.
vv. 24-29	Eliab, son of Helon of Zebulun brings offerings for third day.
vv. 30-35	Elizur, son of Shedeur of Reuben brings offerings for fourth day.
vv. 36-41	Shelumiel, son of Zurishaddai of Simeon brings offerings for fifth day.
vv. 42-47	Eliasaph, son of Deuel of Gad brings offerings for sixth day.
vv. 48-53	Elishama, son of Ammihud of Ephraim brings offerings for seventh day.
vv. 54-59	Gamaliel, son of Pedahzur of Manasseh brings offerings for eighth day.
vv. 60-65	Abidan, son of Gideoni of Benjamin brings offerings for ninth day.
vv. 66-71	Ahiezer, son of Ammishaddai of Dan brings offerings for tenth day.
vv. 72-77	Pagiel, son of Ocran of Asher brings offerings for eleventh day.
vv. 78-83	Ahira, son of Enan of Naphtali brings offerings for twelfth day.
vv. 84-88	Shekel of sanctuary is for altar offering.
v. 89	The Lord spoke to Moses from mercy seat and Moses obeyed.
Chapter 8	**Consecration of Levites**
vv. 1-4	Lighting of lamps by priests
vv. 5-13	Patterns for cleansing of Levites; laying on of hands and wave offerings
vv. 14-19	Levites shielded people from dreadful effects of holiness, which causes plagues.

vv. 20-22	After being cleansed, they go about duties.
vv. 23-26	Levites minister from ages 25 until 50 years.
Chapter 9	**Observance of Passover**
vv. 1-8	If man is unclean from touching dead, he cannot observe Passover.
vv. 9-14	Strangers, unclean and Israelites on journey can keep Passover 1 month later.
vv. 15-23	Cloud by day and fire by night covered Tabernacle.
Chapter 10	**Israelites Depart from Sinai.**
vv. 1-10	Sounding trumpets was a military call, not an assembly call.
vv. 11-36	Israelites were on march with God's presence 11 months after arrival at Sinai.
Chapter 11	**Israel's murmuring in Wilderness and 70 Elders Selected**
vv. 1-3	People complained; God sent fire; people cried out; Moses prayed; fire stopped.
vv. 4-6	People complained of eating nothing but manna.
vv. 7-9	Manna was given to Israelites daily by the Lord.
vv. 10-15	Moses argues with God about murmuring for Egyptian foods.
vv. 16-23	God informs Moses, He will give them meat for 30 days. Moses gathers 70 elders.
vv. 24-25	Some of Moses' spirit is imparted to seventy elders who prophesy.
vv. 26-30	Eldad and Medad, filled with God's spirit and prophesy
vv. 31-35	Rabble who craved quails, died at Kibroth-hattaavah from God's plague.
Chapter 12	**Miriam and Aaron Oppose Moses.**
vv. 1-8	Miriam and Aaron, rebuked by God for murmuring against His prophet, Moses.
vv. 9-16	Miriam punished with leprosy; Moses prays; God heals. She is outside camp 7 days.

Chapter 13	**Twelve Spies Sent to Explore Canaan.**
vv. 1-16	Moses sends spies to check out land of Canaan.
vv. 17-25	The 12 men spy on land and return with fruit after 40 days.
vv. 26-33	Two men give good report but others, bad report, saying giants are too powerful.
Chapter 14	**Lord's Punishment on Israel**
vv. 1-10	Israelites are angry and want to stone Joshua and Caleb.
vv. 11-25	Lord promises faithless Israelites will not enter Promised Land.
vv. 26-35	God says faithless 20 years up will not enter Promised Land; a 40-year penalty.
vv. 36-45	People repent and fight giants; Lord was not with them; they were defeated.
Chapter 15	**Laws Concerning Offerings**
vv. 1-16	Law prescribes cereal and drink offerings with burnt or peace offering to Lord.
vv. 17-26	Unintentional sins are forgiven by atonement sacrifice.
vv. 27-36	Profaning Sabbath intentionally causes person to be stoned by congregation.
vv. 37-41	Tassels on garments help people remember God's commands.
Chapter 16	**Korah's Rebellion**
vv. 1-11	Korah and 250 Levite men seek authority equal to Moses and Aaron.
vv. 12-14	Dathan and Abiram refuse to come when Moses called.
vv. 15-19	Levites have popular support against Aaron and Moses.
vv. 20-24	God is ready to destroy Korah, Dathan and Abiram.
vv. 25-30	Moses prophesizes death of these three men.
vv. 31-35	Earth swallows Korah and fire consumes 250 Levites.
vv. 36-40	Censors of destroyed Levites made into broad plates for covering altar.
vv. 41-50	God's plague kills 14,700 rebels until Aaron makes atonement for people.

Chapter 17	**Aaron's Budding Rod**
vv. 1-5	God says of the 12 rods, Aaron's will bud showing he is to stop murmuring.
vv. 6-9	Aaron's rod budded and produced almonds.
vv. 10-13	Priest can approach Tabernacle; he dies unless he cares for the Holy of Holies.
Chapter 18	**Provision for Priests and Levites**
vv. 1-7	Levites help priests for Tabernacle service. Priests can enter Tabernacle of Witness.
vv. 8-19	Priests and families can eat holy things such as wave, peace and first fruit offerings.
vv. 20-24	Other Levites receive tithes for service in Tent of Meeting.
vv. 25-32	Priests receive tithes from Levites' tithes coming from congregation.
Chapter 19	**Rites for Purifying People Defiled by Corpse**
vv. 1-10	Rite of ashes in water for cleansing the unclean for handling dead heifer
vv. 11-13	Touching a corpse, makes one unclean seven days; water applied or cut off.
vv. 14-19	Uncleanness from corpses can contaminate tent or open vessel.
vv. 20-22	Unclean, not cleansed by water for impurity, shall be cut off from people.
Chapter 20	**Departure from Kadesh in Zin**
v. 1	Miriam is buried in Kadesh. She and older generation do not enter Canaan.
vv. 2-9	Moses is told to speak to rock to get water for murmuring people.
vv. 10-13	Moses strikes rock twice instead of honoring God by speaking to rock.
vv. 14-19	Edom refuses to let Israel pass through land.
vv. 20-29	God tells Moses to bury Aaron after Eleazar is made high priest.

Chapter 21		**Fiery Serpents**
vv. 1-3		Promise to destroy Canaanite cities if the Lord would let Israelites win war.
vv. 4-9		Those bitten by serpents will live, looking at bronze serpent on pole.
vv. 10-15		Quote from "The Book of Wars of the Lord"
vv. 16-20		Quote from "The Song of the Well"
vv. 21-30		Israel fights Sihon and Amorites conquering Amorite cities for themselves.
vv. 31-35		Israelites defeat Og of Bashan taking land as they had Sihon's land at Heshbon.
Chapter 22		**Balak and Balaam**
vv. 1-6		Moabite king invites Mesopotamian diviner to curse invading Israelites.
vv. 7-14		Elders of Midian and Moab offer Balaam money to curse Israel. God says "NO!"
vv. 15-20		Balaam offered more money by other leaders. God tells Balaam to go with them.
vv. 21-30		Angel of God blocks donkey's passage and talks to Balaam through donkey.
vv. 31-35		Balaam, can speak only what God and Angel of the Lord tell him to speak.
vv. 36-41		Balak sacrifices oxen and sheep then sends for Balaam and princes of Moab.
Chapter 23		**Prophecies of Balaam**
vv. 1-12		Balaam blesses Israel saying, "let my end be like Israel's end."
vv. 13-24		Balaam blesses Israel, "God is not man, that He should lie, or son of man, etc."
vv. 25-30		On another mountain, Balak offers seven oxen and seven rams on seven altars.
Chapter 24		**Balaam Foretells Happiness of Israel.**
vv. 1-9		"Blessed everyone who blesses Israel and cursed be everyone who curses Israel."

vv. 10-25	Balaam blesses Israel fourth time and foretells destruction of Canaan.
Chapter 25	**Zeal of Priest Phinehas**
vv. 1-5	Men who intermarried with Moabite women were hung.
vv. 6-9	Phinehas kills Israelite man and Midianite woman, stopping plague; but 24,000 died.
vv. 10-13	Phinehas, for killing wickedness in camp; descendants have perpetual priesthood.
vv. 14-18	God tells Israelites to vex or harass Midianites and smite them.
Chapter 26	**Census for Numbering Israel in Moab**
vv. 1-4	Second census numbered those 20 years and upwards of men able to go to war.
vv. 5-11	Reuben's tribe numbered 43,730 men.
vv. 12-14	Simeon's tribe numbered 22,200 men.
vv. 15-18	Gad's tribe numbered 40,500 men.
vv. 19-22	Judah's tribe numbered 76,500 men.
vv. 23-25	Issachar's tribe numbered 64,300 men.
vv. 26-27	Zebulun's tribe numbered 60,500 men.
vv. 28-34	Manasseh's tribe numbered 52,700.
vv. 35-37	Ephraim's tribe numbered 32,500.
vv. 38-41	Benjamin's tribe numbered 45,600.
vv. 42-43	Dan's tribe numbered 64,400.
vv. 44-47	Asher's tribe numbered 53,400.
vv. 48-50	Naphtali's tribe numbered 45,400.
v. 51	Total of Israel's warriors was 601,730.
vv. 52-56	Land to be divided by lot with bigger sections going to larger tribes.
vv. 57-62	Levite males were numbered from one month upwards and totaled 23,000 but were not "totaled" with other tribes of Israel.
vv. 63-65	Joshua and Caleb numbered in second census. Those 20 and older died.

Chapter 27	**Laws of Inheritance**
vv. 1-4	Five daughters of Zelophehad of Manasseh's tribe ask for land inheritance because they are women without brothers.
vv. 5-11	Land is to remain in tribe and not to pass to another tribe.
vv. 12-17	The Lord prepares Moses for his burial. Moses asks the Lord for his successor.
vv. 18-23	Moses lays hands on Joshua's head and commissions him as leader of Israelites.
Chapter 28	**Daily, Sabbath and Monthly Offerings**
vv. 1-8	Offerings are to be a sweet odor and acceptable to God.
vv. 9-10	Burnt offerings for every Sabbath
vv. 11-15	Since year is based on a lunar calendar, a festival is held at each new moon.
vv. 16-25	Unleavened bread and no laborious work for seven days
vv. 26-31	Offering for a holy convocation or Pentecost
Chapter 29	**Offerings at Appointed Feasts**
vv. 1-6	Instructions on offerings for first day of seventh month (New Year)
vv. 7-11	Day of Atonement offerings
vv. 12-16	First day of Feast of Booth's offering
vv. 17-19	Second day of Feast of Booths
vv. 20-22	Third day of Feast of Booths
vv. 23-25	Fourth day of Feast of Booths
vv. 26-28	Fifth day of Feast of Booths
vv. 29-31	Sixth day of Feast of Booths
vv. 32-34	Seventh day of Feast of Booths
vv. 35-38	Eighth day of Feast of Booths
vv. 39-40	Offering of Feast of Booths (Tabernacles) exceeds any other convocation.
Chapter 30	**Law Concerning Vows Made by Women**
vv. 1-16	Vows by a man or a widow or divorced woman will stand.

Chapter 31	**Holy War against Midianites**
vv. 1-12	In a holy war, all men of Midianites who fought were sacrificed to the Lord.
vv. 13-20	Married women were to be killed as well as boys and men.
vv. 21-24	Laws of purification for material items
vv. 25-31	Law for distribution of goods captured during war
vv. 32-41	Tally of goods is divided among soldiers and priests
vv. 42-47	Tally of goods for congregation and Levites
vv. 48-54	Moses and Eleazar receive gold from officers of war.
Chapter 32	**Land on East Side of Jordan**
vv. 1-5	Reubenites and Gadites request land east of Jordan.
vv. 6-15	Moses rehearses reason people had to wander in wilderness for 40 years.
vv. 16-27	Reubenites and Gadites vow to cross Jordan and fight battles with fellow Israelites.
vv. 28-32	Moses agrees to give land to Reubenites and Gadites if they fight Canaanites.
vv. 33-42	Moses gives land to Gad, Reuben and one-half tribe of Manasseh.
Chapter 33	**Wilderness Journeys Reviewed**
vv. 1-4	Moses begins review with departure from Rameses of Egypt.
vv. 5-37	Israel's wilderness itinerary for 40 years
vv. 38-39	Aaron dies on Mt. Hor at 123 years of age.
vv. 40-49	Moses journals from Kadesh to plains of Moab.
vv. 50-56	Land is divided according to size of tribes.
Chapter 34	**Boundaries of Canaan**
vv. 1-5	Southern and eastern boundaries of Canaan for Israelites
vv. 6-9	Western and northern boundaries of Canaan for Israelites
vv. 10-12	Eastern boundary explained
vv. 13-15	Land given to 9 1/2 of tribes on west of Jordan versus 2 1/2 on east of Jordan.
vv. 16-29	Naming of leaders of each tribe who will divide land

Chapter 35		**Forty-eight Levitical Cities, Including Six Cities of Refuge**
vv. 1-8		Special cities were given because Levites were not entitled to inheritance.
vv. 9-15		Six cities of refuge have three on each side of Jordan River.
vv. 16-21		Punishment for murderers
vv. 22-28		Laws for manslaughter
vv. 29-34		Only blood of a murderer can expiate murder.
Chapter 36		**Inheritance by Marriage**
vv. 1-4		A question is raised about intertribal marriages.
vv. 5-9		Women with property can only marry within their tribe.
vv. 10-13		Women with land married their cousins to keep property within tribe.

DEUTERONOMY
Fifth book Of Moses

Chapter 1	**Israel's History after the Exodus**
vv. 1-8	Moses rehearses events since departure from Sinai. Land extends to Euphrates River.
vv. 9-18	Moses rehearses appointing 70 elders in settling disputes between Israelites.
vv. 19-25	Moses rehearses choosing 12 spies, one from each tribe, to preview land.
vv. 26-33	Moses rehearses people's fear of Amorites though God delivered from Egyptians.
vv. 34-40	Moses rehearses people's murmuring, saying only their children shall possess land.
vv. 41-46	Moses rehearses defeat by Amorites when Israelites went to war without God.
Chapter 2	**Thirty-eight Years Wilderness Wandering**
vv. 1-15	Israelites wandered 38 years until warriors perished and children took their places.
vv. 16-25	God will make enemy fearful of Israelites because battle is the Lord's.
vv. 26-37	Moses rehearses defeat of Sihon of Heshbon, and possessing land given them.
Chapter 3	**Israel Conquers Og of Bashan.**
vv. 1-11	Moses recounts how they destroyed people taking 60 cities from Og in Bashan.
vv. 12-17	Moses recounts giving land east of Jordan to Reubenites, Gadites and 1/2 Manasseh.

vv. 18-22	Moses exhorts 2 1/2 tribes to fight along with other 9 1/2 tribes.
vv. 23-29	Moses retells people he can only see Promised Land and Joshua will lead them.
Chapter 4	**Conclusion of Moses' First Speech**
vv. 1-8	Moses exhorts people to obey God's commands, not adding or taking from them.
vv. 9-14	Moses reminds people to obey Ten Commandments and statutes and ordinances.
vv. 15-24	People are not to worship any graven images but only the Lord.
vv. 25-31	If you serve idols, God will take you out of land.
vv. 32-40	Moses commands people to obey God in order to live in land.
vv. 41-43	Moses sets apart three cities on east of Jordan as cities of refuge.
vv. 44-49	Moses controls east of Jordan after defeating Kings Sihon and Og.
Chapter 5	**Ten Commandments at Sinai**
vv. 1-5	Moses commands people to hear what is to follow.
vv. 6-21	I am God; Name sacred; Sabbath holy; honor parents; no murder; no adultery; not steal; no lie; no covet.
vv. 22-27	People heard God's voice out of fire and lived.
vv. 28-33	Obey and you will live long in land God is giving you.
Chapter 6	**Meaning of First Commandment**
vv. 1-3	Reverent obedience results in divine blessings, long life, fruitfulness and welfare.
vv. 4-9	First commandment on hand, forehead and doorpost for meditating on Law daily.
vv. 10-15	God, Holy and Jealous, will not tolerate idolatry.
vv. 16-19	Israelites fear and obey the Lord; He drives out enemies and gives promised land.

vv. 20-25	Parents are to teach children God's deliverance from Egypt and wilderness.

Chapter 7 — Blessings of Obedience

vv. 1-5	Make no covenants or marriages with Canaanites; destroy their Asherim (gods).
vv. 6-11	God blesses to a thousand generations obedient but destroys those who hate Him.
vv. 12-16	God blesses Israel's obedience, giving fruitfulness, prosperity and protection.
vv. 17-26	Israel, do not fear any nation; the Lord God is with you doing mighty deeds.

Chapter 8 — Wonders of Wilderness Recalled

vv. 1-10	God prospers humility; when nation forgets God, He disciplines as a father his son.
vv. 11-20	Do not forget God or He will treat you as any rebellious nation.

Chapter 9 — Israel's Rebellion at Horeb Remembered

vv. 1-3	As Israel crosses Jordan and God goes before them driving out giants.
vv. 4-5	The Lord drives out wicked nations, not because of Israel's righteousness.
vv. 6-12	God's anger to have destroyed Israel at Horeb for golden calf but Moses interceded.
vv. 13-21	Moses intercedes on Mt.Sinai, keeping God from destroying Aaron and Israel.
vv. 22-24	Moses claims Israel was rebellious against God before leaving Egypt.
vv. 25-29	Moses reminds Israel God brought them out of bondage with an outstretched hand.

Chapter 10 — Covenant Renewed with Second Tablets of Stone

vv. 1-5	Moses retells receiving 2nd tablets of stone. He places them in Ark of Covenant.

vv. 6-9	Eleazar replaces father, Aaron. Levites commissioned to carry Ark of Covenant.
vv. 10-11	God does not destroy Israel. He tells Moses to lead them to Promised Land.
vv. 12-22	Israel is to fear Lord God; walk in Him; love Him; serve Him; keep commandments.
Chapter 11	**Blessings of Obedience in Promised Land**
vv. 1-7	You shall love and obey your Lord; He delivered you from Egypt and wilderness.
vv. 8-12	Promised Land has been blessed by the Lord.
vv. 13-17	A warning to only serve the Lord or perish in this good land.
vv. 18-25	Obey the Lord and He will protect you by putting fear into your enemies.
vv. 26-32	Israelites stand in a time of a solemn decision of divine blessing or judgment.
Chapter 12	**Only One Place of Worship**
vv. 1-14	Each tribe has place for sacrifices and destroy all places of pagan sacrifices.
vv. 15-19	Levites are cared for eat offerings in places prescribed by the Lord.
vv. 20-28	Meat is eaten anywhere unless consecrated and in designated holy places.
vv. 29-32	When entering a land to possess it, do not inquire how pagans served false gods.
Chapter 13	**Idolaters are put to Death**
vv. 1-5	Do not follow anyone who leads you after false gods or into idolatry.
vv. 6-11	Stone anyone who would lead you away from only true God.
vv. 12-18	When city turns to idolatry, it is burned as offering. Devoted things are the Lord's.
Chapter 14	**Clean and Unclean Food**
vv. 1-2	You are holy: do not cut yourselves or shave your foreheads for the dead.

vv. 3-8	You can eat animals that have cloven hooves and chew the cud.
vv. 9-10	You can eat fish that have scales and fins.
vv. 11-20	You cannot eat winged insects or unclean birds such as buzzards or vultures.
v. 21	Cannot eat what dies of itself; can sell to foreigners. Not boil goat in mother's milk.
vv. 22-27	Israel, a steward of God's land. Tithes of produce offered at annual harvest festival.
vv. 28-29	Every 3 years bring produce tithes; store them for Levites, widows, orphans, etc.
Chapter 15	**Year of Release**
vv. 1-6	Sabbatical (seventh) year is like year of jubilee, a time for forgiveness of debts.
vv. 7-11	You shall freely give to your brother, needy and poor in land.
vv. 12-18	Law of Hebrew servitude for six years of labor shall be rewarded.
vv. 19-23	Firstborn males of livestock are consecrated to God. Blood is poured on ground.
Chapter 16	**Three Appointed Feasts**
vv. 1-8	Law of Passover Feast or Feast of Unleavened Bread
vv. 9-12	Law concerning Feast of Weeks, or Pentecost, or Harvest of First Fruits
vv. 13-15	Feast of Ingathering or Tabernacles or Booths is 5 days after Day of Atonement.
vv. 16-17	Males to come before Lord three times each year to observe these appointed feasts.
vv. 18-20	Judges are appointed in every town to deal righteously with people.
vv. 21-22	Prohibitions against Canaanite cultic installations
Chapter 17	**Future Rules for Judges and Kings**
v. 1	No blemished animal is to be sacrificed to the Lord.

vv. 2-7	Anyone found worshipping idols shall be stoned by two or three witnesses.
vv. 8-13	Levitical judges rule in hard cases. People do what judge says or be put to death.
vv. 14-17	If men want king, he must be Israelite without too many horses, wives, silver, gold.
vv. 18-20	When made king, he writes a copy of law; reads it daily; and learns to fear God.
Chapter 18	**Proper Worship of the Lord**
vv. 1-5	Levites have no inheritance; God is their inheritance; they eat "offerings by fire."
vv. 6-8	Town Levites may participate in services at central sanctuary.
vv. 9-14	Israelites not to practice evils of nations God is dispossessing.
vv. 15-22	Test of true prophet is his prophecy will be fulfilled according to the Lord's purpose.
Chapter 19	**Justice in Cities of Refuge: Three cities East and Three West of Jordan River**
vv. 1-10	Three cities in Canaan and 3 east of Jordan River, for refuge of innocent Israelites.
vv. 11-13	If killer is not innocent, elders will give him to avenger of blood.
v. 14	Do not remove ancient landmarks.
vv. 15-21	If evil witness is found by ruling priests, he receives the punishment he planned.
Chapter 20	**Rules for Waging a Holy War**
vv. 1-4	A Holy War is one wherein God fights for His people against enemy.
vv. 5-9	Priests and officers tell soldiers what to do.
vv. 10-18	Palestinian city to be destroyed. Plunder can be taken from non-Palestinian cities.
vv. 19-20	Israelites can only make siege works out of non-fruit-bearing trees.

Chapter 21	**Laws about Life in Land**
vv. 1-9	Law for expiation of murder if killer is unknown; elders absolve by washing hands.
vv. 10-14	Treatment of a female captive whom you desire for a wife
vv. 15-17	Rights of a firstborn son
vv. 18-21	How to deal with a stubborn, rebellious son
vv. 22-23	Hanging criminals on a tree after execution is regarded as greatest disgrace.
Chapter 22	**Laws Concerning Chastity**
vv. 1-4	You are to help restore a fellow Israelite's lost animals.
v. 5	It is an abomination for a male to wear female clothing and vice-versa.
vv. 6-7	If you wish long life, do not take a mother bird along with her eggs or young.
v. 8	A low wall is be built on roof of a new house to keep one from falling.
vv. 9-11	No different seeds in ground; no plowing, ox and ass; no mixture allowed.
v. 12	Tassels are on four corners of cloaks to remind Israelites of the Lord's rulership.
vv. 13-21	Proof of a woman's virginity is questioned in these verses.
v. 22	Adultery is punishable by stoning.
vv. 23-24	Adultery with a betrothed virgin is also punishable by stoning.
vv. 25-27	If a betrothed woman is raped in countryside only attacker is stoned.
vv. 28-29	A man who rapes lady pays 50 shekels of silver, marries her and never divorces her.
v. 30	A man shall not take his stepmother as a wife.
Chapter 23	**People Excluded from Congregation**
v. 1	People with damaged genitals, cannot enter.
v. 2	No bastards till tenth generation shall enter assembly.

vv. 3-6	No Ammonite nor Moabite till tenth generation shall enter assembly.
vv. 7-8	Third generation Egyptian and Edomite enters assembly, not 1st nor 2nd generation.
v. 9	Keep yourselves from every evil thing while in enemy's camp.
vv. 10-11	Camp must be clean for sanitary as well as holy reasons.
vv. 12-14	Daily excrements shall be covered in holes and hidden from eyesight.
vv. 15-16	You are not to return an escaped slave nor oppress him.
vv. 17-18	No monies from prostitution or sale of a dog shall be given to the Lord's house.
vv. 19-20	No interest shall be charged on loan to fellow Israelite, only to foreigners.
vv. 21-23	Vows made to the Lord must be paid.
vv. 24-25	You can eat your neighbor's crops; you cannot carry crops to your house.

Chapter 24	**Laws of Domestic Relations**
vv. 1-4	A former husband cannot remarry a woman he has divorced.
v. 5	A recently married man is free from military duty for one year.
v. 6	Since daily life depends upon bread, a mill cannot be taken as security for a loan.
v. 7	Kidnappers of Israelites must die.
vv. 8-9	In cases of leprosy do what priests command to be done.
vv. 10-13	No taking something pledged from poor; if you take cloak, return it before nightfall.
vv. 14-15	You shall pay poor their wages daily.
v. 16	Parent shall not be put to death for a son's sin or vice versa.
vv. 17-18	Do not take a widow's cloak as a pledge.
vv. 19-22	Leave gleanings in fields for sojourner, fatherless and widows.

Chapter 25	**Laws of Human Relations**
vv. 1-3	A guilty man may not be beaten more than 40 stripes.
v. 4	Do not muzzle an ox treading out grain.
vv. 5-10	A sister-in-law whose husband dies, is to marry brother-in-law to bear children.
vv. 11-12	A woman's hand cut off if she helps husband fight by attacking other's genitals.
vv. 13-16	Do not use false weights and measurements. This will shorten one's life.
vv. 17-19	Hebrews are to destroy Amalek's people for attacks on Israelites.
Chapter 26	**Offerings of First Fruits and Tithes**
vv. 1-4	Entering land, Israelites give some first fruits to priest, who present it at altar.
vv. 5-15	A liturgy for year of tithing
vv. 16-19	"This day" refers to God's demands that He is Lord; Israel is His chosen people.
Chapter 27	**Law to Be Recorded on Mt. Ebal**
vv. 1-8	When you cross over write Law on stones.
vv. 9-10	Moses and priests command Israelites to keep laws and statutes.
vv. 11-14	Some tribes repeat blessings; others repeat cursings.
v. 15	Cursed is man who makes idols.
v. 16	Cursed is person who dishonors parents.
v. 17	Cursed is man who removes boundaries.
v. 18	Cursed is man who misleads blind.
v. 19	Cursed is man taking advantage of a sojourner, orphan or widow.
v. 20	Cursed is he who sleeps with his stepmother.
v. 21	Cursed is he who sleeps with animals.
v. 22	Cursed is he who sleeps with stepsister.
v. 23	Cursed is he who sleeps with his mother-in-law.
v. 24	Cursed is he who kills a neighbor secretly.

v. 25	Cursed is he who kills innocent for money.
v. 26	Cursed is he who does not carry out this Law.
Chapter 28	**Consequences of Disobedience**
vv. 1-6	These blessings come when you obey the Lord.
vv. 7-14	Obey the Lord, follow Him and you will prosper in all you do.
vv. 15-19	These six curses parallel with six previous blessings of verses 7-14.
vv. 20-24	More curses proclaimed for disobedience.
vv. 25-35	More severe curses proclaimed for disobedience.
vv. 36-46	Most severe curses proclaimed for disobedience.
vv. 47-57	Curses become worse as people continue to disobey, viz. eating children.
vv. 58-68	Final curse is to be returned to Egypt as slaves.
Chapter 29	**The Lord's Covenant with Israel**
v. 1	This covenant, made in Moab, is renewal of original made in Horeb (Mt. Sinai).
vv. 2-9	Be careful to obey all words of covenant that you may prosper.
vv. 10-15	Covenant is made with both present and future Israelites.
vv. 16-28	God's warning to cast out rebellious from Promised Land for not keeping covenant.
v. 29	God knows secrets; we know what is revealed in Deuteronomy.
Chapter 30	**Restoration after Repentance**
vv. 1-10	Repent and keep commandments, He will give His blessings and enemies His curses.
vv. 11-14	Keep the Lord's word is in your hearts so you can obey Him.
vv. 15-20	Moses sets life and death before people. They must choose to obey or disobey God.
Chapter 31	**Joshua Commissioned as Moses' Successor**
vv. 1-6	Moses tells people to be strong and of good courage.

vv. 7-8	Moses tells Joshua, be strong and courageous leading people into Promised Land.
vv. 9-13	Joshua is to rehearse the Law to future generations after they possess land.
vv. 14-15	God tells Moses to get Joshua and meet with Him in Tent of Meeting.
vv. 16-22	God commands Moses to write a song. Song helps when they break covenant.
v. 23	God commissions Joshua to lead Israelites into Promised Land.
vv. 24-29	After Moses writing the Law, he commands Levites to put it inside the Ark.
v. 30	Moses speaks words of song he finished writing.
Chapter 32	**Song of Moses (vv. 1-43)**
	Song contrasts the Lord's faithfulness with Israel's faithlessness.
vv. 1-3	Introduction appeals to Israelites.
vv. 4-6	Integrity of God contrasted to perversity of Israel. (Rock is an epithet for the Lord).
vv. 7-14	A recital of the Lord's saving deeds in days of old.
vv. 15-18	Israel, like a well-fed animal, rebelled against his caretaker.
vv. 19-27	God's righteous indignation revealed, not wanting Canaanites thinking victory.
vv. 28-33	Israel's Rock is superior to rock (god) of their enemies.
vv. 34-43	God is all-powerful; He avenges His people and cleanses land of His enemies.
vv. 44-47	Moses commands Israel," Learn and recite this song to live long in Promised Land."
vv. 48-52	God tells Moses to ascend Mt. Nebo to die; Moses did not reverence God as Holy.
Chapter 33	**Moses Blesses Tribes.**
vv. 1-5	The Lord is proclaimed "King" in assembly of Israelite confederacy.

v. 6	Blessing on Rueben to live and be many people.
v. 7	Blessing on Judah against his adversaries.
vv. 8-11	Blessing on Levi as he officiates at altar.
v. 12	Blessing on Benjamin as he is loved by God.
vv. 13-17	Blessing on Joseph's, Ephraim's and Manasseh's natural and military strengths.
vv. 18-19	Blessing on Zebulun from Seas with Issachar from Seas (Mediterranean and Galilee).
vv. 20-21	Blessing on Gad who obtained best land in Transjordan after helping other tribes.
v. 22	Blessing on Dan who has migrated from north of Judah to Mt. Herman.
v. 23	Blessing on Naphtali who is to possess west and south Sea of Galilee.
vv. 24-25	Blessing on Asher who is to be strong and prosperous.
vv. 26-29	God is a refuge with everlasting arms to care for Israel.
Chapter 34	**Death of Moses**
vv. 1-4	God lets Moses see Promised Land but doesn't let him enter.
vv. 5-6	God buries Moses secretly in Land of Moab in valley by Bethpeor.
v. 7	Moses died at 120 of age in good physical condition.
v. 8	Israelites wept for Moses 30 days.
v. 9	Joshua becomes leader whom Moses had prepared for leadership over Israel.
vv. 10-12	Moses was greatest prophet Israel ever had.

JOSHUA

Chapter 1	**Preparations for Conquest of Canaan**
vv. 1-9	God commands Joshua to be strong and possess land promised to Israelites.
vv. 10-11	Joshua commands leaders to prepare for conquering and.
vv. 12-15	Joshua commands armies of 2 1/2 tribes to help other tribes before going to land.
vv. 16-18	Leaders of these 2 1/2 tribes tell Joshua they will obey as he follows God.
Chapter 2	**Rahab protects Israel's two spies.**
vv. 1-7	Rahab hides two spies on her roof.
vv. 8-14	Spies pledge Rahab to spare her family when Israelites invade Jericho.
vv. 15-21	Rahab ties a scarlet cord in window to protect her family during invasion.
vv. 22-24	Spies report to Joshua concerning fears of Jericho's inhabitants.
Chapter 3	**Israel to Cross Jordan on Dry Ground**
vv. 1-6	Joshua gives directions to leaders about crossing Jordan River.
vv. 7-13	Joshua commands priests to take Ark into Jordan River; leaders of 12 tribes follow.
vv. 14-17	Waters of Jordan stop flowing while Israelites pass over on dry ground.
Chapter 4	**Israel to Build Twelve Stone Memorial**
vv. 1-7	Twelve men are chosen to place 12 stones by Jordan as a sign to future generations.

vv. 8-9	Memorial of 12 stones is set in place.
vv. 10-13	Forty thousand Israelites prepare for war.
vv. 14-18	After Ark crosses, river water overflows again.
vv. 19-24	The 12 stones are for future generations to revere God who dried up river.
Chapter 5	**Circumcision and Passover at Gilgal**
v. 1	Amorites and Canaanites become fearful due to God's drying up Jordan River.
vv. 2-7	Young men are now being circumcised.
vv. 8-9	After circumcision men waited until they were healed before warring.
vv. 10-12	Israelites celebrate Passover as manna ceases to be provided.
vv. 13-15	Joshua standing on holy ground, obeys Angel Michael and removes his sandals.
Chapter 6	**Fall of Jericho**
vv. 1-5	Instructions for seven days marching and shouting of 40,000 Israeli warriors.
vv. 6-7	Joshua repeats to priests instructions God gave him for them.
vv. 8-11	Israelites march around Jericho first day then spend night in camp.
vv. 12-14	Following marches and trumpet blowings
vv. 15-21	Seventh day they march around city 7 times. Jerico destroyed except Rahab's family.
vv. 22-25	The two spies rescue Rahab and her family.
vv. 26-27	Joshua pronounces a curse on anyone who rebuilds Jericho.
Chapter 7	**Sin of Achan**
v. 1	Achan takes accursed articles.
vv. 2-5	Army of Ai kills 36 warriors causing discouragement among Israelites.
vv. 6-9	Joshua laments Israel's defeat.
vv. 10-15	God declares destruction by fire to those who have brought shame to Israel.
vv. 16-21	Achan confesses his sin to Joshua.

vv. 22-26	Achan and his family are stoned and burned. God's anger is turned from Israel.
Chapter 8	**Capture and Defeat of Ai**
vv. 1-2	Plans to ambush and destroy Ai
vv. 3-9	Joshua plans for Ai's men to chase Israelites. Israelites ambush and burn Ai.
vv. 10-17	King of Ai and men pursue 5,000 Israelites. Israelites wait in ambush to destroy Ai.
vv. 18-23	Israelites surround Ai, destroying every man and capturing their king.
vv. 24-29	Joshua hangs king and returns his body to destroyed city.
vv. 30-35	Joshua recopies 10 Commandments and rehearses blessings and curses Moses read.
Chapter 9	**Deceit of Gibeonites**
vv. 1-2	Kings in the area decide to fight Joshua and Israel.
vv. 3-15	Against God's directions, Joshua covenants with deceitful Gibeonites (Hivites).
vv. 16-21	These Hivites become slaves, cutting wood and carrying water for Israel.
vv. 22-27	Fearful Hivites explain to Joshua their reason for deceiving elders of Israel.
Chapter 10	**Sun to Stand Still**
vv. 1-5	Five Amorite kings war against Gibeon for making a covenant with Israel.
vv. 6-11	Israel kills many Amorites but God destroys even more by His giant hailstones.
vv. 12-14	Sun (and moon) stay in course until killing of Amorites is complete.
vv. 15-21	Five kings hid in a cave at Makkedah while fighting continued.
vv. 22-27	Five kings killed, hung that evening and returned to cave where they hid.
vv. 28-30	The Israelites destroy Makkedah and Libnah.

vv. 31-32	Israelites destroy Lachish.
vv. 33-37	Gezer, Eglon and Hebron are destroyed.
vv. 38-39	Debir is also destroyed.
vv. 40-43	After defeating all surrounding nations, Joshua and army return to Gilgal.
Chapter 11	**Joshua Defeats Kings of Northern Galilee.**
vv. 1-5	Jabin, King of Hazor, invites other kings in Galilee to join him in opposing Israelites.
vv. 6-9	The Lord gives victory to Joshua over kings of north.
vv. 10-15	The Lord and Moses told Joshua, to destroy and burn cities; not those on mounds.
vv. 16-20	God hardens people against Israel, so He can conquer them through Israelites.
vv. 21-23	Land given to Israel had rest after defeating former residents, Anakim (giants).
Chapter 12	**Summary of Israel's Victories**
vv. 1-6	Kings, Joshua defeated are Sihon, king of Amorites and Og, king of Bashan.
vv. 7-24	Joshua defeated 32 kings west of Jordan River.
Chapter 13	**Land Allotments of Tribes East of Jordan**
vv. 1-7	God promises to banish inhabitants; now land is to be divided among 9 1/2 tribes.
vv. 8-13	Reubenites, Gadites and 1/2 of Manasseh received lands east of Jordan.
v. 14	Levites received no land, only offerings.
vv. 15-23	Borders of Reubenites are stated here.
vv. 24-28	Borders of Gadites are mentioned in these verses.
vv. 29-31	The 1/2 of Manasseh's borders is outlined in these verses.
v. 32	The Lord God of Israel is inheritance of Levites.
Chapter 14	**Hebron is assigned to Caleb.**
vv. 1-5	Leaders of Israel allot land to 9 1/2 tribes excluding Levites.
vv. 6-12	Caleb, at 85 years of age, asks Joshua for hill country where giants live.

vv. 13-14	Joshua gives Hebron to Caleb.

Chapter 15	**Cities Allotted to Judah**
vv. 1-12	Boundaries are defined for tribe of Judah.
vv. 13-19	Caleb gives Achsah to Othniel as wife for taking land from giant Kirjathsepher.
vv. 20-63	Cities given to Judah who does not drive out all Jebusites living in Jerusalem.

Chapter 16	**Cities Allotted to Ephraim**
vv. 1-4	Tribes of Joseph, Manasseh and Ephraim receive their inheritance.
vv. 5-10	Territory of Ephraim where many Canaanites still dwell.

Chapter 17	**Territory of Manasseh**
vv. 1-2	Allotment given to families of Manasseh.
vv. 3-6	Land allotted to daughters of Zelophehad because he had no sons.
vv. 7-13	Manasseh conquers land but does not drive out all Canaanites.
vv. 14-18	Joshua commands people of Joseph to drive out Canaanites in hill country.

Chapter 18	**Cities Allotted to Benjamin**
vv. 1-7	Joshua sends three men from remaining 7 tribes to survey rest of land.
vv. 8-10	Joshua cast lots at Shiloh to determine which tribe would receive what land.
vv. 11-20	Land allotted to tribe of Benjamin with all its boundaries
vv. 21-28	Cities are named that Benjaminites are to possess.

Chapter 19	**Remainder of Land Divided**
vv. 1-9	Simeon receives land from Judah because Judah had too much land.
vv. 10-16	Zebulun receives its inheritance, family by family, with 12 cities.
vv. 17-23	Issachar receives its inheritance with 16 cities.

vv. 24-31	Asher receives 22 cities for inheritance of its families.
vv. 32-39	Naphtali receives 19 cities for its inheritance.
vv. 40-48	Dan takes Leshem and other cities for its inheritance.
vv. 49-51	Conclusion of distribution of land to various tribes
Chapter 20	**Six Cities of Refuge Appointed.**
vv. 1-6	Reasons given for these cities of refuge
vv. 7-9	Names of these six cities of refuge are stated here.
Chapter 21	**Forty-Eight Cities of Levites**
vv. 1-8	Kohathites, Gershonites and Merarites get land from 12 tribes.
vv. 9-12	Levites received pasture lands from Judah and Simeon.
vv. 13-19	More land is given for pasture from Judah, Simeon and Benjamin.
vv. 20-26	Kohathites received lands from Ephraim, Dan and the 1/2 tribe of Manasseh.
vv. 27-33	Gershonites get pasture lands from 1/2 of Manasseh, Issachar, Asher and Naphtali.
vv. 34-40	Merarites were given pasture lands from Zebulun and Gad.
vv. 41-45	All of promises God made to Israel came to pass.
Chapter 22	**Two and One- Half Eastern Tribes Return Home, East of Jordan River**
vv. 1-6	Joshua blesses and sends home 1/2 tribe of Manasseh with Gad and Reuben.
vv. 7-9	Two and half tribes return home with their newly acquired possessions.
vv. 10-12	Conflict between eastern and western tribes due to building altar east of Jordan.
vv. 13-20	Nine and one-half tribes rebuke these two and one-half tribes.
vv. 21-29	Two and one-half eastern tribes defend building altar beside Jordan River.
vv. 30-34	Finally, eastern and western tribes are reconciled.

Chapter 23	**Joshua Exhorts People.**
vv. 1-16	Joshua says if they follow God, blessings come; if they rebel, curses come.
Chapter 24	**Joshua's Final Exhortation and Farewell Address**
vv. 1-13	Joshua calls to remembrance all God did for Israel delivering them from Egypt.
vv. 14-15	Joshua tells people to choose God, "For me and my house, we will serve the Lord".
vv. 16-18	Israelites tell Joshua they will serve God who brought them out of Egypt.
vv. 19-28	Joshua sets a stone as witness to Israelites who profess they will serve the Lord.
vv. 29-33	Joshua dies at 110 years. Bones of Joseph are buried as requested at Shechem.

JUDGES

Chapter 1	**Judah and Simeon Capture Adonibezek.**
vv. 1-7	Jews slew 10,000 Canaanites and cut off big toes and thumbs of Adonibezek.
vv. 8-10	Judah conquered Jerusalem, Hebron, and slew Sheshai, Ahiman and Talmai.
vv. 11-15	Othniel conquered Debir for Caleb and wins his daughter, Achsah, as wife.
vv. 16-21	Judah and Simeon conquered Hormah, Gaza, Askelon and Ekron.
vv. 22-26	Conquests of Joseph over Bethel
vv. 27-28	Manasseh did not drive out Canaanites but did take tribute from them.
v. 29	Ephraim did not drive out Canaanites from Gezer.
v. 30	Zebulun did not drive out Canaanites from Kitron or Nahalol but received tribute.
vv. 31-32	Asher did not drive out Canaanites from Accho, Zidon, Ahlab, Achzib, Helbah,etc..
v. 33	Naphtali did not drive out Canaanites in Bethshemesh and Bethanath.
v. 34	Dan and Joseph made Canaanites pay tribute in Heres, Aijalon and Shaalbim.
Chapter 2	**Israel Rebuked for Disobedience by the Lord's Angel.**
vv. 1-5	Angel of God rebuked Israel for not destroying pagan Canaanite altars.
vv. 6-11	Joshua died; elders died; new generation did not know the Lord.
vv. 11-15	Israelites worshipped pagan gods, becoming apostates.

vv. 16-23	God raised judges for Israel and used Canaanites as "thorns" to help Israel repent.
Chapter 3	**Pagan Nations Used by God to Prove Israel**
vv. 1-7	Canaanites, Sidonians, Hivites, Hittites, Amorites, Perizzites, Jebusites tested Israel.
vv. 8-11	Israel, servant 8 years; cried to God; Othniel delivers them; peace for 40 years.
vv. 12-30	Israel, prisoner 18 years; Benjaminites kill 10,000 Moabites; peace for 80 years.
v. 31	Shamgar slays 600 Philistines with an ox goad.
Chapter 4	**Deborah and Barak's Victory over Sisera**
vv. 1-16	Prophetess Deborah and Barak with 10,000 warriors defeat Jabin and Sisera.
vv. 17-24	Jael, wife of Heber, put spike through Sisera's temple while sleeping in her tent.
Chapter 5	**Song of Deborah and Barak**
vv. 1-31	Deborah and Barak sing over Jabin and Sisera who held Israel captive for 20 years.
Chapter 6	**Midian Invades Israel.**
vv. 1-6	Israel sins; Midianites and Amalekites ravage land; Israel cries out to God for help.
vv. 7-10	God reminds Israelites of His help in past and rebukes them for disobedience.
vv. 11-18	God comes to Gideon to challenge him to rise against his oppressors.
vv. 19-24	Gideon prepares food for Angel of the Lord, Who blesses Gideon with peace."
vv. 25-27	Gideon, with 10 servants and a bull, removes town idols and altar of Baal at night.
vv. 28-32	Joash argues with townsmen for his son, Gideon's life.
vv. 33-35	Gideon calls for other tribes of Israel to join him in battle against Midianites.

vv. 36-40	Gideon gets two fleece signs from God before fighting Midianites and Amalekites.
Chapter 7	**Gideon Selects Army of Three Hundred Men.**
vv. 1-3	Jerubbaal, (Gideon) told by. God tells Gideon to reduce size of Israelite army from 22,000 to 10,000.
vv. 4-8	God further reduces army from 10,000 to 300 men.
vv. 9-14	Gideon is encouraged when he hears fearful conversation of enemy.
vv. 15-18	Gideon instructs 300 men God has given victory. He tells them what to do for battle.
vv. 19-23	Gideon and men win battle because they followed God's instructions.
vv. 24-25	Gideon's men slay the two Midianite princes, Oreb and Zeeb.
Chapter 8	**Gideon Slays Two Midianite Kings.**
vv. 1-3	Tribe of Ephraim criticizes Gideon but he flatters them with encouragement.
vv. 4-9	Gideon and 300 soldiers are refused food by towns of Succoth and Penuel.
vv. 10-12	After 120,000 killed, Gideon attacks Zebah and Zalmunnas' men, routing them.
vv. 13-17	Gideon returns and defeats men of Succoth and Penuel and breaks tower of Penuel.
vv. 18-21	Gideon kills Zebah and Zalmunna.
vv. 22-28	Gideon defeats Midian. Israelites have peace 40 years.
vv. 29-32	Gideon has 70 children and dies of a good old age in Ophrah.
vv. 33-35	Israel turns from God, forgetting what Gideon did for Israel.
Chapter 9	**Abimelech, Gideon's Son, Rules over Israel.**
vv. 1-6	Abimelech kills 68 of his brothers and became king in Shechem.
vv. 7-15	Jotham rebukes Shechemites for Abimelech by quoting prophetic riddle.

vv. 16-21	Jotham prophesizes judgment upon Shechem while Abimelech flees.
vv. 22-25	Men of Shechem deal treacherously with Abimelech by robbing passers-by.
vv. 26-29	Gaal conspires against Abimelech by winning people of Shechem over to him.
vv. 30-33	Zebul, ruler of Shechem, warns Abimelech about Gaal's insurrection against him.
vv. 34-41	Abimelech and Zebul drive out Gaal and his men from Shechem.
vv. 42-45	Abimelech continues battle next day by razing city and salting it.
vv. 46-49	Abimelech and his men set fire to Tower of Shechem killing 1000 people.
vv. 50-57	Abimelech tried to burn tower, woman drops millstone killing Abimelech.
Chapter 10	**Tola and Jair, Minor Judges of Israel**
vv. 1-2	Tola judges Israel for 23 years.
vv. 3-5	Jair, had thirty sons, ruled as judge in Israel for 22 years.
vv. 6-9	Israel oppressed 18 years, angering God by worshipping neighbor's pagan gods.
vv. 10-16	God exhorts Israel He will deliver no more saying, "Serve idols and cry to them."
vv. 17-18	Ammonites and Israelites prepare for battle against each other.
Chapter 11	**Jephthah Delivers Northeast Israel (Gilead).**
vv. 1-3	Jephthah, son of harlot fathered by Gilead, thrust out of family, lived at Tob.
vv. 4-11	Jephthah entreated to return to Gilead and be leader against Ammonites.
vv. 12-28	Jephthah sends messengers to King of Ammonites not to battle Israelites.
vv. 29-33	Jephthah makes a foolish vow to God but is blessed in victory over Ammonites.

vv. 34-40	Jephthah's daughter is offered as a sacrifice to God due to this foolish vow.
Chapter 12	**Jephthah's War with Ephraim**
vv. 1-6	Jephthah and Gileadites slay 42,000 men of Ephraim.
v. 7	Jephthah rules in Israel for six years and is buried in a city of Gilead.
vv. 8-10	Ibzan of Bethlehem judged Israel seven years. He had 30 sons and 30 daughters.
vv. 11-12	Elon judged Israel for 10 years, died and was buried at Aijalon in Zebulun.
vv. 13-15	Abdon, son of Hillel, who had 40 sons and 30 grandsons, judged Israel eight years.
Chapter 13	**Birth of Samson**
v. 1	Again, Israel sinned against God; He let Philistines rule them for 40 years.
vv. 2-7	Angel of Lord appeared to Manoah's wife saying she would have Nazarite son who would be a Nazarite.
vv. 8-14	Angel of God tells couple what to do regarding food and drink during pregnancy.
vv. 15-20	Manoah prepares burnt and cereal offering. Angel of God ascends in flames.
vv. 21-25	Samson born and Spirit of the Lord begins to stir in him at Mahanehdan.
Chapter 14	**Samson and Woman of Timnath**
vv. 1-3	Samson wants to marry Philistine woman.
v. 4	God uses incident to make war with Philistines, setting Israel free again.
vv. 5-9	Samson kills lion and eats honey found later in lion's carcass.
vv. 10-14	During wedding feast Samson gives riddle to 30 males for wager of 60 garments.
vv. 15-19	Samson's wife gives riddle to countrymen; Samson kills 30 Philistines to pay debt.

v. 20	Samson's wife is given to best man at wedding, in Samson's absence.
Chapter 15	**Samson's Revenge on Philistines**
vv. 1-3	Samson discovers his wife has been given to a Philistine while he was gone.
vv. 4-8	Samson burns grain fields of Philistines using 300 foxes' tails set on fire.
vv. 9-13	Three thousand men from Judah take Samson, bound by new ropes to Philistines.
vv. 14-17	Samson kills 1000 Philistines with the jawbone of an ass (donkey).
vv. 18-20	Samson is refreshed by water from God after battle and rules Israel 20 years.
Chapter 16	**Delilah's Betrayal of Samson**
vv. 1-3	Samson removes gate off wall and carries it to top of hill.
vv. 4-9	Delilah trys to find Samson's strength. Philistines offer her 1100 pieces of silver.
vv. 10-12	Samson lies to Delilah about his source of strength.
vv. 13-14	Again, Samson mocks Delilah as she seeks his source of strength.
vv. 15-17	Delilah presses Samson; he tells secret is his hair has never been cut.
vv. 18-22	Samson's hair is shorn; he is blinded; taken captive to Gaza to grind at mill.
vv. 23-27	Samson, taken to supported by two pillars. Philistines mock Samson.
vv. 28-31	Samson dies with Philistines killing more in death than in lifetime.
Chapter 17	**Micah's Image and Hired Levite Priest**
vv. 1-6	Micah steals 1100 pieces of silver from mother. He returns it and she makes idol.
vv. 7-13	Levite becomes Micah's priest for 10 pieces of silver, clothes with room and board.

Chapter 18	**Danites Steal Micah's Levitical Priest.**
vv. 1-6	Five Danite spies, seeking residence for tribe, inquire of Levite about God's will.
vv. 7-10	Five spies report that land of Laish is ripe for taking by Danites.
vv. 11-13	Dan's tribe of 600 warriors arrive at house of Micah.
vv. 14-20	Danites take Levite and Micah's images with them.
vv. 21-26	Micah follows Danites to retrieve idols but they were too strong for him.
vv. 27-31	Danites capture Laish and rename it Dan. Jonathan (son of Gershon) made priest.
Chapter 19	**Levite's Concubine and Benjamin's Crime**
vv. 1-9	Levite and concubine tarry too long with his father-in-law.
vv. 10-15	Levite journeys as far as Gibeah, a town of Benjaminites.
vv. 16-21	An old man from Ephraim invites Levite and group into his house.
vv. 22-26	Levites' concubine is sexually abused all night by Benjaminites until she dies.
vv. 27-30	Levite takes body to his house dividing it into 12 pieces to send through Israel.
Chapter 20	**Israel Wars against Benjamin.**
vv. 1-7	Israelite men numbering 400 gather at Mizpeh to hear about abused concubine.
vv. 8-11	Israelites prepare for war against Gibeah of Benjamin.
vv. 12-17	Benjaminites would not deliver Gibeah for their crime so war is imminent.
v. 18	Judah is selected by God to go first in battle against Benjamin.
vv. 19-28	Benjaminites slay 22,000 men of Judah and Israel.
vv. 24-28	Next battle Benjaminites kill 18,000. Israelites fast, pray, weep and offer sacrifices.
vv. 29-35	Third battle Israelites slaughter 25,100 Benjaminites; God gave them victory.

vv. 36-48	Israelites kill all but 600 Benjaminite warriors who fled to Rimmon.
Chapter 21	**Israel Seeks Wives for Benjaminites.**
vv. 1-7	Israelites mourn because 600 Benjaminites had no wives to keep their tribe alive.
vv. 8-12	Jabesh-gilead men did not fight Benjamin so were destroyed except 400 virgins.
vv. 13-15	The 600 Benjaminites marry four hundred virgins but need 200 more wives.
vv. 16-25	Remaining 200 Benjaminites catch 200 wives at "Feast of the Lord" at Shiloh.

RUTH

Chapter 1	**Naomi's Misfortunes and Ruth's Loyalty**
vv. 1-5	Naomi loses her husband and two sons in Moab.
vv. 6-14	Orphah returns to her people. Ruth joins Naomi's people.
vv. 15-18	Ruth returns with Naomi to Israel.
vv. 19-21	Naomi confesses that God has dealt strongly with her.
v. 22	Naomi and Ruth return to Bethlehem at beginning of barley harvest.
Chapter 2	**Ruth Gleans in Field of Boaz**
vv. 1-7	Boaz inquires about Ruth.
vv. 8-13	Boaz blesses Ruth because of her faithfulness to Naomi.
vv. 14-16	Boaz further blesses Ruth by giving her extra grain.
vv. 17-23	Ruth follows Naomi's instructions gleaning wheat and barley in Boaz's field.
Chapter 3	**Ruth Claims Boaz as Kinsman.**
vv. 1-5	Ruth does what Naomi instructs her.
vv. 6-13	Ruth does what Boaz coaches her to do.
vv. 14-18	Boaz continues to bless Ruth.
Chapter 4	**Boaz Marries Ruth.**
vv. 1-6	Boaz is permitted to redeem Elimelech's land and marry Ruth.
vv. 7-12	Boaz redeems Elimelech's land and receives blessings from people.
vv. 13-22	Hebrew Boaz and Gentile Ruth have sons Obed, Jesse and David.

1 SAMUEL

Chapter 1	**Birth of Samuel**
vv. 1-2	Elkanah's two wives, Hannah (childless) and Peninnah (with children)
vv. 3-8	Elkanah consoles Hannah who has not yet borne any children.
vv. 9-18	Hannah vows to give man child to God if He gives her a son. Eli blesses her desire.
vv. 19-28	Hannah gives Samuel to God to serve with Eli as a temple priest.
Chapter 2	**Sins of Eli's Two Sons**
vv. 1-11	Hannah praises God and leaves Samuel in temple to minister to the Lord.
vv. 12-17	Eli's two priestly sons treat burnt offerings with contempt.
vv. 18-21	Eli blessed Elkanah and wife who have five children after lending Samuel to God.
vv. 22-26	Eli reproves his two sons for their wickedness, but they refuse to obey him.
vv. 27-36	Eli is warned of sons' death and demise of family's priestly reign.
Chapter 3	**Call of Samuel**
vv. 1-9	God calls Samuel three times before Eli explains it is God calling him.
vv. 10-14	God tells Samuel that He will soon judge sins of Eli's household.
vv. 15-18	Samuel tells Eli what God said.
vv. 19-21	Samuel is established as a prophet of God.

Chapter 4	**Philistines defeat Israel.**
vv. 1-4	Israel loses 4,000 men in battle against Philistines.
vv. 5-9	Israelites bring Ark of Covenant into their war camp.
vv. 10-11	Israelite's 30,000 men die; Ark captured by Philistines; Hophni and Phinehas die.
vv. 12-18	Eli, aged 98, falls backward and dies of a broken neck on hearing capture of Ark.
vv. 19-22	Phinehas' wife dies, giving birth to a son named Ichabod.
Chapter 5	**Ark Among Philistines**
vv. 1-5	Ark causes Philistine god, Dagon, to fall, breaking off its head and hands.
vv. 6-12	Philistines fear Ark being afflicted with tumors and dying of bubonic plague.
Chapter 6	**Philistines Return Ark.**
vv. 1-9	Philistine priests tell leaders to send golden guilt offering with Ark back to Israel.
vv. 10-16	Two milk cows take Ark to Beth-shemesh in Israel.
vv. 17-18	Golden tumors placed by stone in field of Joshua at Beth-shemesh beside Ark.
vv. 19-21	Because 70 men looked into the Ark, they died.
Chapter 7	**Repentance and Victory at Mizpeh**
vv. 1-2	Ark taken to Kiriath-jearim to Abinadab's son to watch it. Ark stays for 20 years.
vv. 5-11	Samuel offers burnt offerings; cries to God Who delivers them.
vv. 12-14	Peace lasted between Israel, Philistia and Amorites rest of Samuel's judgeship.
vv. 15-17	Samuel built an altar to God in Ramah, his hometown.
Chapter 8	**Israel Wants King.**
vv. 1-3	Samuel appoints his two sons judges over Israel but they are unrighteous.
vv. 4-9	People want a king since Samuel's sons are corrupt judges.

vv. 10-18	Samuel warns people how it will affect them to have a king.
vv. 19-22	People insist on having a king to rule over them.

Chapter 9 — **Saul is Chosen as Israel's King.**

vv. 1-2	Saul, son of Kish, a Benjaminite, is handsome and taller than other young men.
vv. 3-4	Saul is sent to locate his father's donkeys.
vv. 5-10	They travel to Samuel's city to inquire about lost donkeys.
vv. 11-14	They see Samuel enroute to high place to make a sacrificial offering to God.
vv. 15-21	Samuel tells Saul donkeys are found. God says Saul will be Israel's captain.
vv. 22-24	Samuel gives best meat portion for Saul and servant during feast.
vv. 25-27	Samuel prepares to inform Saul what God has given him.

Chapter 10 — **Saul Anointed and Installed as King**

vv. 1-8	Samuel prophesies to Saul about future. Saul waits seven days till Samuel returns.
vv. 9-13	Saul prophesies as Samuel had predicted earlier.
vv. 14-16	Saul explains what Samuel revealed while sharing with his uncle.
vv. 17-19	Samuel prepares people at Mizpeh to receive their first king.
vv. 20-24	Samuel presents Saul from tribe of Benjamin as king of Israel.
vv. 25-27	Some men accept Saul while others reject him as their king.

Chapter 11 — **Saul Defeats Ammonites.**

vv. 1-4	Nahash, Ammonite leader, covenants with Jabesh-gilead if men will lose right eyes.
vv. 5-11	Saul defeats Ammonites and delivers Jabesh-gilead.
vv. 12-15	Samuel confirms Saul as King at Gilgal and Israelites rejoice.

Chapter 12 — **Samuel Rebukes Israel for Wanting a King.**

vv. 1-5	Israelites confess to Samuel that he has been righteous with them.

vv. 6-18	Samuel rebukes Israelites for wanting a king instead of God to rule them.
vv. 19-25	God is giving Israelites a king but exhorts them to put God first.

Chapter 13 — Saul's Disobedience to God at Gilgal

vv. 1-4	Saul summons Israelites to battle at Gilgal against Philistines.
vv. 5-7	Israelite army distressed when they see size of Philistine army.
vv. 8-12	Saul excuses himself to Samuel since he made an illegal priestly sacrifice.
vv. 13-18	Samuel reproves Saul telling him God will take his rule and give it to another.
vv. 19-23	Israelites have very little fighting equipment.

Chapter 14 — Jonathan's Victory over Philistines

vv. 1-5	Jonathan and armor-bearer plan to engage Philistines in warfare.
vv. 6-15	Jonathan and armor-bearer kill 20 Philistines causing them to panic.
vv. 16-23	Israelites scatter Philistines at Michmash.
vv. 24-30	Saul curses anyone breaking fast, but Jonathan breaks fast ignorantly.
vv. 31-35	People sin by eating meat with the blood in it.
vv. 36-42	Jonathan, because he ate forbidden food, proves to be guilty.
vv. 43-46	Soldiers plead for Jonathan so Saul spares Jonathan's life.
vv. 47-52	Saul's victories and family are mentioned in these verses.

Chapter 15 — Saul's Disobedience and Rejection as King

vv. 1-5	Saul prepares to battle Amalekites.
vv. 6-9	Saul spares best of cattle along with King Agag.
vv. 10-16	Samuel rebukes Saul for unfaithfulness to God.
vv. 17-23	Saul is rejected as king because of his greedy disobedience.
vv. 24-31	Saul confesses sin in humiliation.
vv. 32-35	Samuel slays Agag and God regrets that Saul was king.

Chapter 16	**Samuel Anoints David as King.**
vv. 1-5	God rejects Saul telling Samuel to anoint a son from Jesse's household.
vv. 6-13	Samuel anoints David king of Israel, Jesse's youngest and eighth son.
vv. 14-23	David becomes Saul's armor-bearer and harpist.
Chapter 17	**David Kills Goliath.**
vv. 1-11	Goliath, over nine feet tall, challenges Israel to send a soldier to fight him.
vv. 12-16	Goliath challenges Israel for 40 days.
vv. 17-18	Jesse sends David with provisions to his three older soldier brothers.
vv. 19-23	David hears Goliath's challenge.
vv. 24-27	David learns that the man who kills Goliath will be enriched by Saul.
vv. 28-30	Eliab rebukes David for asking questions about Goliath and war.
vv. 31-40	David prepares to fight Goliath.
vv. 41-47	David and Goliath verbally challenge each other in front of their armies.
vv. 48-49	David strikes Goliath in head with rock from sling, killing him.
vv. 50-54	David brings head of Goliath to Jerusalem.
vv. 55-58	David is taken by Abner to meet King Saul.
Chapter 18	**Saul Becomes Jealous of David.**
vv. 1-5	Saul sets David over Israelite army and Jonathan becomes David's covenant friend.
vv. 6-9	David receives more acclaim than Saul, making him jealous.
vv. 10-11	Evil spirit in Saul attempts to kill David with javelin.
vv. 12-16	Saul is afraid of David because God is with him.
vv. 17-19	Merab, Saul's eldest daughter, is given in marriage to Adriel instead of David.

vv. 20-30	Michal is given to David by Saul in marriage for 200 Philistine foreskins.
Chapter 19	**Saul Seeks to Kill David.**
vv. 1-7	Jonathan intercedes for David before King Saul and David is restored.
vv. 8-10	David again flees from Saul.
vv. 11-17	Michal helps David escape from King Saul.
vv. 18-24	Saul with his messengers prophesy before Samuel as they seek David.
Chapter 20	**Friendship Between David and Jonathan**
vv. 1-11	David shares with Jonathan his fear of Saul.
vv. 12-17	David and Jonathan renew their covenant of friendship with each other.
vv. 18-23	Jonathan warns David by shooting three arrows.
vv. 24-25	David's seat at the table was empty.
vv. 26-29	Jonathan excuses David's absence to King Saul.
vv. 30-34	Saul hurls spear to disgrace Jonathan for protecting David.
vv. 35-42	Jonathan and David weep knowing that Saul is intent on killing David.
Chapter 21	**David Flees to Nob and Later to Gath.**
vv. 1-6	Priest Ahimelech gives David "Bread of the Presence" to eat.
v. 7	Doeg, Edomite chief of Saul's herdsmen, saw what priest did for David.
vv. 8-9	David receives sword of Goliath from Ahimelech.
vv. 10-15	David feigns madness before King Achish of Gath.
Chapter 22	**David Escapes to Cave of Adullam.**
vv. 1-2	David leads 400 malcontent men.
vv. 3-5	David takes his parents to Moab as he flees to Judah.
vv. 6-10	Doeg testifies to Saul against Ahimelech, priest of Nob.
vv. 11-19	Saul orders Doeg to kill Ahimelech, 84 priests and people of Nob, city of priests.

vv. 20-23	Abiathar, son of Ahimelech escapes to warn David.
Chapter 23	**David Delivers City of Keilah.**
vv. 1-5	David defeats Philistines who are robbing Keilah.
vv. 6-14	The Lord tells David and now 600 men to flee Keilah, escaping Saul.
vv. 15-18	Jonathan encourages David by renewing their covenant.
vv. 19-24	Ziphites tell Saul where David is hiding.
vv. 25-29	Saul, nearing David, returns to Israel to fight attacking Philistines.
Chapter 24	**David Spares Saul's Life.**
vv. 1-7	David will not kill King Saul because Saul is God's anointed.
vv. 8-15	David explains why Saul's life is spared.
vv. 16-22	Saul acknowledges David will one day be king of Israel.
Chapter 25	**David, Nabal and Abigail**
v. 1	Samuel dies and is buried at Ramah.
vv. 2-8	David asks provisions from Nabal for a feast day.
vv. 9-13	Nabal refuses provisions. David leads 400 of his men to fight Nabal and his men.
vv. 14-17	A servant warns Abigail how Nabal answered David's men.
vv. 18-22	Abigail hastens to meet David giving him provisions his 600 men.
vv. 23-31	Abigail intercedes for foolish Nabal, giving honor to David.
vv. 32-35	David accepts Abigail's apology for Nabal's arrogance.
vv. 36-38	God smites Nabal and he dies.
vv. 39-42	Abigail becomes David's wife.
vv. 43-44	David takes another wife. Saul gives Michal to Palti, son of Laish.
Chapter 26	**David Again Spares Saul's Life.**
vv. 1-5	Saul encamps around David.
vv. 6-12	David takes Saul's spear but spares his life.
vv. 13-16	David chides Abner for not guarding King Saul.

vv. 17-20	David pleads with Saul to stop pursuing him.
vv. 21-25	Saul acknowledges sin against David and goes home.
Chapter 27	**David Lives among Philistines.**
vv. 1-4	David escapes to Philistine land.
vv. 5-7	David lives in Ziklag for 16 months.
vv. 8-12	Achish thinks David is against Israelites but he's fighting Philistines.
Chapter 28	**Saul Consults Medium of Endor.**
vv. 1-2	Achish takes David to be bodyguard as he fights Israelites.
vv. 3-7	Saul seeks a witch for counsel since God won't speak with him.
vv. 8-14	Witch brings Samuel's spirit up from grave.
vv. 15-19	Samuel prophesies Saul's defeat and death by Philistines.
vv. 20-25	Saul is refreshed and revived by food before leaving.
Chapter 29	**Philistines Reject David's Help.**
vv. 1-5	Other Philistines distrust David.
vv. 6-11	Achish dismisses David and men to return to Ziklag.
Chapter 30	**David and Amalekites**
vv. 1-6	David returns home finding disaster but strengthens himself in the Lord.
vv. 7-10	David asks God's permission to pursue Amalekites.
vv. 11-15	David gets directions to Amalekites from Egyptian servant.
vv. 16-20	David recovers captives and spoils from Amalekites.
vv. 21-25	David shares loot with 200 men who stayed behind with baggage.
vv. 26-31	David shares plunder with friends in cities of Judah.
Chapter 31	**Death of Saul and His Sons**
vv. 1-7	Philistines defeat Israelites and kill Saul's sons; Saul and armor-bearer die- suicide.
vv. 8-13	Valiant men of Jabesh-gilead take bodies of Saul and sons to bury them in Jabesh.

2 SAMUEL

Chapter 1	**Lament Over Saul and Jonathan**
vv. 1-10	Amalekite takes news of Saul and Jonathan's death to David.
vv. 11-16	David has young men kill Amalekite for slaying. King Saul.
vv. 17-27	David sings a song honoring King Saul and Prince Jonathan.
Chapter 2	**David made King over Judah.**
vv. 1-4	David is anointed king in Hebron.
vv. 5-7	David credits men of Jabesh-gilead for honorably burying Saul and sons.
vv. 8-11	Abner makes Saul's son, Ishbosheth, king of Israel.
vv. 12-17	Abner's men are beaten by David and Joab's army.
vv. 18-23	Abner slays Asahel, Joab's younger brother.
vv. 24-28	Joab stops pursuing Abner and Benjaminites.
vv. 29-32	David lost 20 men but Abner lost 360 Benjaminites.
Chapter 3	**David grows stronger; Saul's household becomes weaker.**
v. 1	David's army grows stronger.
vv. 2-5	David's six sons are born by his six wives.
vv. 6-11	Abner rejects Ishbosheth as king of Israel.
vv. 12-16	David demands first wife, Michal, returned to him.
vv. 17-19	Abner asks Israel and Benjamin to accept David as king.
vv. 20-21	David and Abner meet peacefully.
vv. 22-25	Joab reproaches David for allowing Abner to leave peacefully.
vv. 26-30	Joab and Abishai deceitfully slay Abner. David curses Joab's family.
vv. 31-39	David weeps and fasts for Abner. Israelites respect him for honor given Abner.

Chapter 4	**Ishbosheth murdered by Israelites and Revenged by David.**
vv. 1-3	Ishbosheth's courage fails, hearing of Abner's death.
v. 4	Mephibosheth's nurse flees, carrying him and falls, crippling him.
vv. 5-8	Rechab and Baanah slay Ishbosheth and carry his head to David.
vv. 9-12	David has these two men slain then buries Ishbosheth in Abner's tomb at Hebron.
Chapter 5	**David is Made King of all Israel.**
vv. 1-5	David anointed king, reigning 7 1/2 years in Judah and 33 years over all Israel.
vv. 6-10	David defeats Jebusites making Jerusalem city of David.
vv. 11-12	King Hiram of Tyre helps David build Jerusalem.
vv. 13-16	David takes wives and concubines in Jerusalem. He has a total 17 children.
vv. 17-21	David defeats Philistines at Baal-perazim.
vv. 22-25	David again defeats Philistines as the Lord gives him victory.
Chapter 6	**Ark is brought to Jerusalem.**
vv. 1-5	David with 30,000 men brings Ark of the Covenant from Abinadab's house.
vv. 6-11	Uzzah steadies Ark when oxen stumbled. God slays Uzzah for touching Ark.
vv. 12-15	Later people rejoice when David brings Ark from Obed-edom's house to Jerusalem.
vv. 16-19	David dances before the Lord in a linen ephod while Michal despises him.
vv. 20-23	God shuts Michal's womb for despising one who worships Him with all his might.
Chapter 7	**God's Covenant with King David**
vv. 1-3	David tells Nathan he wants to build a house for the Ark of the Lord.

vv. 4-17	God secures David's throne forever through his descendants.
vv. 18-29	David worships God for promising him a throne on earth forever.

Chapter 8 — **David Extends His Kingdom.**

v. 1	David subdues Philistines.
v. 2	Moabites become servants of David.
vv. 3-8	David defeats Hadadezer and slays 22,000 Syrians helping Hadadezer.
vv. 9-12	Toi, king of Hamath sends gifts to David for defeating his enemy, Hadadezer.
vv. 13-14	David slays 18,000 Edomites.
vv. 15-18	David sets chosen men as officials in his government.

Chapter 9 — **David's Kindness to Mephibosheth**

vv. 1-8	David restores all of Saul's land to Mephibosheth.
vv. 9-13	Lame Mephibosheth eats at David's table. Ziba becomes Mephibosheth's servant.

Chapter 10 — **Defeat of Ammonites and Syrians**

vv. 1-5	Ammonites shame David's messengers to comfort Hanun during his father's death.
vv. 6-8	Ammonites seek help from other kings as they prepare for war against David.
vv. 9-14	Joab and Abishai defeat Ammonites and Syrians.
vv. 15-19	David slays 700 charioteers, 40,000 Syrian horsemen and army leader, Shobach.

Chapter 11 — **David's Sin against Uriah**

v. 1	When Israel goes to war David remains in Jerusalem.
vv. 2-5	Bathsheba provokes David. They commit adultery and she conceives a son.
vv. 6-13	Uriah will not sleep with his wife since other soldiers are fighting Ammonites.
vv. 14-21	Joab puts Uriah where Ammonites could kill him.
vv. 22-25	David receives message from Joab that Uriah is dead.

vv. 26-27	David marries Bathsheba. God is displeased with David's actions.

Chapter 12 — **Nathan Rebukes King David.**

vv. 1-6	Nathan quotes parable to David, who orders man to restore 4x to poor man.
vv. 7-14	Nathan accuses David; he acknowledges his sin; God judges David; the baby dies.
vv. 15-23	David fasts and prays until baby dies. Afterward, David eats a meal.
vv. 24-25	God forgives David. Second baby lives who later becomes king.
vv. 26-31	David subdues Ammonites and puts them to work at forced labor.

Chapter 13 — **Ammon's Abuse of Tamar**

vv. 1-6	Ammon strategizes to get Tamar into his bedroom.
vv. 7-14	Ammon rapes Tamar, his half-sister.
vv. 15-19	Tamar leaves Ammon's house in disgrace.
vv. 20-22	Absalom hates his half-brother, Ammon, for raping his sister, Tamar.
vv. 23-29	Absalom has Ammon murdered at his banquet.
vv. 30-33	Jonadab, Absalom's cousin, tells uncle King David that Ammon is dead.
vv. 34-36	King David and servants weep at message of Ammon's death by Absalom.
vv. 37-39	King David mourns for Absalom who fled to Geshur for three years.

Chapter 14 — **Joab's Scheme for Absalom's Return**

vv. 1-3	Joab plans to manipulate King David by using a woman mourner.
vv. 4-7	Woman creates a parable to tell King David as requested by Joab.
vv. 8-11	Woman gets David's protection against injustice in her parable.

vv. 12-17	Woman explains parable to David saying two sons are Ammon and Absalom.
vv. 18-20	David knows that Joab uses woman for Absalom's return.
vv. 21-24	David tells Joab to bring Absalom to Jerusalem but refuses to see Absalom.
vv. 25-27	People admire Absalom for his good looks.
vv. 28-33	Absalom finally gets to see King David, his father.
Chapter 15	**Absalom Revolts Against David.**
vv. 1-6	Absalom steals affection of Israel from King David.
vv. 7-12	Absalom plans a scheme against David to become King of Israel.
vv. 13-18	King David and his people flee from his son, Absalom.
vv. 19-23	David leaves Jerusalem. Ittai and others devoted to David flee with him.
vv. 24-29	David tells Priest Zadok to keep Ark of the Covenant in Jerusalem till he returns.
vv. 30-31	Ahithophel conspires with Absalom against King David.
vv. 32-37	Hushai confuses Ahithophel's counsel to Absalom as he enters Jerusalem.
Chapter 16	**Injustices of Ziba and Shimei**
vv. 1-4	Ziba accuses his master; David hastily gives Mephibosheth's property to Ziba.
vv. 5-8	Shimei curses David as he and his people flee Jerusalem.
vv. 9-14	David restrains his men from killing Shimei.
vv. 15-19	Counselor Hushai ingratiates himself to Absalom in order to help David.
vv. 20-23	Ahithophel counsels Absalom to take David's concubines.
Chapter 17	**Hushai Frustrates Ahithophel's Counsel.**
vv. 1-4	Ahithophel counsels Absalom to take 12,000 men and kill David while he is weary.
vv. 5-14	Hushai's counsel defeats Ahithophel's, causing Absalom to attack later.

vv. 15-20	Hushai's message reaches Ahimaaz, hiding until Absalom ceases searching for him.
vv. 21-22	Two men warn David to cross Jordan River to be safe from Absalom's men.
v. 23	Ahithophel realizing his counsel is not followed, returns home and hangs himself.
vv. 24-26	Absalom puts Amasa in charge of army to pursue David by crossing Jordan.
vv. 27-29	Shobi, David's friend, brings food and provisions to David and his men.
Chapter 18	**David's Troops Defeat Absalom's.**
vv. 1-5	David divides his army into three groups, sending them to battle.
vv. 6-8	David's men defeat Israel, killing 20,000 in the forest of Ephraim.
vv. 9-15	Joab and his ten armor-bearers kill Absalom while he was caught in a tree.
vv. 16-18	Joab's men bury Absalom in a pit, heaping stones over him.
vv. 19-23	Joab sends two runners with a message to King David concerning battle.
vv. 24-27	Watchman observes two runners and tells King David.
vv. 28-30	Ahimaaz reports on battle but has no knowledge of Absalom's death.
vv. 31-33	David grieves when the Cushite tells him of Absalom's death.
Chapter 19	**David Ceases Mourning and Returns to Jerusalem.**
vv. 1-8	Joab rebukes David for making soldiers feel sad for winning battle.
vv. 9-10	Defeated Israelites desire to bring King David back to Jerusalem.
vv. 11-15	Judah crosses Jordan River to escort David back to Jerusalem as their king.

vv. 16-23	David spares Shimei who had cursed him as David fled Jerusalem.
vv. 24-30	Mephibosheth explains that Ziba, his servant, deceived him as well as King David.
vv. 31-40	David blesses 80-year-old Barzil'lai, for providing food to his men as they fled city.
vv. 41-43	Judah and Israel debate who should have brought David back to Jerusalem.
Chapter 20	**Sheba Revolts Against David.**
vv. 1-3	Sheba, a Benjaminite, and men of Israel withdraw from David.
v. 3	David encloses his ten concubines Absalom molested. He cares for them as widows.
vv. 4-10	David appoints Amasa head of army not Joab, who kills Amasa.
vv. 11-13	Joab and Abishai pursue Sheba, son of Bichri.
vv. 14-22	A woman saves city by inciting people to kill Sheba; she gives his head to Joab.
vv. 23-26	Again, Joab is in command of Israel's army.
Chapter 21	**War with Philistines**
vv. 1-6	Saul's killing innocent Gibeonites results in 7of Saul's descendants being hung.
vv. 7-9	Two sons and 5 grandsons were hung by Gibeonites. David spared Mephibosheth.
vv. 10-14	David takes bones of 7 men with Saul and family and buries all in tomb of Kish.
vv. 15-17	Abishai saves David in battle with Philistines by killing giant Ishbi-benob.
vv. 18-22	David's servants kill giants in other wars with Philistines.
Chapter 22	**David's Song of Deliverance**
vv. 1-6	David praises God for delivering him from King Saul.
vv. 7-16	David cries to God to scatter his enemies.
vv. 17-20	God delivers David because He delights in David.

vv. 21-25	God recompenses David for his uprightness.
vv. 26-31	God protects all who put their trust in Him.
vv. 32-43	God our Lord delivers us from our enemies.
v. 44-46	God delivers from strife with people.
vv. 47-49	God delivers from men of violence.
vv. 50-51	God shows His steadfast love to His anointed ones.
Chapter 23	**David's Mighty Men**
vv. 1-7	David sings hymn of praise concerning God's covenant with his household.
v. 8	Josheb-Basshe-beth killed 800 men at one time.
vv. 9-10	Eleazar stood with David defying Philistines when other Israelites withdrew.
vv. 11-12	Shammah stood and slew Philistines when others withdrew.
vv. 13-17	These three men risked their lives, bringing David water from Bethlehem.
vv. 18-19	Abishai, who slew 300 men, was chief of 30 but did not attain to first three.
vv. 20-23	Benaiah, leader of David's bodyguard, slew two Moabites, an Egyptian and a lion.
vv. 24-39	David lists 37 of his finest warriors in Israel's army.
Chapter 24	**David's Census of Israel**
vv. 1-9	God moves David to number warriors; Israel has 800,000 men and Judah 500,000.
vv. 10-14	David's choice: 3 years famine, 3 months fleeing enemy or 3 days plague for census.
vv. 15-17	David repents of taking census when he sees the Lords's angel killing his people.
vv. 18-25	David builds altar and sacrifices burnt offerings to God, thus stopping plague.

1 KINGS

Chapter 1	**Solomon, Not Adonijah, Anointed King.**
vv. 1-4	David grows old; servants get Abishag to warm but not sleep with David.
vv. 5-8	Adonijah endeavors to make himself successor to King David.
vv. 9-10	Adonijah invites brothers except Solomon to his inaugural ceremony.
vv. 11-14	Nathan warns Bathsheba that Adonijah is seeking to be king instead of Solomon.
vv. 15-21	Bathsheba tells David what Adonijah is doing to make himself king.
vv. 22-27	Prophet Nathan warns David that Adonijah is proclaiming himself Israel's king.
vv. 28-31	David swears to Bathsheba that Solomon will be next king of Israel.
vv. 32-37	David gathers leaders, exhorting them to anoint Solomon, proclaiming him king.
vv. 38-40	Solomon rides on David's mule as Zadok, Nathan, Benaiah proclaim Solomon king.
vv. 41-48	Jonathan warns Adonijah that David has proclaimed Solomon as next king.
vv. 49-53	Adonijah bows to King Solomon and is fearful for his life.
Chapter 2	**Death of King David**
vv. 1-4	David counsels Solomon concerning kingdom's future.
vv. 5-9	David warns Solomon against Joab and Shimei who treated David deceitfully.
vv. 10-12	David dies at age 70 after ruling over Hebron and Jerusalem.

vv. 13-18	Adonijah asks Bathsheba for David's former concubine, Abishag.
vv. 19-25	Solomon kills Adonijah for requesting David's concubine who belongs to the king.
vv. 26-27	Solomon sends Abiathar into exile and removes his priesthood.
vv. 28-35	Benaiah slays Joab and Zadok replaces Abiathar as priest.
vv. 36-38	Solomon orders Shimei to stay in Jerusalem or he will die.
vv. 39-46	Benaiah slays Shimei who disobeys Solomon by leaving city.
Chapter 3	**Solomon's Prayer for Understanding**
vv. 1-2	Solomon takes an Egyptian wife; Israelites continue worshipping idols.
vv. 3-9	Solomon asks God for wisdom to govern Israel.
vv. 10-14	God blesses Solomon with riches, wisdom and long life.
v. 15	Solomon makes a banquet for his servants.
vv. 16-22	Two harlots argue before Solomon as to ownership of live son.
vv. 23-28	King Solomon discerns rightful mother.
Chapter 4	**Solomon's Organization of His Kingdom**
vv. 1-6	Officials both civil and religious are named in these verses.
v. 7-19	Solomon appoints 12 officers to provide food for each month of year.
vv. 20-21	People of Judah and Israel are happy with their new king.
vv. 22-28	These verses list daily provisions of food for Solomon and his servants.
vv. 29-34	Solomon's wisdom surpasses all wisdom of eastern kings and wise men.
Chapter 5	**Solomon's Agreement with King Hiram**
vv. 1-6	Solomon requests King Hiram to cut cedar trees for building temple in Jerusalem.
vv. 7-12	Solomon provides food for Hiram who in turn provides wood for Solomon's temple.

vv. 13-18	Solomon recruits thousands of workers to build temple.
Chapter 6	**Solomon Builds Temple.**
vv. 1-6	Description of temple is recorded in these verses.
v. 7	No sound of building tools was heard at temple site.
vv. 8-10	Temple was furnished with beautiful beams of cedar.
vv. 11-13	The Lord promises to dwell with Israelites as long as they obey Him.
vv. 14-22	Temple was overlaid with cedar and cypress wood as well as gold.
vv. 23-28	Cherubim were made of olive wood and overlaid with pure gold.
vv. 29-30	Walls were of carved figures and floor overlaid with gold.
vv. 31-32	Entrance to sanctuary had doors of olive wood overlaid with gold.
vv. 33-36	Walls and doors had carvings of cherubim, palm trees and flowers overlaid with gold.
vv. 37-38	Solomon built temple in 7 years.
Chapter 7	**Other Buildings of Solomon**
v. 1	Solomon finishes his own house in 13 years.
vv. 2-5	He built house from forest of Lebanon; it was partly used to store weapons.
v. 6	He made a porch of pillars connecting house of forest with porch of judgment.
v. 7	He made a porch of judgment where he sat to make judicial decisions.
v. 8	Solomon's palace probably joined porch of judgment.
vv. 9-12	These buildings were made of costly stones.
vv. 13-14	Hiram from Tyre, did bronze work (Not same man as King Hiram).
vv. 15-22	Hiram constructs two pillars of bronze 18 feet around and 35 feet high.
vv. 23-26	"Molten Sea" is 45 feet in circumference, holding 18,000 gallons of water for priests.

vv. 27-37	The 10 stands support 10 washbasins or lavers.
vv. 38-39	Each laver held 240 gallons of water.
vv. 40-44	Hiram finished his work by making pots, shovels and basins.
vv. 45-47	Due to so many bronze vessels, Solomon left them all un-weighed.
vv. 48-50	Solomon finished making all of vessels that were in house of the Lord.
v. 51	Solomon brought things David dedicated, storing them in house of the Lord.
Chapter 8	**Solomon Dedicates Temple.**
vv. 1-11	Cloud fills temple; Solomon sacrifices, preparing to dedicate house of the Lord.
vv. 12-21	Solomon dedicates temple that he built for God to inhabit.
vv. 22-30	Solomon entreats God to hear his prayer, forgiving from His heavenly dwelling.
vv. 31-32	Judge innocent and guilty, vindicating righteous and condemning unrighteous.
vv. 33-34	When Israel repents and turns back to God, please restore Israel to their land.
vv. 35-36	When Israel repents and turns again to You, please let rain fall upon their land.
vv. 37-40	If famine, plague or pestilence come, please forgive and restore us to our land.
vv. 41-43	Bless foreigners who come to Israel to learn of God when they pray to You.
vv. 44-45	Bless army of Israel when they pray to You in battle.
vv. 46-53	Forgive all coming to You asking for forgiveness; for all have sinned.
vv. 54-61	Solomon asks God to help their cause as they walk in His commandments.
vv. 62-64	King's peace offerings are 22,000 oxen and 120,000 sheep for temple dedication.
vv. 65-66	This feast was celebrated for 7 days all over Israel.

Chapter 9	**God's Covenant with Solomon**
vv. 1-9	God promises to bless or curse, depending on what Solomon does in obedience.
vv. 10-14	King Hiram does not appreciate 20 cities Solomon gives him instead of money.
vv. 15-22	Solomon made Amorites, Hittites, Perizzites, Hivites and Jebusites forced slaves.
v. 23	Solomon used 550 chief officers of Israel to oversee all workers.
v. 24	Pharaoh's daughter leaves Jerusalem to live in palace Solomon built for her in Millo.
v. 25	Solomon offers burnt and peace offerings on altar three times each year.
vv. 26-28	Solomon's and Hiram's sailors go to Ophir to get 31,500 pounds of gold.
Chapter 10	**Queen of Sheba Visits Solomon.**
vv. 1-5	Solomon answers Queen of Sheba's questions until she had no more spirit in her.
vv. 6-10	Queen of Sheba gives Solomon 9000 pounds of gold and spices for his treasuries.
vv. 11-12	Hiram's navy brought Solomon quantities of almug wood and precious stones.
vv. 13-14	Solomon gave to Queen of Sheba all she desired before returning to her country.
vv. 14-22	Gold for Solomon yearly was 49,950 pounds or 20 billion dollars plus valuables.
vv. 23-25	Each year kings came to meet Solomon presenting gifts to him.
vv. 26-29	Solomon had 1400 chariots and 12,000 horsemen.
Chapter 11	**Solomon's Apostasy and God's Anger**
vv. 1-8	Solomon disobeys God, worshipping idols that turn him from God.

vv. 9-13	God promises to take kingdom from Solomon for this apostasy.
vv. 14-22	God raises Hadad the Edomite to war against Solomon.
vv. 23-25	God raises Rezon, King of Damascus, to come against Solomon.
vv. 26-40	Ahijah tells Jeroboam he will rule 10 tribes due to Solomon's apostasy.
vv. 41-43	Solomon reigned 40 years and at his death, Rehoboam becomes king.

Chapter 12 — Israel Revolts Against Rehoboam.

vv. 1-5	Israelites ask Rehoboam to lighten heavy load Solomon placed on them.
vv. 6-11	Rehoboam forsakes counsel of elders and accepts counsel of younger men.
vv. 12-15	The Lord leads Rehoboam to give wrong counsel to Israel.
vv. 16-20	Jeroboam is made king of Israel; Rehoboam, king only of Judah.
vv. 21-24	Rehoboam prepares 180,000 warriors; Shemaiah tells him this revolt is from God.
vv. 25-33	Jeroboam continues turning Israelites from God.

Chapter 13 — Prophets Turn Against Jeroboam.

vv. 1-10	A prophet pronounces doom over Jeroboam's altars.
vv. 11-19	Elder prophet deceives God's prophet sent from Judah.
vv. 20-25	Elder prophet prophecies doom to younger prophet from Judah; a lion kills him.
vv. 26-32	Elder prophet buries man of God from Judah in his tomb.
vv. 33-34	Jeroboam consecrates anyone who desires to be a priest in Israel.

Chapter 14 — Jeroboam Is Condemned.

vv. 1-3	Jeroboam sends his wife to Prophet Ahijah to learn outcome of sick son, Abijah.
vv. 4-16	Prophet Ahijah tells Jeroboam's wife their son shall die; Israel shall be defeated.

vv. 17-20	Child dies and after 22 years, Jeroboam dies; Nadab, his son, reigns in Israel.
vv. 21-24	Rehoboam dies at age 58 after ruling Judah for 17 years.
vv. 25-28	Shishak, King of Egypt, raids treasures of palace and gold shields from guardroom.
vv. 29-31	After Rehoboam dies, his son, Abijam, rules Judah.
Chapter 15	**War between Israel and Judah**
vv. 1-8	Abijam rules Judah three years and dies; Asa, his son, reigns in Abijam's place.
vv. 9-15	Asa rules Judah for 41 years, wholly following after God.
vv. 16-24	Asa with aid from Syria stops Israel from building a fortress in Ramah.
vv. 25-26	Nadab follows Jeroboam as Israel's king, reigning only 2 years.
vv. 27-30	God uses Baasha, son of Ahijah, to kill Nadab and Jeroboam's heirs to throne.
vv. 31-34	Baasha rules Israel 24 years, ruling as an evil king as Jeroboam, preceding him.
Chapter 16	**Reigns of Baasha, Elah, Zimri and Omri**
vv. 1-4	Jehu prophesies against Baasha and tells of his doom.
vv. 5-7	Baasha dies and his son Elah rules Israel.
vv. 8-10	Zimri, officer of half of Israel's chariots, assassinates Elah who only rules 2 years.
vv. 11-14	God fulfills His Word by having Zimri kill all of Baasha's descendants.
vv. 15-20	Zimri rules 7 days, and dies; Omri attacks Zimri's city to kill him.
vv. 21-24	Omri kills Tibni, becomes king, for 12 years. He makes Samaria capital of Israel.
vv. 25-29	Omri dies then his son, wicked king Ahab, reigns in Samaria.
vv. 29-34	Ahab is most evil king to date. His wife, Jezebel, a Sidonian, is also very evil.

Chapter 17	**Elijah and Famine in Israel**
vv. 1-7	Elijah tells Ahab of coming drought; rain will come only by Elijah's word.
vv. 8-16	Elijah, a widow and her son have oil and meal during famine.
vv. 17-24	Elijah prays for widow's dead son who comes back to life.
Chapter 18	**Contest on Mount Carmel**
vv. 1-6	Ahab and Obadiah search for springs to water Ahab's livestock.
vv. 7-16	Elijah exhorts Obadiah to bring King Ahab for meeting.
vv. 17-19	Elijah challenges Ahab to bring Jezebel's 850 prophets to Mr. Carmel.
vv. 20-29	Baal's 450 prophets receive no response for fire upon sacrificed bull.
vv. 30-35	Elijah asks people to pour water three times over his sacrifice.
vv. 36-40	God sends fire upon Elijah's sacrifice. Elijah slays 450 prophets of Baal.
vv. 41-46	God sends rain upon land as Elijah outruns Ahab's chariot to Jezreel.
Chapter 19	**Elijah Flees from Jezebel to Mount Horeb.**
vv. 1-3	Elijah flees to Beersheba in Judah since Jezebel vows to kill him.
vv. 4-8	Elijah, nourished with meal cakes and water; he stays 40 days on Mount Horeb.
vv. 9-18	Elijah anoints Hazael as Syria's king, Jehu as Israel's king and Elisha as Prophet.
vv. 19-21	Elijah casts his mantle over Elisha as he follows Elijah.
Chapter 20	**Benhadad Wars against Ahab.**
vv. 1-6	Benhadad tells Ahab "the gold, silver and your fairest wives are mine!"
vv. 7-12	Ahab exhorts Benhadad to not boast of victory until after a battle, not before.

vv. 13-15	Israeli Prophet tells Ahab to organize governors and warriors to begin battle.
vv. 16-18	Ahab's servants with soldiers go to fight Benhadad with 32 kings and soldiers.
vv. 19-22	Israel defeats Benhadad but Syrians will return in spring for another siege.
vv. 23-25	Benhadad replaces kings with commanders planning war in spring in the valley.
vv. 26-30	Israelites kill 100,000 Syrians; 27,000 die in Aphek as wall falls on them.
vv. 31-34	Ahab spares Benhadad's life after concessions are made to Israel.
vv. 35-43	Prophet pronounces doom on Ahab and Israel for letting Benhadad escape alive.

Chapter 21 — **Ahab and Naboth's Vineyard**

vv. 1-4	Naboth refuses to sell his vineyard to Ahab because it is his inheritance.
vv. 5-7	Jezebel reassures Ahab she will get Naboth's vineyard for him.
vv. 8-14	Jezebel has Naboth killed on false charges resulting in his being stoned to death.
vv. 15-16	Jezebel tells Ahab that Naboth is dead.
vv. 17-19	Elijah tells Ahab dogs will lick Ahab's blood where Naboth was killed.
vv. 20-24	Elijah pronounces severe judgment on family of Ahab and Jezebel.
vv. 25-26	No king and queen were as evil as Ahab and Jezebel; she incited him to do evil.
vv. 27-29	Ahab humbled himself before God. This judgment came in the days of his son.

Chapter 22 — **Death of Ahab**

v. 1-4	Ahab and Jehoshaphat plan to battle Syria and retake Ramoth-Gilead.

vv. 5-12	The 400 false prophets tell Ahab what he desires to hear about victory over Syria.
vv. 13-23	Micaiah prophesies Ahab's defeat and death; false prophets have lying spirits.
vv. 24-28	Micaiah put in prison because he prophesies truthfully to King Ahab.
vv. 29-36	A stray arrow causes Ahab to die in his chariot.
vv. 37-40	Ahab is buried in Samaria and Ahaziah reigns in Ahab's place.
vv. 41-44	Jehoshaphat ruled 25 years over Judah, serving God.
vv. 45-46	Jehoshaphat exterminated cult of male prostitutes in Judah.
vv. 47-50	Jehoram reigned after Jehoshaphat died.
vv. 51-53	Ahaziah an evil king like Ahab and Jezebel served Israel as king two years.

2 KINGS

Chapter 1	**Death of Ahaziah**
vv. 1-4	Elijah rebukes Ahaziah's messengers who inquired of god of Ekron, Baalzebub.
vv. 5-8	Messengers tell Ahaziah that he will die.
vv. 9-10	Elijah sends fire killing 50 soldiers of Ahaziah.
vv. 11-12	Another 50 soldiers sent to capture Elijah are consumed by fire.
vv. 13-16	Elijah spares third captain's 50 men and reports to Ahaziah.
vv. 17-18	Jehoram succeeds brother, King Ahaziah, of Israel who had no son.
Chapter 2	**Angels Take Elijah to Heaven.**
vv. 1-11	Elijah goes to heaven in whirlwind. Elisha seeks double portion of Elijah's spirit.
vv. 12-18	Elisha divides Jordan with Elijah's mantle.
vv. 19-25	Elisha recognized as God's prophet of authority.
Chapter 3	**Jehoram Reigns in Israel.**
vv. 1-3	Jehoram sins less than father and mother.
vv. 4-8	Israel and Judah agree to fight Moab who has rebelled against Israel.
vv. 9-12	Kings of Israel and Judah seek Elisha's counsel concerning war with Moab.
vv. 13-20	Elisha predicts victory over Moab.
vv. 21-27	Moab is defeated because Israelites obey God's prophet.
Chapter 4	**Widow's Oil and Shunammite Woman's Son**
vv. 1-7	God's miracle of filling oil pots for widow pays her rent.
vv. 8-17	Elisha prays for Shunammite woman to have a child.

vv. 18-26	Shunammite woman believes even though her son is dead, he will be restored.
vv. 27-31	Gehazi precedes Elisha, prays for boy, with no results.
vv. 32-37	Elisha raises the boy from death.
vv. 38-41	Elisha cures poisonous food in the pot.
vv. 42-44	God meets needs of all the people.
Chapter 5	**Cure of Naaman's Leprosy**
vv. 1-5	King of Syria prepares letter for King of Israel.
vv. 6-7	King of Israel fears a war with Syria.
vv. 8-14	Naaman humbles himself and healed of leprosy.
vv. 15-19	Elisha refuses Naaman's gifts.
vv. 20-27	Gehazi's greedy lying causes him and descendants to be lepers.
Chapter 6	**Syrian Army Blinded and Captured.**
vv. 1-7	Ax head made to float.
vv. 8-14	King of Syria tries to capture Prophet Elisha.
vv. 15-19	Elisha prays, Syrians blinded and led to Samaria.
vv. 20-23	Elisha and King of Israel feed captives and send them home.
vv. 24-29	Siege of Samaria by King Benhadad of Syria
vv. 30-33	Benhadad seeks Elisha's life. Elisha prophesies this fact.
Chapter 7	**Elisha Prophesies Food for Samaria.**
vv. 1-4	Elisha prophesies food tomorrow. God allows four lepers to discover food.
vv. 5-8	God puts fear in Syrians. They flee and lepers find spoils.
vv. 9-15	Israel's king sends messengers to confirm report of four lepers.
vv. 16-20	Officer who doubted Elisha's prophecy dies as crowd tramples him to get spoils.
Chapter 8	**Again Elisha helps Shunammite Woman.**
vv. 1-6	Shunammite woman has property restored after seven-year famine.
vv. 7-15	Elisha predicts Benhadad's death and Hazael's wicked rule over Syria.

vv. 16-24	Jehoram, age 32, reigns over Judah eight years, while Joram reigns in Israel.
vv. 25-27	Ahaziah, age 22, rules over Israel one year as a wicked king.
vv. 28-29	Joram wounded as he and Ahaziah war against Hazael of Syria.
Chapter 9	**Jehu Anointed King Over Israel.**
vv. 1-3	Elisha commands prophet to go to Ramoth-gilead to anoint Jehu as king of Israel.
vv. 4-10	Young prophet flees after telling Jehu to slay Ahab and household.
vv. 11-13	Jehu proclaimed king of Israel.
vv. 14-16	Jehu commands servants to let no one leave Ramoth-gilead towarn Jezreel.
vv. 17-20	Jehu rides to Jezreel, meeting two of Joram's messengers en route.
vv. 21-26	Jehu's arrow kills Joram. He is cast on Naboth's land where Jezebel killed Naboth.
vv. 27-29	Ahaziah is killed and carried to Jerusalem for burial.
vv. 30-37	Jezebel is killed. Her body eaten by dogs of Jezreel.
Chapter 10	**Jehu Destroys House of Ahab and Worshippers of Baal.**
vv. 1-11	Jehu and elders of Samaria slay Ahab's descendants in Jezreel and Samaria.
vv. 12-14	Jehu slays 42 kinsmen of Ahaziah.
vv. 15-17	Jehu and Jehonadab go to Samaria, slaying all Ahab's grandchildren.
vv. 18-24	Jehu gathers the Baal worshippers into one place.
vv. 25-31	Jehu's 80 soldiers slay all of Israel's Baal worshippers and burning house of Baal.
vv. 32-36	Jehu reigns in Israel 28 years. Jehoahaz, his son, becomes king.
Chapter 11	**Reign and Death of Athaliah**
vv. 1-3	Athaliah kills all but one of her grandchildren. Jehosheba hides Joash 6 years.

vv. 4-8	Jehoiada has rulers over hundreds to protect Joash, the young king.
vv. 9-11	Captains of 100s with spears and shields guard Joash.
vv. 12-15	Joash proclaimed king of Judah.
vv. 16-21	Joash or Jehoash at age seven, begins reining after Athaliah is slain.
Chapter 12	**Jehoash Reigns over Judah.**
vv. 1-3	Jehoash reigns 40 years, beginning in the seventh year of Jehu's reign in Israel.
vv. 4-8	Priests are told to repair temple of the Lord.
vv. 9-16	Monies brought into temple are given to workers to repair God's house.
vv. 17-21	Jehoash gives Syria money to not destroy Jerusalem. Jehoash murdered by servants.
Chapter 13	**Jehoahaz, Jehoash and Elisha's Death**
vv. 1-9	Jehoahaz sins like Jeroboam; God delivers him into Syria's hands.
vv. 10-13	Jehoash reigns wickedly over Israel for 16 years and dies.
vv. 14-19	Elisha rebukes Joash for smiting ground with arrows only three times.
vv. 20-21	Man buried in Elisha's tomb revives and returns to life.
vv. 22-23	God restrains Hazael from oppressing Israel because of His covenant.
vv. 24-25	Joash beats Syria thrice, retaking his cities from Benhadad of Syria.
Chapter 14	**Amaziah of Judah wars with Jehoash (Joash) of Israel.**
vv. 1-6	Amaziah kills Joash's murderers when he becomes king of Judah.
v. 7	Amaziah kills 10,000 Edomites in Valley of Salt.
vv. 8-10	Amaziah challenges Jehoash (Joash), king of Israel.
vv. 11-14	Jehoash wins battle and loots temple in Jerusalem.
vv. 15-16	Jehoash dies; Jeroboam rules in Israel's capital of Samaria.

vv. 17-22	Amaziah is murdered and his 16-year-old son, Azariah, is king in Judah.
vv. 23-27	Jeroboam reigns 41 years over Israel.
vv. 28-29	Zachariah replaces Jeroboam at death.
Chapter 15	**Azariah Reigns over Judah.**
vv. 1-7	Leperous Azariah rules for 52 years. Son, Jotham, rules after Azariah's death.
vv. 8-12	Zechariah, son of Jeroboam, rules 6 months. God's promise to Jehu is fulfilled.
vv. 13-16	Shallum kills Zechariah. Menahem of Israel kills Shallum.
vv. 17-22	Menahem extracts 75,000 pounds of sliver from Israelites to appease Assyria.
vv. 23-26	Pekahiah reigns 2 years in Israel before murdered by Pekah and 50 Gileadites.
vv. 27-28	Pekah begins ruling Israel for 20 years.
vv. 29-31	Pekah loses Naphtali to Assyria. Hoshea murders Pekah, ruling after him.
vv. 32-28	Jotham rules 16 years in Judah before Ahaz begins rule in Judah.
Chapter 16	**Ahaz Attacked by Pekah and Rezin.**
vv. 1-4	Wicked Ahaz reigns 16 years over Judah.
vv. 5-9	Rezin of Syria is killed when he attacks Damascus to rescue Ahaz of Jerusalem.
vv. 10-16	King Ahaz has an altar built in Jerusalem like altar in Assyria.
vv. 17-20	Ahaz closes temple forcing Jews to worship at pagan shrines; Hezekiah, next king.
Chapter 17	**Hoshea is last king in Israel.**
vv. 1-6	Shalmaneser puts Hoshea in prison for seeking aid from Egypt.
vv. 7-18	Fall of Samaria and captivity of Israel
vv. 19-23	Israelites are exiled into Assyria.

vv. 24-28	Assyria sends Samaritan priests to Israel to teach new inhabitants laws of Israel.
vv. 29-34	New inhabitants brought with them idols for worship.
vv. 35-40	People refuse God and continue worshipping idols.
v. 41	Descendants also worship idols.
Chapter 18	**Hezekiah's Reign and Reform over Judah**
vv. 1-12	Hezekiah obeys God as did King David.
vv. 13-25	Sennacherib doesn't accept Hezekiah's offer and plans to invade Judah.
vv. 26-37	Assyrians try to intimidate Judah into surrendering.
Chapter 19	**Hezekiah Consults Isaiah.**
vv. 1-7	Isaiah encourages Hezekiah and Judah not to fear Assyrians.
vv. 8-19	After Assyria writes Hezekiah, he prays to God for protection.
vv. 20-28	Hezekiah defies Sennacherib and prophesies against Assyria.
vv. 29-37	God protects Judah by slaying 185,000 Assyrians. Sennacherib is killed by his sons.
Chapter 20	**Hezekiah's Sickness and Recovery**
vv. 1-7	Hezekiah's deathly illness leaves him. God gives him 15 extra years to live.
vv. 8-11	Sign Hezekiah would be healed, sundial goes backward 10 degrees.
vv. 12-15	Hezekiah shows envoys from Babylon everything in storehouse.
vv. 16-19	Isaiah pronounces judgment on future princes of Hezekiah.
vv. 20-21	Manasseh succeeds father, Hezekiah, as king of Judah.
Chapter 21	**Manasseh Rules Judah.**
vv. 1-9	Manasseh causes more evil in Judah than people God drove out in Canaan.
vv. 10-15	God's prophets warn of Judah's impending judgments.
v. 16	Manasseh sheds innocent blood all over Jerusalem.
vv. 17-18	Manasseh reigns 55 years in Jerusalem and dies at 67 years.

vv. 19-26	Amon rules two years and murdered at age 24 by servants.
Chapter 22	**Josiah Rules Judah.**
vv. 1-2	Josiah, a godly king, begins reign of Judah at eight years and dies at 39 years.
vv. 8-10	Hilkiah, high priest, finds scroll of law in temple.
vv. 11-13	Josiah orders priests and prophets to inquire of God concerning scroll.
vv. 14-20	God tells Josiah He will not harm Judah while Josiah lives because he repented.
Chapter 23	**Reforms of Josiah**
vv. 1-3	King, priests, prophets and people covenant to obey God's Word in scroll.
vv. 4-14	Josiah destroys high places of foreign gods as he honors God.
vv. 15-20	Josiah honors God's prophets and slays priests of ungodly high places.
vv. 21-23	After time, Judah resumes keeping Passover.
vv. 24-25	No other king put away evil as did Josiah.
vv. 26-27	Though Josiah is a good king, God purposed to remove Judah as He did Israel.
vv. 28-30	Pharaoh Necho slays Josiah; he is buried in Jerusalem.
vv. 31-35	Necho of Egypt puts Jehoahaz in prison. makeing Jehoiakim king of Judah.
vv. 36-37	Ungodly Jehoiakim, like Jehoahaz, reigns from age 25 to 36 years as king of Judah.
Chapter 24	**Nebuchadnezzar Conquers Jerusalem.**
vv. 1-7	Nebuchadnezzar takes Judah from Necho, punishing Judah for evils of Manasseh.
vv. 8-9	Evil king Jehoiachin at 18, rules three months in Jerusalem.
vv. 10-17	Jeconiah, yields to Nebuchadnezzar; deported to Babylon; Zedekiah is king.
vv. 18-20	Zedekiah, another evil king, at 21 rules for 11 years in Jerusalem.

Chapter 25	**Jerusalem is Besieged and Burned.**	
vv. 1-7	Zedekiah rebels; Jerusalem besieged; king flees, blinded and taken to Babylon.	
vv. 8-12	Nebuchadnezzar's captain goes to Jerusalem; burns buildings; deports all but poor.	
vv. 13-17	Bronze, silver and gold in temple are broken and carried to Babylon by Chaldeans.	
vv. 18-21	Leaders are slain in Riblah by Nebuchadnezzar and others exiled.	
vv. 22-26	Ishmael goes to Jerusalem killing King Gedaliah and men. Ishmael flees to Egypt.	
vv. 27-30	Evil-Marduk rules after Nebuchadnezzar, dealing favorably with Jehoiachin.	

1 CHRONICLES

Chapter 1	**Place of Israel Among Nations**
vv. 1-4	Descendants of Adam listed
vv. 5-7	Descendants of Japheth or Indo- Europeans
vv. 8-16	Descendants of Ham or Ancient Egypt and Philistia
vv. 17-23	Descendants of Shem (Semites)
vv. 24-27	Shem's Line to Abraham (Hebrews)
vv. 28-33	Descendants of Ishmael and Keturah
vv. 34-37	Descendants of Esau (Edom) and Israel
vv. 38-42	Descendants of Seir (Esau)
vv. 43-50	Kings who reigned in Edom earlier.
vv. 51-54	Chiefs who ruled in Edom.
Chapter 2	**Descendants of Judah**
vv. 1-2	Sons of Jacob (Israel)
vv. 3-4	Sons of Judah, five in all
vv. 5-8	Sons of Perez, Zerah, Carmi and Ethan
vv. 9-17	Sons of Hezron through David's family
vv. 18-20	Caleb, son of Hezron, and his descendants
vv. 21-24	History of Hezron and Caleb
vv. 25-41	History of childless people and others only with daughters
vv. 42-50	Descendants of Caleb (the brother of Jerahmeel)
vv. 51-55	Sons of Hur, the eldest of Epahrathah
Chapter 3	**Descendants of David and Solomon**
vv. 1-9	Sons of David in Hebron and Jerusalem
vv. 10-24	Descendants of Solomon

Chapter 4	**Descendants of Judah and Simeon**
vv. 1-23	Sons of Judah are listed.
vv. 24-43	Sons of Simeon are listed.
Chapter 5	**Descendants of Reuben, Gad and Half Tribe of Manasseh**
vv. 1-10	Sons of Reuben are listed.
vv. 11-17	Descendants of Gad
vv. 18-26	History of the two and one-half tribes
Chapter 6	**Lineage of Levites**
vv. 1-15	High priestly line
vv. 16-30	Levitical line
vv. 31-48	Temple singers and keepers
vv. 49-53	Descendants of Aaron
vv. 54-60	Cities of Kohathites
vv. 61-65	Cities of other Kohathites
vv. 66-70	Some Kohathites and Cities of Refuge
vv. 71-81	Gershonites and pasture lands
Chapter 7	**Descendants of Issachar, Benjamin, Naphtali, Ephraim and Asher**
vv. 1-5	Sons of Issachar
vv. 6-12	Sons of Benjamin
v. 13	Sons of Naphtali
vv. 14-19	Sons of Manasseh
vv. 20-29	Sons of Ephraim
vv. 30-40	Sons of Asher
Chapter 8	**Descendants of Benjamin**
vv. 1-32	Sons of Benjamin
vv. 33-40	Sons of Saul
Chapter 9	**Ones Who Returned from Babylon**
vv. 1-9	Genealogies of Israel and Judah
vv. 10-13	Priests in Jerusalem
vv. 14-16	Levites in Jerusalem

vv. 17-27	Gatekeepers in Jerusalem
vv. 28-32	Servers in Temple of Jerusalem.
vv. 33-34	Singers in Jerusalem
vv. 35-44	Sons of Saul

Chapter 10 — Death of Saul and Sons

vv. 1-7	Saul falls upon his sword.
vv. 8-12	Valiant men honor bodies of Saul and sons to Jabesh, fasting for seven days.
vv. 13-14	God gives kingdom to David.

Chapter 11 — David Made King of Israel

vv. 1-3	David anointed king at Hebron.
vv. 4-9	David captures Zion.
vv. 10-11	Chiefs of David's mighty men
vv. 12-14	Next to mighty are valiant men
vv. 15-19	Three mighty men
vv. 20-21	Abishai, chief of thirty
vv. 22-25	Benaiah, David's bodyguard
vv. 26-47	Valiant men of armies

Chapter 12 — Army of King David

vv. 1-7	Men who join David at Ziklag
vv. 8-15	Gadites, strong warriors
vv. 16-18	Men from Benjamin and Judah
vv. 19-22	Men from Manasseh
vv. 23-37	Men numbered 340,822, helping David at Hebron.
vv. 38-40	Men making David king over all Israel.

Chapter 13 — David's Desire to Bring Ark to Jerusalem

vv. 1-4	David plans to bring Ark of Covenant to Jerusalem.
vv. 5-8	People rejoice as Ark is transported.
vv. 9-14	God slays Uzzah for touching Ark.

Chapter 14 — David's Family and Defeat of Philistines

vv. 1-2	Hiram's kindness to David
vv. 3-7	Children born to David in Jerusalem

vv. 8-12	David defeats Philistines.
vv. 13-17	David's fame spreads to all nations.

Chapter 15 — Ark Comes to Jerusalem.
vv. 1-15	David prepares to bring Ark of Covenant to Jerusalem.
vv. 16-24	David commands singers of Levites to raise sounds of joy.
vv. 25-28	Singers respond with great sounds of joy as Ark returns.
v. 29	Michal despises David for his dancing in city.

Chapter 16 — David's Sacrifices and Thanksgivings
vv. 1-3	Burnt and peace offerings given.
vv. 4-6	David appoints Levites to minister before Ark.
vv. 7-36	David's psalm of thanksgiving
vv. 37-43	Levites appointed for Ark.

Chapter 17 — David Forbidden to Build Temple
vv. 1-2	David's desire for temple to honor God
vv. 3-15	David cannot build temple but Solomon can.
vv. 16-27	David's prayer and thanksgiving

Chapter 18 — David Extends His Kingdom.
vv. 1-8	Victories over Philistia, Moab, King Hadadezer of Zobah and Syria
vv. 9-11	Tori, king of Hamath congratulates David for defeating Hadadezer.
vv. 12-13	Abishai defeats the Edomites.
vv. 14-17	David reigns with justice, equity and righteousness.

Chapter 19 — Defeat of Ammonites and Syrians
vv. 1-5	David's messengers humiliated.
vv. 6-15	David defeats Ammonites.
vv. 16-18	David defeats Syrians.
v. 19	Hadadezer makes peace with David.

Chapter 20 — War With Philistines
vv. 1-3	Joab and David capture Rabbah.
vv. 4-8	Philistine giants are slain.

Chapter 21	Census, Plague and Altar
vv. 1-6	David numbers Israel and Judah.
vv. 7-13	David chooses his punishment.
vv. 14-17	The Lord sends a pestilence upon Israel.
vv. 18-27	David builds an altar.
vv. 28-30	David fears Angel of Lord.

Chapter 22	David's Charge to Solomon
v. 1	David chooses site and building of God's house.
vv. 2-5	David collects materials for building of temple.
vv. 6-16	David commands Solomon to build temple costing $3,120,000,000 just for gold.
vv. 17-19	David charges leaders of Israel to help Solomon in building God's temple.

Chapter 23	David Makes Solomon King.
v. 1	David anoints Solomon King.
vv. 2-6	David organizes priests and Levites into a workforce.
vv. 7-11	Sons of Gershon, organized as overseers.
vv. 12-20	Sons Kohath, organized into overseer positions.
vv. 21-23	Sons of Merari, numbered.
vv. 24-32	Levites, given duties and responsibilities.

Chapter 24	Divisions of Priests and Services
vv. 1-6	David organizes priests to their appointed services.
vv. 7-19	Priests, organized into 24 divisions of services in temple.
vv. 20-31	Other Levites are numbered.

Chapter 25	Divisions of Musicians
vv. 1-8	David and leaders separate musicians for duties.
vv. 9-31	David organizes other musicians for services.

Chapter 26	Organization of Gatekeepers and Treasurers
vv. 1-11	Gatekeepers are named.
vv. 12-19	Duties are mentioned.
vv. 20-21	Levites of treasuries are mentioned.

vv. 22-28	Levites used spoils from battles to maintain temple.
vv. 29-32	Those for outside duties are to tend to interests of religious establishment.
Chapter 27	**David Organizes Military and Civil Affairs.**
v. 1	Lists leaders serving David
vv. 2-15	Leaders serve a month with 24,000 men, making 12 leaders and 288,000 warriors.
vv. 16-24	Leaders, named who are of 12 tribes and over priestly leaders.
vv. 25-31	David sets leaders of treasuries and agricultural departments.
vv. 32-34	Other leaders assigned to David's sons and army.
Chapter 28	**David Instructs Solomon Concerning Temple.**
vv. 1-8	David declares Solomon to build temple; David cannot, because of wars.
vv. 9-10	"Solomon, obeying God, kingdom will be established. You are to build temple."
vv. 11-19	David gives Solomon detailed account of building furniture in temple.
vv. 20-21	Everyone under Solomon's command in building temple
Chapter 29	**Installation of Solomon and Death of David**
vv. 1-5	David gives wealth and challenges others to give to build temple and furniture.
vv. 6-9	Leaders give for building God's house.
vv. 10-13	David thanks leaders for building temple.
vv. 14-19	David blesses God asking Him to direct Solomon in building temple.
vv. 20-22a	David and Israel worship God, offering burnt sacrifices, to Him.
vv. 22b-25	Solomon made king and Zadok, priest.
vv. 26-30	David reigns 40 years, dying at 70 years of age.

2 CHRONICLES

Chapter 1	**Solomon Prays and Receives Wisdom.**
v. 1	Solomon establishes himself as king of Israel.
vv. 2-6	Solomon offers 1,000 burnt offerings upon altar in high place at Gibeon.
vv. 7-13	God promises wisdom, riches and long life to Solomon.
vv. 14-17	Solomon imports many horses and chariots from Egypt.
Chapter 2	**Preparations for Building Temple**
vv. 1-10	Solomon organizes 150,000 workers and 3,600 supervisors for work of temple.
vv. 11-12	Huram, King of Tyre, responds to King Solomon's letter for workers and materials.
vv. 13-16	Huram agrees with Solomon for materials and payments for other supplies.
vv. 17-18	Solomon uses aliens in Israel to work and supervise laborers.
Chapter 3	**Solomon Begins Building Temple.**
vv. 1-2	Solomon begins construction in the fourth year second month of reign.
vv. 3-7	Much gold used to overlay interior.
vv. 8-9	Fine gold covers most holy place.
vv. 10-14	Two cherubim of wood are overlaid with fine gold.
vv. 15-17	Two pillars are named Jachin and Boaz.
Chapter 4	**Furnishings of Temple**
vv. 1-6	Altar and ten lavers are made.
vv. 7-10	The 10 golden lampstands, 10 tables, 100 basins, courts and doors are made.
vv. 11-18	Huram made pots, shovels, basins for temple.

vv. 19-22	Solomon made all furnishings for house of the Lord.
Chapter 5	**Ark Brought into Temple.**
v. 1	Solomon uses everything David collected for house of God.
vv. 2-14	Ark is placed in temple; priests and Levites praise God as smoke fills temple.
Chapter 6	**Solomon's Prayer of Dedication**
vv. 1-11	Solomon blesses assembly of Israel and the Lord God.
vv. 12-17	Solomon entreats God to keep David's descendants on throne.
vv. 18-21	He prays God hears and forgives when Israel strays from God.
vv. 22-23	"Judge the guilty and reward the righteous," prays Solomon.
vv. 24-25	When Israel is defeated and returns to God, forgive and restore them to their land.
vv. 26-27	When Israel repents of sin, let rain come upon the land.
vv. 28-31	When Israel sins and plagues come, forgive and restore.
vv. 32-33	When foreigners pray toward temple, hear and bless them.
vv. 34-35	Bless our armies when they pray toward this place.
vv. 36-42	Remember our captives in foreign lands when they repent and pray.
Chapter 7	**God Answers Solomon's Prayer.**
vv. 1-3	God sends consuming fire on burnt sacrifices.
vv. 4-6	Solomon offers 22,000 oxen and 120,000 sheep to God.
v. 7	Offerings are abundant. Solomon devotes middle of temple court for burnt offerings.
vv. 8-10	Solomon keeps the feast for seven days.
vv. 11-18	God answers Solomon's prayer, challenging Israel to follow God and be blessed.
vv. 19-22	If Israel turns from God, they will become a by-word to surrounding nations.
Chapter 8	**Solomon's Activities and Fame**
vv. 1-2	Solomon rebuilds cities King Huram (Hiram) gave him.

vv. 3-10	Solomon uses foreigners for slave labor and Israelites for soldiers.
v. 11	Solomon builds house for Pharaoh's daughter.
vv. 12-15	Solomon divides ministry between priests, Levites and gatekeepers.
v. 16	Solomon completes construction of temple.
vv. 17-18	Solomon receives 450 talents of gold from Ophir.
Chapter 9	**Queen of Sheba Visits Solomon.**
vv. 1-4	Queen of Sheba, amazed at Solomon's wisdom and wealth.
vv. 5-9	Queen of Sheba gives Solomon 120 talents of gold with precious gifts.
vv. 10-11	King Huram (Hiram) provides wood for Solomon's steps and musical instruments.
v. 12	Solomon gives Queen of Sheba more than she gave him.
vv. 13-21	Solomon's wealth and annual income are stated here.
vv. 22-28	Solomon's wealth and wisdom are known by surrounding kingdoms.
vv. 29-31	Solomon rules 40 years and dies.
Chapter 10	**Reign of Rehoboam**
vv. 1-5	Jeroboam and fellow Israelites ask Rehoboam to lighten tax burden.
vv. 6-11	Rehoboam takes counsel of young rebels and makes burden heavier.
vv. 12-15	God's word comes to pass, using Rehoboam's young counselors.
vv. 16-19	Israel rebels against King Rehoboam.
Chapter 11	**Rehoboam Counseled Not to Fight Israel's Ten Tribes.**
vv. 1-4	God says, "Don't go to war against Israel."
vv. 5-12	Rehoboam fortifies cities of Judah and Benjamin.
vv. 13-17	Jeroboam rejects Levites who go to Rehoboam to worship God.
vv. 18-23	Rehoboam's family mentioned here.

Chapter 12	**Shishak Invades Judah.**
v. 1	Rehoboam forsakes God's law.
vv. 2-8	Shishak is used of God to humble Rehoboam.
vv. 9-12	Shishak takes all gold Solomon acquired.
vv. 13-14	Rehoboam reigns 17 years. He did not wholly serve the Lord.
vv. 15-16	Rehoboam dies at age 58 and buried in Jerusalem.
Chapter 13	**Reign of Abijah in Judah**
vv. 1-2	Abijah reigns three years in Jerusalem.
vv. 3-7	Abijah speaks to warriors of Jeroboam from Mount Zemaraim.
vv. 8-12	Abijah proclaims God is with Judah and against Israel.
vv. 13-22	God gives victory to Judah; Jeroboam never recovers from Israel's defeat.
Chapter 14	**Reign of Asa in Judah**
vv. 1-8	Asa served God; Judah has peace for 10 years.
vv. 9-15	Asa's Lord God defeats army of Zerah (Ethiopian), carrying spoils to Jerusalem.
Chapter 15	**Asa's Reforms in Judah**
vv. 1-7	Prophet Azariah challenges Asa to continue seeking God and His blessings.
vv. 8-15	Judah, Benjamin and people of other tribes covenant to be faithful to God.
vv. 16-19	Asa has peace many years; he banishes Queen Maacah, his mother, for her idolatry.
Chapter 16	**Asa's War with Baasha of Israel**
vv. 1-6	Asa makes league with Benhadad of Syria to war against Baasha of Israel.
vv. 7-10	Hanani is incarcerated by Asa for joining with Syria instead of trusting Yahweh.
vv. 11-14	Asa sought physicians instead of God; he died in the 41st year of his reign.

Chapter 17	**Reign of Jehoshaphat**
vv. 1-6	Jehoshaphat honors God by demolishing high places and Asherim in Judah.
vv. 7-9	Jehoshaphat sends princes, priests and Levites throughout Judah to teach the Law.
vv. 10-19	Jehoshaphat fortifies cities; nations fear God due to Judah's reverencing Him.
Chapter 18	**Jehoshaphat's Alliance with Ahab**
vv. 1-3	Ahab asks Jehoshaphat to join him against Ramoth-gilead in battle.
vv. 4-11	False prophets of Israel tell Ahab and Jehoshaphat they will defeat Syria.
vv. 12-22	Micaiah prophesies Syria will defeat Ahab in battle.
vv. 23-27	Ahab incarcerates Micaiah for prophesying truth which he refuses to hear.
vv. 28-34	Ahab is fatally wounded in battle by a Syrian's arrow.
Chapter 19	**Jehu Rebukes Jehoshaphat**
vv. 1-3	Jehu rebukes Jehoshaphat for aiding Ahab, wicked king of Israel.
vv. 4-7	Jehoshaphat warns judges to be righteous with people of Judah.
vv. 8-11	Jehoshaphat appoints Levites and priests to judge fairly in disputed cases.
Chapter 20	**Deliverance from Moab and Ammon**
vv. 1-4	After invasion of enemies, Jehoshaphat proclaims a fast for God's deliverance.
vv. 5-12	Jehoshaphat gets "prayers" against warring Ammonites, Moabites and Meunites.
vv. 13-17	Jahaziel, a Levite, prophesies that God will fight for Judah.
vv. 18-19	Jehoshaphat and Levites worship and praise God for salvation of Judah.
vv. 20-23	Jehoshaphat proclaims victory as God causes enemies to fight among themselves.

vv. 24-30	Judah spends 3 days collecting spoils, blessing God, returning with joy and peace.
vv. 31-34	Jehoshaphat was 60 years of age when he died.
vv. 35-37	Jehoshaphat and wicked king, Ahaziah, lose all ships in joint- shipping venture.
Chapter 21	**Jehoram Reigns in Judah.**
vv. 1-7	Jehoram kills brothers and nephews when he is king for next eight years.
vv. 8-10	Jehoram has forsaken God's laws; Edom and Libnah revolt against Judah.
vv. 11-15	Elijah prophesies plague on Jehoram due to his evil ways.
vv. 16-17	God causes Philistines and Arabs to invade Judah, taking Jehoram's possessions.
vv. 18-20	Jehoram's bowels come out of body as he dies because of evil ways.
Chapter 22	**Ahaziah Reigns Wickedly in Judah.**
vv. 1-6	Ahaziah at 42 years of age rules Judah for one year.
vv. 7-9	Jehu slays Ahaziah and brothers, fulfilling prophecy.
vv. 10-12	Athaliah rules Judah six years; Joash is hidden by Jehoshabeth and Priest Jehoiada.
Chapter 23	**Joash Crowned King of Judah.**
vv. 1-7	Jehoiada enthrones Joash as king of Judah with help of leaders and Levites.
vv. 8-11	Jehoiada, his sons, the Levites and leaders proclaim Joash as "King of Judah."
vv. 12-15	Athaliah is slain outside house of the Lord.
vv. 16-21	Joash ushered into palace and sits upon throne of David.
Chapter 24	**Joash Repairs Temple.**
vv. 1-3	Joash beginning at 12 years, reigns 40 years in Jerusalem.
vv. 4-7	Joash begins repairing temple of worship in Judah.
vv. 8-14	More money came than needed to rebuild temple. Extra money bought dishes and vessels for burnt offerings.

vv. 15-16	Good Priest Jehoiada dies at 130 years.
vv. 17-19	After Jehoiada's death Joash turns from God to idolatry.
vv. 20-22	Zechariah, Jehoiada's son, prophesies judgment against Joash and is stoned to death.
vv. 23-24	God helps Syrians to defeat Joash due to idolatry.
vv. 25-27	Joash, king of Judah, slain for killing Zechariah.

Chapter 25 — Amaziah Reigns in Judah.

vv. 1-4	Amaziah kills men who murdered his father, Joash.
vv. 5-13	Amaziah, rebuked for not hiring Israelites who kill 3,000 Jews going back to Israel.
vv. 14-16	Amaziah refuses counsel of prophet sent to rebuke him for worshipping idols.
vv. 17-19	Amaziah's pride causes him to seek war with Israel.
vv. 20-24	Joash, king of Israel, defeats Amaziah, breaks Jerusalem's walls and spoils city.
vv. 25-28	Amaziah killed at age 54 in Lachish, ruled 29 years and buried in Jerusalem.

Chapter 26 — Uzziah Reigns, Prospers and Disobeys.

vv. 1-5	Uzziah at 16 becomes king; prospers seeking God; he reigns in Judah for 52 years.
vv. 6-15	Uzziah had a great army of 307,500 men. His fame reached Egypt.
vv. 16-21	Uzziah being proud, tries offering priestly incense; God smites him with leprosy.
vv. 22-23	Uzziah dies a leper and is buried.

Chapter 27 — Reign of King Jotham in Judah

vv. 1-9	"Jotham became mighty because he prepared his ways before the Lord His God."

Chapter 28 — Ahaz Reigns in Judah.

vv. 1-4	Ahaz, made king at age 20, reigns 16 years in Jerusalem. He worships idols.
vv. 5-7	Because of idolatry, he loses wars to Syria, Israel and Zichri of Ephraim.

vv. 8-15	Israelites return 200,000 captives and spoils to Judah.
vv. 16-21	Ahaz disgraced by God for Philistines, Edomites and Assyrians fighting Judah.
vv. 22-27	Ahaz becomes more rebellious, evil and wicked till death.
Chapter 29	**Hezekiah's Reign and Revival**
vv. 1-2	Hezekiah rules Judah for 29 years, beginning at age 25. He was a good king.
vv. 3-11	Hezekiah orders Levites to be sanctified, reopen and restore temple worship.
vv. 12-19	Priests and Levites tell king temple is ready for use.
vv. 20-24	Burnt and sin offerings are made for all Israel.
vv. 25-30	Priests, Levites, princes and King Hezekiah bow and worship God.
vv. 31-36	Restoration of temple is completed and offerings to God are huge in quantity.
Chapter 30	**Preparation and Celebration of Passover**
vv. 1-9	Hezekiah invites northern tribes of Israel to celebrate Passover with Judah.
vv. 10-12	Few of Israel's northern tribes come to Jerusalem to celebrate Passover.
vv. 13-22	Passover festival lasts seven days and is blessed by God.
vv. 23-27	People observe Passover Feast for seven more days and God unites their hearts.
Chapter 31	**Hezekiah's Provisions for Priests and Levites**
v. 1	Benjamin, Ephraim and Manasseh destroy idols in high places of Judah,
vv. 2-10	God prospers priests and Levites with abundance after contributions to Him.
vv. 11-19	Hezekiah reforms Judah and establishes divisions of priests and Levites.
vv. 20-21	Hezekiah prospered because he sought to serve God with whole heart.

Chapter 32	**Sennacherib Invades Judah.**
vv. 1-8	Hezekiah fortifies city, produces mass weapons, encouraging commanders for war.
vv. 9-15	As Sennacherib invades Lachish, envoys tell Hezekiah it's useless to resist him.
vv. 16-19	Envoy speaks in Hebrew to frighten commanders on Jerusalem walls.
vv. 20-23	Hezekiah prays; God sends angel who destroys 186,000 of Sennacherib's men.
vv. 24-26	Hezekiah's pride brings God's wrath upon Judah. He repents and God delays wrath.
vv. 27-31	Riches and honors are given to Hezekiah as he follows God.
vv. 32-33	Hezekiah dies with honor and evil Manasseh becomes king of Judah.
Chapter 33	**Manasseh's Abominations, Captivity and Restoration**
vv. 1-9	Manasseh is king at 12, ruling 55 years in Jerusalem. He was evilest king of Judah.
vv. 10-13	Manasseh, captured by Assyrians, repents and restored king of Jerusalem.
vv. 14-17	Manasseh reinstates temple worship and offerings to God.
vv. 18-20	Manasseh dies in good standing with Judah and buried in Jerusalem.
vv. 21-25	Amon at 22, reigns two years and slain by servants due to his evilness.
Chapter 34	**Book of Law is Found.**
vv. 1-7	Josiah at age eight reigns 31 years. He purges Israel and Judah from idolatry.
vv. 8-13	Josiah and officials repair temple in Jerusalem.
vv. 14-18	Priest Hilkiah finds Book of the Law in temple. Shaphan reads it before King Josiah!
vv. 19-21	Josiah commands priests and Levites to seek God concerning Book of the Law.

vv. 22-28	Huldah tells priests God will judge Judah. Faithful Josiah will not see judgment.
vv. 29-33	Josiah gathers his people to serve God and keep His laws.
Chapter 35	**Keeping Passover**
vv. 1-6	Josiah prepares Judah to keep Passover.
vv. 7-9	King, princes and chiefs of Levites give 1000s of lambs and bulls for Passover Feast.
vv. 10-15	Priests and Levites do all that is necessary for the Passover Feast.
vv. 16-19	No Passovers since Samuel's are as great as Josiah's.
vv. 20-26	Josiah dies from arrow wound by King Necho's archers and buried in Jerusalem.
Chapter 36	**Last Kings of Judah**
vv. 1-3	Jehoahaz at 23 is king for three months until Nehco takes him captive to Egypt.
vv. 4-8	Eliakim's name is changed to Jehoiakim Nebuchadnezzar takes him to Babylon.
vv. 9-10	Jehoiachin at 8 reigns for 3 months; because of evils, deported to Babylon.
vv. 11-14	Zedekiah at 21, appointed king of Judah. He and priests do evil in sight of God.
vv. 15-16	God's wrath is against Judah for not listening to prophets and returning to God.
vv. 17-21	Chaldeans burn Jerusalem and people are exiled to Babylon for 70 years.
vv. 22-23	After 70 years Cyrus, king of Persia, sends Jews to Jerusalem to rebuild temple.

EZRA

Chapter 1	**Proclamation of Cyrus as Exiles Return to Jerusalem**
v. 1	God stirs Cyrus's spirit to make a proclamation regarding Jews.
vv. 2-4	Royal decree given by Cyrus
vv. 5-11	Jews given finances, gold, goods, animals, temple properties to be returned.
Chapter 2	**First Wave of Exiles Return to Jerusalem.**
vv. 1-2	Exiles by Nebuchadnezzar return to Jerusalem and towns in Judah.
vv. 3-35	Famous people from Israel numbered by families
vv. 36-39	Sons of priests numbered
vv. 40-42	Sons of Levites numbered
vv. 43-54	Sons of temple servants numbered
vv. 55-58	Solomon's servants numbered
vv. 59-63	These numbered cannot prove priestly genealogy and cannot temple food.
vv. 64-37	Exiles of first wave total 42,360, plus 7,337 servants plus 200 singers.
vv. 68-69	Money given by heads of families in Jerusalem to rebuild house of God.
v. 70	Priests and Levites live in Jerusalem. Singers, gatekeepers and servants live in towns.
Chapter 3	**Beginning of Rebuilding Temple**
vv. 1-7	Renewal of altar and Feast of Tabernacles
vv. 8-9	Sons of priests and Levites have oversight of rebuilding temple.

vv. 10-13	People shout and weep when foundation of temple is laid.
Chapter 4	**Adversaries Seek to Stop Work.**
vv. 1-3	Locals desire to rebuild temple but exiles refuse their help.
vv. 4-5	Locals thwart rebuilding temple from Cyrus' reign until Darius.
v. 6	Locals write Ahasuerus to stop Jews from rebuilding.
vv. 7-16	Opposition writes King Artaxerxes saying Jerusalem a rebellious city not be rebuilt.
vv. 17-22	King Artaxerxes says rebuilding should cease until he gives a decree.
vv. 23-24	Work ceases until reign of Darius, king of Persia.
Chapter 5	**Rebuilding Jerusalem Resumes**
vv. 1-2	Governor and prophets encourage rebuilding of temple.
vv. 3-5	Opposition tries to stop rebuilding temple.
vv. 6-17	Letter sent by opposition to King Darius to halt labor.
Chapter 6	**Darius' Decree to Rebuild Temple**
vv. 1-5	Scroll with Cyrus' decree to rebuild temple found in Achmetha.
vv. 6-12	Darius' decree is powerful in helping Jews rebuild temple.
vv. 13-15	Temple finished in sixth year of Darius' reign.
vv. 16-18	Israelites celebrate with priests and Levites finished house of God in Jerusalem.
vv. 19-22	Priests and Levites cleanse themselves and celebrate Passover.
Chapter 7	**Ezra Comes to Jerusalem.**
vv. 1-6	Ezra, descendent of Moses, favored by king of Persia (Iran), Artaxerxes
vv. 7-10	Ezra studies Law to teach statutes and ordinances in Israel.
vv. 11-20	King Artaxerxes tells Ezra whatever needed for temple comes from royal treasury.
vv. 21-24	Artaxerxes tells neighboring nations to help with Jews' rebuilding of temple.

vv. 25-26	Artaxerxes orders Ezra to punish resisters to God's commandments and ordinances.
vv. 27-28	Ezra thanks God for favor with f King Artaxerxes to rebuild temple.
Chapter 8	**Those Who Return with Ezra**
vv. 1-14	Men named who return with Ezra.
vv. 15-20	Ezra requests Levites and temple servants to return with him.
vv. 21-23	Ezra and people humble themselves by fasting.
vv. 24-30	Ezra gives gold and silver to priests and Levites for Jerusalem.
vv. 31-34	They arrive in Jerusalem with precious metals for temple.
vv. 35-36	Returning exiles offer burnt offerings to God.
Chapter 9	**Lamentations of Ezra over Mixed Marriages**
vv. 1-9	Ezra asks God's forgiveness of people's faithlessness in mixed marriages.
vv. 10-15	Ezra pleads before a loving God for people's sins.
Chapter 10	**Foreign Wives and Children Set Aside**
vv. 1-5	Elders plead with Ezra they will leave foreign wives and children.
vv. 6-8	Declaration for returning exiles to assemble at Jerusalem or forfeit properties.
vv. 9-15	Opposition given concerning putting away foreign wives.
vv. 16-17	Priests check all who have foreign wives.
vv. 18-44	Names listed of those putting aside foreign wives and children

NEHEMIAH

Chapter 1	**Arrival of Nehemiah in Jerusalem**
vv. 1-3	Nehemiah, in Susa, learns problems of Jews remaining in Jerusalem.
vv. 4-11	Nehemiah prays, fasts and intercedes for Israelites' sin, breaking God's covenant.
Chapter 2	**Nehemiah's Mission to Jerusalem**
vv. 1-8	Nehemiah granted by Artaxerxes to return and rebuild Jerusalem's walls
vv. 9-10	Sanballat and Tobiah are displeased with Nehemiah's visit to Jerusalem.
vv. 11-16	Nehemiah inspects walls and gates.
vv. 17-20	Sanballat, Tobiah and Geshem mock Jews' rebuilding walls and gates.
Chapter 3	**Working on Walls of Jerusalem**
vv. 1-2	Eliashib, high priest and brethren, rebuild Sheep Gate.
vv. 3-5	Sons of Hassenaah rebuild Fish Gate.
vv. 6-12	Old Gate is repaired with city's walls.
v. 13	Valley Gate is repaired.
v. 14	Dung Gate is repaired.
vv. 15-27	Fountain Gate and walls are further repaired.
vv. 28-32	Horse Gate, East Gate, and Muster Gate are repaired with adjoining walls.
Chapter 4	**Further Opposition to Rebuilding**
vv. 1-5	Builders return words of ill omen to trouble makers.
v. 6	Walls are joined together.
vv. 7-9	Builders set guards by walls, praying for protection.

vv. 10-14	Nehemiah exhorts Jews to fight those trying to kill or destroy walls.
vv. 15-20	Trumpeters sound warning of enemy attacks; others gather at place of attack.
vv. 21-23	Workers sleep clothed inside walls, ready for battle.
Chapter 5	**Economic Troubles and Interest Abolished**
vv. 1-5	Judah cries out due to famine and financial struggles.
vv. 6-13	Nehemiah curses nobles for interest rates on mortgaged Jewish properties.
vv. 14-19	Nehemiah never demanded what Artaxerxes' subjects owed him.
Chapter 6	**Plots of Sanballat, Tobiah and Geshem**
vv. 1-9	Sanballat, Tobiah and Arab Geshem seek to lure Nehemiah to Ono to harm him.
vv. 10-14	Shemaiah hired unsuccessfully to put fear into Nehemiah.
vv. 15-19	Wall around Jerusalem finished in 52 days despite Tobiah's scare tactics.
Chapter 7	**List of Returning Exiles**
vv. 1-4	Nehemiah appoints rulers for Jerusalem.
vv. 5-6	Transition verses introducing genealogies
vv. 7-38	List of men of Israel
vv. 39-42	List of priests numbered.
vv. 43-45	Levites numbered in this list.
vv. 46-56	Temple servants named.
vv. 57-60	Sons of Solomon's servants mentioned and 392 numbered.
vv. 61-65	Men in these verses not documented could not serve in priesthood at this time.
vv. 66-69	Whole assembly numbered 42,360 plus 7,337 servants and 245 singers.
vv. 70-72	Total amount of gold, silver and priestly garments listed.
v. 73	Priests, Levites, gatekeepers, singers, and temple servants lived in their towns.

Chapter 8	**Ezra Reads Law to People.**
vv. 1-8	Scribe Ezra reads to people Law of Moses by Water Gate every morning.
vv. 9-12	People celebrate by eating and drinking as they hear Law read.
vv. 13-18	People celebrate Feast of Booths (Tabernacles) seven days; first since days of Joshua.
Chapter 9	**Public Confession of Sin**
vv. 1-5	Jews separate from foreigners; they fast, pray and confess sins of Israel.
vv. 6-8	Ezra proclaims the Lord's goodness praising God in prayer.
vv. 9-15	Ezra blesses God for all He has done for Israel.
vv. 16-25	Ezra resumes blessing God for faithfulness when Israel was unfaithful.
vv. 26-31	Ezra continues praising God for being gracious and merciful to Israel.
vv. 32-37	Ezra pleads Israel's cause to God when enslaved and seeks restoration.
v. 38	Israelite princes, Levites and priests make covenant with God to obey laws.
Chapter 10	**Those Who Sealed Covenant**
vv. 1-27	Governor, officials, priests, Levites and chiefs of people set seals on covenant.
vv. 28-31	People agree not to intermarry, buy on Sabbath or holidays and let land rest 7th year.
vv. 32-39	Tithe of tithe goes to house of God, chambers and storehouse.
Chapter 11	**List of Those Living in Jerusalem**
vv. 1-2	One of every 10 is to live in Jerusalem while others live in towns.
vv. 3-6	Listed are leaders living in Jerusalem
vv. 7-9	Sons of Benjamin listed who live in Jerusalem.
vv. 10-14	Priests' families are listed who live in Jerusalem.

vv. 15-18	Levites are listed in Jerusalem.
vv. 19-21	Gatekeepers are also listed.
vv. 22-24	Uzzi was overseer of Levites.
vv. 25-36	Villages occupied by Israelites are listed. |//
Chapter 12	**Dedication of Wall**
vv. 1-7	Chief priests and Levites who came with Zerubbabel are listed.
vv. 8-11	Levites are listed by genealogy.
vv. 12-21	Priests listed by heads of fathers' houses
vv. 22-26	Levites again listed
vv. 27-30P	Priests and people are purified with gates and walls.
vv. 31-37	Leaders march along top of walls in procession.
vv. 38-43	People offer abundant sacrifices and greatly rejoice.
vv. 44-47	Portions from Israel were given to singers, gatekeepers, Levites and priests.
Chapter 13	**Nehemiah's Reforms**
vv. 1-3	Ammonites, Moabites nor foreigners cannot enter assembly of God.
vv. 4-9	Nehemiah, angry with Eliashib for favoring his relative, Tobiah.
vv. 10-14	Nehemiah restores Levites to temple and demands provisions for them.
vv. 15-18	Nehemiah rebukes Israelites for profaning Sabbath.
vv. 19-22	Nehemiah puts Levites at gates keeping wares from entering Jerusalem on Sabbath.
vv. 23-27	Nehemiah rebukes those who marry pagans.
vv. 28-29	Nehemiah chases away priest who is son-in-law of Sanballat.
vv. 30-31	Nehemiah cleanses Judah of foreign culture, helping priests and Levites in work.

ESTHER
Hadassah

Chapter 1	**Ahasuerus Makes Royal Feast.**
vv. 1-9	After ruling three years, Ahasuerus (Xerxes I), holds a seven-day banquet.
vv. 10-12	Vashti refuses obedience to king.
vv. 13-22	Court's wise men counsel Ahasuerus to replace Vashti, putting another in her place.
Chapter 2	**Vashti deposed and Esther Made Queen.**
vv. 1-4	Ahasuerus told to seek another queen.
vv. 5-11	Esther is taken into palace to be judged as next queen.
vv. 12-14	After one year Esther goes before king for inspection.
vv. 15-18	Esther is chosen as crowned queen.
vv. 19-22	Mordecai reports an assassination attempt by two eunuchs on king's life.
Chapter 3	**Haman's Plot to Destroy Jews.**
vv. 1-6	Haman desires to destroy Mordecai and Jews.
vv. 7-11	Haman receives king's authority to destroy all Jews in Persian kingdom.
vv. 12-15	King issues proclamation to kill Jews and take properties 13th of Adar.
Chapter 4	**Esther Promises Intercession for Jews.**
vv. 1-3	Jews mourn and fast for deliverance.
vv. 4-14	Esther willing to go before king on behalf of Jews.
Chapter 5	**Courage of Esther**
vv. 1-8	Esther prepares dinner for Ahasuerus and Haman.

vv. 9-14	Haman makes gallows to hang Mordecai.
Chapter 6	**Haman Forced to Honor Mordecai**
vv. 1-11	Haman honors Mordecai in open square before people.
vv. 12-14	Zeresh, Haman's wife, predicts that Mordecai will prevail.
Chapter 7	**Haman Ordered to be Hanged**
vv. 1-6	Esther tells Ahasuerus of Haman's wicked plans for destruction of Jews and herself.
vv. 7-10	Haman hanged on his gallows.
Chapter 8	**Jews are permitted to Avenge Themselves.**
vv. 1-2	Haman's house given to Esther who appoints Mordecai over it.
vv. 3-8	Esther and Mordecai permitted to write letter, sealed by the king's ring.
vv. 9-14	This decree written for Jews in defense against enemies on 13th of Adar.
vv. 15-17	Jews celebrate edict of king protecting Jews in 127 provinces.
Chapter 9	**Jews Defeat Their Enemies.**
vv. 1-10	Jews slay 500 enemies in Susa including Haman's 10 sons.
vv. 11-15	Next day Jews slay 300 enemies, hanging Haman's 10 sons on gallows.
vv. 16-19	Jews in towns near Susa slay 75,000 enemies.
vv. 20-22	The 14th and 15th of Adar, celebrated by Jews.
vv. 23-28	Jews keep Feast of Purim (Feast of Lots) each year.
vv. 29-32	Two days are observed by authorities honoring Queen Esther and Mordecai.
Chapter 10	**The Greatness of Mordecai**
vv. 1-3	Mordecai made second to King Ahasuerus, helping Jews live in peace.

JOB

Chapter 1	**Job's Piety and Satan's Challenge**
vv. 1-5	Job, rich man, offers sacrifices for family.
vv. 6-12	God allows Satan to do all he desires to Job but cannot kill him.
vv. 13-19	Satan destroys Job's children, most servants, livestock and fortunes.
vv. 20-22	Job honors God though losing his children.
Chapter 2	**Job's Afflictions and Patience**
vv. 1-6	Satan has permission to tempt Job further by afflicting his body.
vv. 7-8	Satan afflicts Job's body with loathsome sores.
vv. 9-10	It is difficult for Job's wife to see Job's suffering.
vv. 11-13	Eliphaz, Bildad, and Zophar seeing Job's affliction, do not speak for seven days.
Chapter 3	**Job Laments His Birth.**
vv. 1-10	Job regrets birth as one of doom and gloom due to suffering by Satan.
vv. 11-19	Job would rather have died at birth than to suffer as he is at present.
vv. 20-26	Job realizes what he has feared has now come upon him.
Chapter 4	**Eliphaz Affirms Divine Justice.**
vv. 1-6	Eliphaz rebukes Job for not taking advice he had given others.
vv. 7-11	Job, "whatever you sowed, you are reaping."
vv. 12-21	No man is pure before his Creator.

Chapter 5	**Man is Born for Trouble.**
vv. 1-7	Sparks from a fire fly upward, so does man having troubles in life.
vv. 8-16	God takes care of His people.
vv. 17-27	God chastises but He also heals.
Chapter 6	**Job Reproaches His Friends.**
vv. 1-7	Job's taste for food is gone.
vv. 8-13	Job desires God would crush him.
vv. 14-23	Job claims his friends are no help in time of need.
vv. 24-30	"Your reproof is of no value to me," says Job.
Chapter 6	**Life is Hard and Transient.**
vv. 1-6	Man's days are hard and disappear quickly.
vv. 7-10	When a man dies, he is soon forgotten.
vv. 11-21	Why does God think about mankind, anyway?
Chapter 8	**Bildad Affirms Divine Justice.**
vv. 1-7	Job, if you repent of your words, God will help you.
vv. 8-10	Our days are few and we know so little.
vv. 11-19	Men who forget God lose confidence.
vv. 20-22	God will restore and encourage you.
Chapter 9	**Job Acknowledges God's Power.**
vv. 1-12	How can man be just before an awesome God?
vv. 13-24	Do not compare man great Creator - God.
vv. 25-35	Job tells Eliphaz there is no umpire between the two of them.
Chapter 10	**Job Protests God's Treatment**
vv. 1-17	Job sees God far off but still prays to Him.
vv. 18-22	Leve me so I can go to land of doom and gloom.
Chapter 11	**Zophar Accuses Job of Iniquity.**
vv. 1-6	Job is rebuked for claiming he is clean before God.
vv. 7-12	God is too distant for man to understand His ways.
vv. 13-20	If your heart is right, your life will be brighter than before.

Chapter 12	**Job Affirms God's Omnipotence.**
vv. 1-6	Job thinks "Why do I suffer when wicked seem to prosper?"
vv. 7-25	God knows no obstacles as Job acknowledges Him as "Omnipotent God."
Chapter 13	**Job Defends His Integrity.**
vv. 1-12	Job charges friends as "worthless physicians" knowing suffering, not pain.
vv. 13-28	Job's concern is silence of God in face of his suffering.
Chapter 14	**Job Speaks of Life's Woes.**
vv. 1-6	Job begs God to treat man with more compassion and mercy.
vv. 7-17	Man can only live once; but, if a tree is cut, it may sprout again.
vv. 18-22	Job feels pain and mourns for himself showing frailty of man!
Chapter 15	**Eliphaz Rebukes Job.**
vv. 1-6	Eliphaz again accuses Job, attacking Job's wisdom.
vv. 7-16	Job is accused of forgetting his human limitations.
vv. 17-35	Eliphaz denounces wicked saying they do not prosper in contrast to Job's reply.
Chapter 16	**Job Complains of God's Hostility.**
vv. 1-5	Job rebukes Eliphaz and the others.
vv. 6-17	Job knows nothing about God and devil; he believes God is afflicting him.
vv. 18-22	Job maintains he has right to cry out to God for his innocence.
Chapter 17	**Job Appeals to God.**
vv. 1-2	Job says he is ready for grave while accusers watch him die.
vv. 3-5	He criticizes friends who have failed him.
vv. 6-16	Job loses hope and his thoughts turn to dying.
Chapter 18	**Bildad Speaks of Lot of Wicked.**
vv. 1-4	Bildad rebukes Job for implying friends are stupid.

vv. 5-21	Bildad believes suffering does not happen to righteous as does Job.

Chapter 19 — **Job Speaks of Friends' Cruelty.**

vv. 1-12	Job claims their words are cruel as strikes upon his body.
vv. 13-22	Job's experience is a foreshadow of what Jesus must suffer from His society.
vv. 23-29	Job believes one day, he will be vindicated standing before God – Redeemer.

Chapter 20 — **Zophar Speaks of Wicked.**

vv. 1-11	Zophar maintains a wicked man will be punished despite his appeals to God.
vv. 12-29	Wicked will ultimately be struck down and eventually lose their wealth.

Chapter 21 — **Job Bemoans e Prosperity of Wicked.**

vv. 1-16	Job states that many wicked live and die in natural, physical prosperity on earth.
vv. 17-26	Man cannot tell God how to judge wicked or righteous on earth.
vv. 27-34	Job never discovers why righteous suffer but he does not believe theology of friends.

Chapter 22 — **Eliphaz Accuses Job of Wickedness.**

vv. 1-20	Eliphaz assumes Job is siding in with prosperous wicked.
vv. 21-30	Job, "If you humble yourself and repent, God will deliver you."

Chapter 23 — **Job Yearns for Access to God.**

vv. 1-7	"If I could plead before God, He would acquit me," says Job.
vv. 8-17	Job says the presence of God is more terrible to him than nearness of death.

Chapter 24 — **Job Complains of God's Indifference to Wickedness.**

vv. 1-12	"Many poor, afflicted people seem to get no help from God," says Job.

vv. 13-17	Some crimes occur in daylight, but majority occur in darkness.
vv. 18-20	"You say, God's justice may be delayed, but it never fails," Job says to Eliphaz.
vv. 21-25	God will judge wicked, but in this life His punishment is not always seen.

Chapter 25 — How Can Man be Justified with God?

vv. 1-6	Bildad states that unclean man cannot be righteous before God.

Chapter 26 — Job Reproves Bildad and Praises God.

vv. 1-14	Job puts down Bildad and praises God's might and wisdom.

Chapter 27 — Job Truthfully Maintains Innocence.

vv. 1-6	Job will die before agreeing he is untruthful.
vv. 7-23	Job states the wickedly wealthy without God will lose all and end in misery.

Chapter 28 — Wisdom is God's Gift.

vv. 1-6	Human technology is powerless compared to divine knowledge.
vv. 7-8	Birds and animals cannot understand divine wisdom.
vv. 9-11	Man can do much, but cannot understand divine wisdom.
vv. 12-19	Man cannot understand nor value the gift of divine wisdom.
vv. 20-22	Wisdom is hidden from all creation.
vv. 23-28	Only God knows value of wisdom and understanding.

Chapter 29 — Job Speaks of Past Wealth and Happiness.

vv. 1-20	Job revered by all people and blessed by God in the past.
vv. 21-25	Job was honored in the past before his present sufferings.

Chapter 30 — Job Bemoans His Present Condition.

vv. 1-8	Those who once honored Job no longer respect him.
vv. 9-23	Good days now gone; Job awaits God's time for his death.
vv. 24-31	Job pleads for God's mercies, but they seem not heard.

Chapter 31 — Job Speaks of His Integrity.

vv. 1-4	Asserting his integrity Job reviews his past morality.

vv. 5-8	If he is wrong, let someone else collect his prosperity instead of Job.
vv. 9-12	Job never coveted a man's wife which is a "heinous crime."
vv. 13-15	Job has never taken advantage of his servants but has shown kindness to them.
vv. 16-23	Job's fear of God never let him ignore a poor person, widow, or orphan.
vv. 24-28	Job claims his wealth has not made him proud.
vv. 29-37	Job's confidence in his goodness has not been shaken.
vv. 38-40	If Job has done wrongly, may his fields produce thorns, not grain.
Chapter 32	**Elihu is Angry with Job and His Friends.**
v. 1	Job's friends stop answering because he is righteous in his own mind.
vv. 2-3	Elihu is angry with Job and his friends.
vv. 4-14	Elihu gives reasons for not speaking earlier.
vv. 15-22	Elihu has to speak due to opinions he must give.
Chapter 33	**Elihu Reasons with Job.**
v. 1	Elihu addresses Job.
vv. 2-8	He tells Job he is another human made by God.
vv. 9-13	Elihu rehearses Job's claims about his innocence before God.
vv. 14-22	God speaks to man in various ways.
vv. 23-30	God sends messengers to man, correcting him from errors.
vv. 31-33	Elihu admonishes Job to listen.
Chapter 34	**God Cannot Be Unjust.**
vv. 1-2	Elihu addresses all four men.
vv. 3-9	He rehearses Job's justification of himself.
vv. 10-15	If God should withdraw His breath mankind would perish.
vv. 16-37	Elihu tells all four that Job needs to confess and trust God.
Chapter 35	**Elihu Exhorts Job to Trust God.**
vv. 1-3	Elihu rehearses Job's statements.

vv. 4-9	"Job, what good is your righteousness before God?"
vv. 10-16	Job replies, "Elihu justifies himself in vain."

Chapter 36 — **Elihu Shows God's Justice.**

vv. 1-4	Elihu justifies his answers.
vv. 5-15	God judges men by goodness or wickedness.
vv. 16-25	God is no respecter of persons.
vv. 26-33	God is too great for man to comprehend Him.

Chapter 37 — **The Greatness of God**

vv. 1-5	Listen to the thunder of God's voice.
vv. 6-13	Elihu rehearses God's power over nature.
vv. 14-24	God orders nature to obey Him.

Chapter 38 — **God Questions Job About His Mighty Creation.**

v. 1	God talks now to Job.
vv. 2-21	God questions Job about His marvelous works.
vv. 22-41	God asks Job about heavens and care for His animals.

Chapter 39 — **God's Greatness Manifested in His Creation.**

vv. 1-4	"Can you, Job, explain animals deliver their young?"
vv. 5-12	"Can you, Job, explain why animals live in rural areas, instead of cities?"
vv. 13-18	God withholds wisdom from ostriches.
vv. 19-25	God made horses not to fear in battles.
vv. 26-30	"Can you, Job, understand ways of hawks and eagles?"

Chapter 40 — **God's Power, Revealed in Large Animals.**

vv. 1-2	Can Job instruct God?
vv. 3-5	Job apologizes for his ignorance before God.
vv. 6-14	God instructs Job to be humble.
vv. 15-24	"Dinosaurs eat grass and mightily move their huge tails," God tells Job.

Chapter 41 — **God's Power, Revealed in Leviathans.**

vv. 1-10	God describes fierceness of water creatures like "crocodiles" or "sea dinosaurs."

vv. 11-34	Science proved dinosaurs can produce flames from hydrogen and carbon in nostrils.
Chapter 42	**God Accepts Job and Blesses Him.**
vv. 1-6	Job repents to God now seeing God's glory and greatness.
vv. 7-8	God rebukes Eliphaz and friends for not doing what Job did.
v. 9	Three men offer sacrifices of seven bulls and seven rams.
vv. 10-12	God blesses Job with twice as much as he previously owned.
vv. 13-15	Job has three daughters and seven sons. Daughters receive the same inheritance as sons.
vv. 16-17	Job lives 140 years after his tribulations.

PSALMS

Chapter 1	**Wisdom Psalm Contrasting Fate of Righteous and Wicked**
vv. 1-3	Blessed a man, meditating on God's law shall prosper.
vv. 4-6	Wicked man's way shall perish.
Chapter 2	**Royal Psalm Enthroning God's King on Zion.**
vv. 1-3	Heathens conspire against God and His appointed King.
vv. 4-6	God sits His Messianic King on Throne in Zion (Jerusalem).
vv. 7-9	God's King will crush His enemies.
vv. 10-11	Kings, be wise and submit to the Lord with reverence to be blessed of God.
Chapter 3	**Psalm of Lament and Prayer of Trust in God (as David flees Absalom).**
vv. 1-2	People are saying David is helpless against Absalom.
vv. 3-4	David laments but trusts in God to deliver him.
vv. 5-6	David declares confidence in God, his Protector.
vv. 7-8	David concludes with first of 71 "Selahs" in Psalms.
Chapter 4	**A Lamenting Prayer for Deliverance from Personal Enemies**
v. 1	David pleads God's gracious answer to his prayer of distress.
vv. 2-3	David reaffirms that God hears his prayers.
vv. 4-5	One can be angry without sinning and trust God.
vv. 6-7	David confesses his joy in the Lord.
v. 8	David trusts God for a good night's sleep.
Chapter 5	**Prayerful Lament for Deliverance from Personal Enemies**
vv. 1-3	David begins day, meditating on God.
vv. 4-6	David declares God's hatred of wickedness.

vv. 7-8	David declares God's love and his desire to worship God.
vv. 9-10	David implores God to judge wicked.
vv. 11-12	The Lord protects righteous in times of trouble.
Chapter 6	**Lamenting Prayer for Healing (First of Seven Penitential Psalms)**
vv. 1-3	David attributes affliction to sin; he confesses his sin.
vv. 4-5	David claims no praising in Sheol, place of dead.
vv. 6-7	David's affliction causes moaning.
vv. 8-10	David proclaims God has heard and will deliver him.
Chapter 7	**Lamenting Prayer from Personal Enemies**
vv. 1-2	Save me God, my enemies seek to destroy me.
vv. 3-5	David asks God to punish him if he wronged others.
vv. 6-8	Prayer for intervention in David's trial
vv. 9-11	God is a Righteous Judge.
vv. 12-16	God punishes the unrepentant.
vv. 17	David promises praise to the Most High.
Chapter 8	**God's Glory and Man's Dignity**
v. 1	God's name is above all names.
v. 2	Matthew 21:15-16 is fulfillment of this verse as Christ enters Jerusalem on a colt.
vv. 3-4	Man is seen as weak and as second only to God in glory and dignity.
vv. 5-8	All life is under man's dominion.
v. 9	God's name is great on earth.
Chapter 9	**Prayerful lamentation for deliverance**
vv. 1-2	David promises to praise God.
vv. 3-4	He praises God for righteous judgment.
vv. 5-6	God removes names of wicked.
vv. 7-8	God judges righteously.
vv. 9-10	God blesses those who seek Him.
vv. 11-12	God knows cry of afflicted.
vv. 13-14	David recounts present situation.

vv. 15-16	Wicked reap what they sow.
vv. 17-18	Wicked go to Sheol and poor have hope.
vv. 19-20	God judges nations!
Chapter 10	**Prayer to Overthrow Wicked.**
vv. 1-2	Wicked be caught in schemes.
vv. 3-4	Wicked proclaims "There is no God."
vv. 5-6	Wicked believe no suffering of adversity.
vv. 7-8	Wicked plot murder of innocent.
vv. 8-9	Wicked scam poor.
vv. 10-11	Hapless think God forgets them.
vv. 12-13	Why do wicked renounce God?
v. 14	God helps fatherless.
vv. 15-16	God destroys wicked from land.
vv. 17-18	God blesses fatherless and oppressed.
Chapter 11	**Confidence in God for Justice**
vv. 1-7	God judges wicked and blesses righteous.
Chapter 12	**David's Prayer for Deliverance from His Enemies.**
vv. 1-2	Save me, God, from unfaithful people.
vv. 3-4	Save me, God, from flatterers.
vv. 5-6	God promises to help poor and needy.
vv. 7-8	Protect us God, from prowling, invasive, wicked people who come at us.
Chapter 13	**Prayer for Help from Enemies**
vv. 1-2	When will you help me, God?
vv. 3-4	Help, lest my enemies prevail.
vv. 5-6	I will praise God because He blesses me.
Chapter 14	**Condemnation of Cynical, Unrighteous Age**
vv. 1-4	All are corrupted atheists.
vv. 5-7	Unrighteous shall be terrified; for God is with righteous.
Chapter 15	**Admission into God's Holy Temple**
v. 1	Who shall dwell in Holy Temple?

vv. 2-5	Qualities of those who can enter God's Holy Temple.
Chapter 16	**Song of Trust in God**
v. 1	Good is only in the Lord.
vv. 3-4	Holy ones are delightful to God and David.
vv. 5-6	The Lord blesses David.
vv. 7-8	David keeps the Lord close to himself.
vv. 9-10	God saves David from pit.
V. 11	In God's presence is fullness of joy.
Chapter 17	**Prayer from Personal Enemies**
vv. 1-5	God, I have tried to follow You, always.
vv. 6-7	Keep me from enemies as I call upon you, my Lord.
vv. 8-9	Keep me safe, O Lord, from those around me.
vv. 10-12	David describes accusers as lions eager to destroy him.
vv. 13-14	Confront and overthrow my enemies, God!
v. 15	When I awake, I shall see my deliverance.
Chapter 18	**David Thanks God for Delivering Him from Saul.**
	(2 Samuel Chapter 22).
vv. 1-3	God's readiness to help David
vv. 4-6	Difficulties from which David is delivered.
vv. 7-19	God's intervention in battle
vv. 20-27	David attributes God's favor to keeping commandments.
vv. 28-30	Confidence increased with God's help.
vv. 31-42	Account of battle and subsequent victory
vv. 43-45	David becomes ruler over a peaceful kingdom.
vv. 46-50	Concluding hymn of praise and thanksgiving to God for victory
Chapter 19	**Praise to God as Creator and Lawgiver**
vv. 1-4	Works of creation tell of God's glory.
vv. 5-6	Sun is as a glorious bridegroom.
vv. 7-13	David delights in God's words, wanting to be a blameless servant.
v. 14	Let my thoughts and words be acceptable to my King!

Chapter 20	**Prayer for Victory in Battle**
vv. 1-3	May God remember good works.
vv. 4-5	May He meet all needs.
vv. 6-8	We boast in name of our God.
v. 9	Give us victory O Lord when we call.
Chapter 21	**Thanksgiving after Victory**
vv. 1-7	God is praised for answered prayer.
vv. 8-12	God will destroy all enemies.
v. 13	God exalted for great strength
Chapter 22	**Prayer for Deliverance from Mortal Illness**
	(Crucifixion Psalm)
vv. 1-5	Cry for help (Mark 15:34)
vv. 6-8	Mocker says God has deserted him.
vv. 9-11	He remembers God's past help.
vv. 12-13	His tormentors act like animals.
vv. 14-15	David recounts fever and weaknesses.
v. 16	Enemies howl like mad dogs.
vv. 17-18	Enemies divide clothing for themselves.
vv. 19-21	Prayer for deliverance from slanderers
vv. 22-24	When he recovers, he will offer vow of thanksgiving in temple.
vv. 25-31	He will sing hymn of praise to Deliverer.
Chapter 23	**Expression of God's Protection**
vv. 1-4	God compared to a Shepherd.
vv. 5-6	God compared to a gracious Host.
Chapter 24	**Upon Entering Sanctuary**
vv. 1-2	God acknowledged as Creator
v. 3	Who is admitted into temple?
vv. 4-6	Moral ones admitted into temple.
vv. 7-10	Choir wants admittance into God's presence inside temple.

Chapter 25	**Prayer for Deliverance from Enemies**
vv. 1-3	Let not my enemies exult over Your people.
vv. 4-7	Remember me, God, because of Your goodness.
vv. 8-10	God blesses those keeping covenant.
vv. 11-15	God protects those who fear Him.
vv. 16-18	O Lord, forgive my sins.
vv. 19-21	Save me, O Lord, as I wait upon You.
v. 22	Help Israel, O Lord, from troubles.
Chapter 26	**Prayer for Deliverance from Enemies**
vv. 1-3	Cry for vindication from unjust charge (1 Kings 8:31-32)
vv. 4-5	He claims innocence (Psalms 4:2-4).
vv. 6-7	He is clean and praises God (Deut. 21:6-8, Psalms 51:7).
vv. 8-10	Prayer for God's help from evil men (Isaiah 4:5, Ezekiel 43:4-5)
vv. 11-12	David is righteous and blesses God.
Chapter 27	**Act of Devotion and Prayer for Deliverance**
vv. 1-6	Song of trust for God's protection
vv. 7-14	Cry for help with expression of confidence in God's goodness
Chapter 28	**Prayer for Deliverance from Enemies**
vv. 1-5	Cry for vindication and justice for evildoers
vv. 6-9	Psalmist is grateful for God's mercy.
Chapter 29	**Hymn to God of the Storm**
vv. 1-2	Call to worship God
vv. 3-9	God's voice is seen in thunder, waters and lightning flashes.
vv. 10-11	Above the storm God reigns as King.
Chapter 30	**Thanksgiving for Healing**
vv. 1-3	God praised for psalmist's recovery from illness
vv. 4-7	He urges congregation to praise God for loving favor.
vv. 8-10	He asserts case for life and health to God, his Physician.
vv. 11-12	He praises God for changing mourning into joyful dancing.

Chapter 31		**Prayer for Deliverance from Enemies**
vv. 1-8		Cry and gratitude for His help
vv. 9-24		Cry and gratitude for help as one waits on Him.
Chapter 32		**Thanksgiving for Healing**
vv. 1-2		God is praised for psalmist's healing.
vv. 3-5		Healing came after acknowledging himself as sinner.
vv. 6-7		God preserves and encompasses us from troubles.
vv. 8-9		Be open before God and receive instruction.
vv. 10-11		God's love surrounds those who trust Him.
Chapter 33		**Hymn to God as Creator of History**
vv. 1-3		Call to worship the Lord
vv. 4-5		The Lord loves righteousness and justice.
vv. 6-9		Lord spoke heavens, earth and hosts into existence by word and breath of mouth.
vv. 10-19		God rules over destinies of nations.
vv. 20-22		Israel puts her complete trust in God.
Chapter 34		**Thanksgiving for Deliverance from Trouble**
vv. 1-3		Brief hymn of exaltation to the Lord
vv. 4-10		Lord cares for those who trust in Him.
vv. 11-18		Lord hears righteous but not evildoers.
vv. 19-22		God delivers His people from many afflictions.
Chapter 35		**Plea for Deliverance and Vindication**
vv. 1-6		Cry for vindication and vengeance
vv. 7-10		Vengeance for enemies and praise for God
vv. 11-18		He thanks the Lord as God rescues him from enemies.
vv. 19-29		Psalmist praises the Lord when enemies are defeated.
Chapter 36		**Liturgy of Lamentation**
vv. 1-4		Wicked are inspired by transgression.
vv. 5-9		Psalmist describes God's character.
vv. 10-11		Prayer for deliverance
v. 12		Assurance of prayer being answered

Chapter 37	**Retribution for Wicked**
vv. 1-7	Wait upon the Lord for blessing righteous and destroying wicked.
vv. 8-19	God blesses His people and cuts off wicked.
vv. 20-31	Righteous are led by the Lord.
vv. 32-40	God delivers righteous out of hands of wicked.
Chapter 38	**Prayer for Healing When Sick**
vv. 1-2	Psalmist cries to God for help.
vv. 3-4	He acknowledges his sickness and sin.
vv. 5-11	God, you know all of my circumstances.
vv. 12-16	God, I am helpless but You can help me.
vv. 17-22	God, I confess my iniquity. Only You can deliver me.
Chapter 39	**Prayer for Healing in Sickness**
vv. 1-3	He controls feelings during sickness so to discourage enemies.
vv. 4-6	All human life is short.
vv. 7-11	Prayer for healing
vv. 12-13	He wants respite from illness before passing to grave.
Chapter 40	**Thanksgiving for Deliverance from Trouble**
vv. 1-3	Psalmist recounts his experience.
vv. 4-10	Fulfillment of vow is speaking of God's goodness to His people.
vv. 11-17	He recites situation, praying for deliverance by God's strength.
Chapter 41	**Prayer for Healing from Sickness**
vv. 1-3	The Lord blesses those who consider the poor.
vv. 4-9	Being mortally ill, his best friend turns against him.
vv. 10-13	He is pleased knowing God loves and blesses him.
Chapter 42	**Preparation for a Pilgrimage**
vv. 1-5	My soul shall not be sad but it shall hope in God.
vv. 6-8	My soul is cast down but God commands His steadfast love toward me.

vv. 9-10	God is my Rock though enemies taunt me asking "Where is your God?"
v. 11	I am cast down but I do hope in God.

Chapter 43 — **Prayer for Healing in Preparation for a Pilgrimage**

vv. 1-2	Vindicate me God. I take refuge in You.
vv. 3-4	Help me, God, and I will praise You.
v. 5	My "disquieted soul", shall praise God.

Chapter 44 — **Prayer for Deliverance from National Enemies**

vv. 1-3	Father, we know what you did to other nations and planting us in the land.
vv. 4-8	God is our King and we shall boast in Him.
vv. 9-12	God has let our enemies overtake us.
vv. 13-16	Taunters have shamed and discouraged us.
vv. 17-19	We have not forgotten You, Oh Lord.
vv. 20-22	We are as sheep for the slaughter.
vv. 23-26	Help us, God, because of Your steadfast love.

Chapter 45 — **Ode for Royal Wedding**

v. 1	My heart is overflowing as a poet's.
vv. 2-9	Bridegroom is a king of Israel.
vv. 10-13a	Tyre's Phoenician queen is to be loyal to her king-husband.
vv. 13b-15	Wedding procession takes place here.
vv. 16-17	Poet promises king prominence.

Chapter 46 — **Song Celebrating God's Victory over Nations**

vv. 1-3	Regardless of circumstances our confidence is in God.
vv. 4-7	World totters but God sustains us.
vv. 8-11	Relax, God controls everything.

Chapter 47 — **Celebration of God's Enthronement as King over all**

vv. 1-4	Rejoice, God chose us as His people.
vv. 5-7	Worship the King of whole earth.
vv. 8-9	Worship God Who is highly exalted.

Chapter 48	**Celebrating Beauty and Security of Zion**
vv. 1-3	Great is God and His city.
vv. 4-8	Kings attacking Jerusalem are scattered.
vv. 9-11	This causes rejoicing in temple.
vv. 12-14	Tell next generation about our God.
Chapter 49	**Meditation on Life and Wealth**
vv. 1-4	Writer summons his audience together.
vv. 5-6	Why should one fear the powerful?
vv. 7-12	No one can take wealth with him.
vv. 13-14	Death is end for all men on earth.
v. 15	Writer is delivered from trouble but he will die on earth.
vv. 16-20	Do not fear wealthy for they will die as all others.
Chapter 50	**Liturgy of Divine Judgment**
vv. 1-6	God will judge His faithful ones.
vv. 7-13	God doesn't need sacrifices; He owns everything.
vv. 14-15	God wants thanksgiving and praise.
vv. 16-21	God rebukes people for their evils.
vv. 22-23	God blesses those who honor Him!
Chapter 51	**Prayer for Healing and Moral Renewal**
vv. 1-2	Prayer for moral and physical deliverance
vv. 3-5	Confession of the psalmist's sinful nature from birth
vv. 6-12	Renewal prayer for deliverance
vv. 13-17	God accepts broken and contrite spirit from people.
vv. 18-19	This added to modify above anti-sacrificial spirit of verses 16-17.
Chapter 52	**God's Judgment against a Tyrant**
vv. 1-4	Description of writer's enemy
vv. 5-7	No refuge in man's wealth
vv. 8-9	Psalmist is confident of deliverance.
Chapter 53	**Condemnation of Unrighteous Age**
v. 1	None who do good.
v. 2	God seeks those who do good.

v. 3	None do good, says psalmist.
v. 4	Evil doers have no understanding.
v. 5	God rejects ungodly.
v. 6	One day Israel will be restored, says hopeful psalmist.
Chapter 54	**Prayer for Deliverance from Enemies**
vv. 1-2	Cry for help
v. 3	"Insolent men are seeking my life."
v. 4-5	God will help me against enemies.
vv. 6-7	God delivered me; I will praise Him.
Chapter 55	**Prayer for Help from Enemies**
vv. 1-2	Cry for help
vv. 3-15	Enemy is a former close friend. He returns curses to those cursing him.
vv. 16-19	God always helps me.
vv. 20-23	God casts down enemies; I will trust Him.
Chapter 56	**Prayer for Deliverance from Enemies**
vv. 1-2	Cry for God's help
vv. 3-4	I trust God. What can enemies do?
vv. 5-7	Put down these fighting me, O God.
vv. 8-11	What can man do? I trust God!
vv. 12-13	I will pay vows to God; he delivered me from death.
Chapter 57	**Prayer for Deliverance from Enemies**
vv. 1-3	I cry to God who protects me.
vv. 4-6	Certainty that God hears prayer for help.
vv. 7-11	Thanksgiving vow to God for His goodness.
Chapter 58	**Prayer for Punishment of Wicked**
vv. 1-5	This language counters curses spoken over psalmist.
vv. 6-9	This is curse against enemies.
vv. 10-11	Deliverance from God is certain.
Chapter 59	**Prayer for Deliverance from Enemies**
vv. 1-2	Cry for help from enemies
vv. 3-7	Prayer against "howling dogs"

vv. 8-10	Psalmist's expression of trust
vv. 11-15	Appeal for retribution against enemies
vv. 16-17	Vow to praise his God
Chapter 60	**Prayer for Help Against National Enemies**
vv. 1-3	Israel's situation following defeat by Edomites
vv. 4-5	"Thy beloved" refers to David or to Israel.
vv. 6-8	God claims all nations mentioned here.
vv. 9-12	Prayer for victory by God's help, not man's
Chapter 61	**David's Prayer for Protection**
vv. 1-2	Cry for help in distress
vv. 3-5	Expression of trust in God
vv. 6-7	Prayer for king on pilgrimage
v. 8	He pays vows by praising God.
Chapter 62	**My Soul Waits for God.**
vv. 1-2	David says, "He waits for Salvation in silence."
vv. 3-4	Enemies bless outwardly but curse inwardly.
vv. 5-7	My refuge and hope are in God.
vv. 8-10	Trust not in men nor riches but only in God.
vv. 11-12	Love belongs to God who has all power.
Chapter 63	**David's Psalm in Judean Wilderness**
vv. 1-4	God better than life; I praise Him.
vv. 5-8	I joyfully meditate on Him who upholds me.
vv. 9-11	King rejoices in God while enemies go to their fate.
Chapter 64	**Cry for Help and Praise to God**
vv. 1-6	Spare me, O Lord, from enemies.
vv. 7-9	God takes down wicked; all men will think about Him.
v. 10	Righteous take refuge in God.
Chapter 65	**God's Bounty in Nature**
vv. 1-4	We praise God and are content in His temple.
vv. 5-8	God answers with deliverance; we shall revere Him.
vv. 9-13	God cares for earth in every manner.

Chapter 66		**Praise for God's Mighty Deeds**
vv. 1-4		Give praise to our great, powerful God.
vv. 5-7		See what God has done for Israel.
vv. 8-12		God brought us through water.
vv. 13-15		I pay vows of offerings to God.
vv. 16-19		God hears prayer; I am clean before Him.
v. 20		Praise God; He heard prayer and did not reject me.
Chapter 67		**God's Equity Blesses Earth.**
vv. 1-3		Bless us, and we will praise You.
vv. 4-5		Praise God who judges with equity.
vv. 6-7		Let earth praise God for increased productivity.
Chapter 68		**God of Sinai, Now in His Sanctuary**
vv. 1-3		Let righteous be jubilant before God.
v. 4		Sing to God who rides above clouds.
vv. 5-6		God blesses needy and reproaches rebellious.
vv. 7-10		When God goes before Israelites, they have provision and security.
vv. 11-14		At God's command enemies flee.
vv. 15-16		God's Sinai is His abode above other mountains.
vv. 17-18		God goes from Sinai into holy place.
vv. 19-20		God, our Salvation, leads us safely.
vv. 21-23		God shatters leadership of enemies.
vv. 24-27		Processions of God enter sanctuary.
vv. 28-31		God's strength conquers foes.
vv. 33-35		Almighty God, gives empowerment to His people.
Chapter 69		**Cry of Distress**
vv. 1-3		Hear me, O Lord, I am awaiting your help.
vv. 4-5		I have done wrong, O Lord; still, I trust in You.
vv. 6-8		Father, let not my follies discourage others.
vv. 9-12		They ridicule me though I have repented.
vv. 13-15		Keep me safe from enemies.
vv. 16-18		Answer and help me, O Lord.

vv. 19-21	They reproach and insult me, O Lord.
vv. 22-28	Erase their names, O Lord; they persecute your servant.
v. 29	Your salvation, O Lord, sets me on high.
vv. 30-33	The Lord helps the oppressed and needy.
vv. 34-36	Those who love God will dwell in holy city, Jerusalem.
Chapter 70	**Another Cry for Help**
vv. 1-3	God, let shame be those who seek my life.
vv. 4-5	Hasten to help me, God.
Chapter 71	**Prayer of Old Man**
vv. 1-3	God, save me; You are my Refuge.
vv. 4-6	I praise You, O Lord, for your presence.
vv. 7-11	Help old man, God, whom foes hate.
vv. 12-16	I will tell Your mighty deeds to others, O Lord.
vv. 17-19	As old man, I proclaim Thy might.
vv. 20-21	Thou will revive and honor me.
vv. 22-24	I praise Thee, O Lord, for shaming foes.
Chapter 72	**Reign of Solomon, "In Righteousness"**
vv. 1-4	David cries for Solomon's righteousness in ruling.
vv. 5-7	May Solomon's rule be righteous and peaceful.
vv. 8-11	May kingdoms honor Solomon.
vv. 12-14	King helps poor and needy.
vv. 15-17	David's confession of kingship of Israel
vv. 18-20	A doxology of blessing the Lord of Israel
Chapter 73	**End of Wicked**
vv. 1-3	I was envious, seeing wicked prosper.
vv. 4-9	Wicked people are arrogant.
vv. 10-14	I suffer while wicked strut.
vv. 15-20	God wipes wicked away in one stroke.
vv. 21-26	Thou, O Lord, my Strength and Deliverer.
vv. 27-28	I will tell of God's wonderful works.
Chapter 74	**Appeal to God Against Enemy**
vv. 1-3	Remember Lord, enemy has destroyed sanctuary.

vv. 4-11	Why wait Lord, when enemy is devastating Your people?
vv. 12-17	Hymn-like interlude, celebrating God as Creator
vv. 18-19	Remember O God and forget not Israel.
vv. 20-21	Remember covenant O God and let poor and needy praise Thy Name.
vv. 22-23	Arise O God and chastise those scoffing at Your Name.

Chapter 75 — God of Judgment

v. 1	Thank You, O Lord, for deeds.
vv. 2-3	Priest or prophet says, "God will judge one day with equity."
vv. 4-8	God will judge boastful wicked.
vv. 9-10	I l rejoice for God takes off horns of wicked.

Chapter 76 — God's Ultimate Victory over Nations

vv. 1-3	In Zion, God defeats enemies.
vv. 4-6	Hymn to victorious God of Israel.
vv. 7-9	God arises to establish righteous judgment.
vv. 10-12	God turns evil to His good purposes; praise the Lord!

Chapter 77 — Meditations on God's Mighty Deeds

vv. 1-2	I cry but my soul is not comforted.
vv. 3-10	Psalmist's agony is intense; he questions God's justice and love.
vv. 11-15	Asaph encourages himself, recalling God's past deeds.
vv. 16-20	Asaph quotes a hymn praising God for creation and Israel's history.

Chapter 78 — God's Guidance of His People

vv. 1-4	Exhortation concerning God's deeds for His people.
vv. 5-8	Parents are to teach children laws of God.
vv. 9-16	Here is noted defection of Ephramites.
vv. 17-20	Faithlessness of Israel is described.
vv. 21-31	God destroys those demanding meat in wilderness.
vv. 32-55	God cared for Israel and devastated Egypt with ten plagues.
vv. 55-66	People provoke God but He protects them from enemies.
vv. 67-72	God rejects Israel and blesses Judah.

Chapter 79	**Lament Over Destruction of Jerusalem**
vv. 1-4	Cry for actions from Judah's enemies.
vv. 5-7	How long O God, will You wait to avenge us?
vv. 8-13	Avenge us, O God; we will praise You.
Chapter 80	**Prayer for Restoration**
vv. 1-2	Help us, Shepherd of Israel.
v. 3	Restore and save us Lord!
vv. 4-6	Our enemies laugh at us Lord.
v. 7	Restore and save us God.
vv. 8-13	Israel, once cared for now, forsaken.
vv. 14-18	Rescue us Lord and we will serve You.
v. 19	Restore us Lord, and save us.
Chapter 81	**God's Goodness and Israel's Waywardness**
vv. 1-5	Hymn-like summons to worship at Feast of Tabernacles
vv. 6-10	Priest or prophet reminding people of God's blessings and their disobedience.
vv. 11-16	Israel's prosperity depends on willingness to obey God.
Chapter 82	**God's Judgment on Pagan Gods**
vv. 1-2	God judges all gods.
vv. 3-4	Minister justly to the oppressed.
v. 5	False gods govern earth unjustly.
vv. 6-7	Children of a god die like other people.
v. 8	Prayer for God's righteous judgment
Chapter 83	**Prayer for Help against National Enemies**
vv. 1-8	God, our enemies are conspiring against Israel.
vv. 9-12	God, judge these opposing nations as You judged other nations.
vv. 13-18	God, let opposing nations know You are Most High God!
Chapter 84	**God's Dwelling Place is Lovely**
vv. 1-2	Sons of Korah hunger for temple of God.
vv. 3-4	Blessed are God's temple dwellers.
vv. 5-7	Joys of pilgrimage through Baca

vv. 8-9	Look upon and bless Israel, O Lord.
vv. 10-12	Life in God's temple is best life.
Chapter 85	**God Removed His Anger from Israel.**
vv. 1-3	God's favor to Israel remembered
vv. 4-7	Prayer for God's favor again to Israel
vv. 8-9	God blesses those returning to Him.
vv. 10-13	Oracle of assurance declared
Chapter 86	**Show Us Thy Steadfast Love.**
vv. 1-7	Gracious God, help in my troubles.
vv. 8-13	Great God, deliver me from death.
vv. 14-17	Faithful God, comfort me in presence of enemies.
Chapter 87	**The Lord Loves Gates of Zion.**
vv. 1-3	God loves Zion above all Israel cities.
vv. 4-6	God notes Zion's people are all over the earth.
v. 7	Worshippers agree Zion is City of God.
Chapter 88	**Prayer for Healing from Sickness**
vv. 1-2	Saddest Psalm of all due to hopelessness
vv. 3-7	Psalmist overwhelmed by God's chastisement
vv. 8-12	God, why don't You hear my prayers?
vv. 13-18	God, have You forgotten me?
Chapter 89	**King Prays for Deliverance from Enemies.**
vv. 1-4	David recalls God's covenant with him.
vv. 5-18	Hymn extols God's power and faithfulness.
vv. 19-37	God is faithful and establishes David's throne forever.
vv. 38-45	King is defeated in battle. It seems God has forsaken His covenant.
vv. 46-48	How long will you keep from helping me?
vv. 49-52	Prayer that God keeps promise to help David's descendant.
Chapter 90	**Prayer of Moses, a Man of God** **The Oldest Psalm**
vv. 1-2	God, You have been here always!
vv. 3-4	Time is nothing to You, O Lord!

vv. 5-6	Man comes and goes like grass.
vv. 7-8	We can hide nothing from You, O Lord!
vv. 9-10	At most our life is only eighty years.
vv. 11-12	Teach us to number our days for wisdom's sake.
vv. 13-17	God, establish the labor of our hands.
Chapter 91	**Abiding in Shadow of Almighty**
vv. 1-6	In God's presence we are protected from men, demons and natural disasters.
vv. 7-8	God's protection amazes mankind.
vv. 9-10	By making God our refuge, we are safe.
vv. 11-13	His angels will protect you.
vv. 14-16	God blesses faithful believers.
Chapter 92	**Song for Sabbath**
vv. 1-4	God, You make me glad.
vv. 5-9	God, evildoers shall be scattered.
vv. 10-15	Psalmist exults in Lord's vindication, an answer to prayers.
Chapter 93	**Hymn Extolling God as King**
vv. 1-2	The Lord reigns from everlasting.
vv. 3-4	God's rule is His control over powers of chaos.
v. 5	God is praised because law and temple are dependable.
Chapter 94	**Cry for Help from Evil Men**
vv. 1-3	God, how long shall wicked exult?
vv. 4-7	Wicked do evil saying You don't notice!
vv. 8-11	God notices everything, O foolish people.
vv. 12-15	God s righteously with His people.
vv. 16-23	God will wipe out wicked.
Chapter 95	**Outline of Celebrating God as King**
vv. 1-5	Let's worship our God, the King.
vv. 6-7	As His sheep let's bow before Him.
vv. 8-11	Do not harden hearts as at Meribah; they died in wilderness.
Chapter 96	**Hymn Celebrating God's Kingship**

vv. 1-6		Worship God of all earth; other gods are powerless.
vv. 7-9		Worship with an offering.
vv. 10-13		God judges world righteously.

Chapter 97 — The Lord God Reigns.

vv. 1-5	All nature bows before God.
vv. 6-9	God is exalted above all gods.
vv. 10-12	Rejoice, God preserves righteous.

Chapter 98 — Future of God's Kingship on Earth

vv. 1-3	The Lord has victory over all earth.
vv. 4-6	Rejoice before God, the King!
vv. 7-9	The Lord righteously judges earth.

Chapter 99 — Celebration of God's Kingship

vv. 1-5	Worship God, for He is Holy!

Chapter 100 — All Nations Are to Praise God

vv. 1-2	Joyfully serve and sing to God.
v. 3	Know God as Lord and enjoy being His people.
v. 4	Give thanks, praise and bless His Holy Name.
v. 5	The Lord is good with enduring love to all.

Chapter 101 — King Pledges to Rule Justly

vv. 1-2	I will sing to Thee of loyalty and justice.
v. 3	I will keep my heart fixed on my Lord.
v. 4	I will do nothing with evil ways.
v. 5	I will abhor slandering, arrogant people.
v. 6	The blameless shall minister to me.
v. 7	Deceiving liars shall not dwell with me.
v. 8	I will not allow evildoers to enter Jerusalem.

Chapter 102 — An Afflicted Person's Prayer

vv. 1-2	Quickly answer request, O Lord.
vv. 3-11	Enemies regard hurting psalmist as forsaken by God.
vv. 12-17	He offers hymn of praise to God.
vv. 18-22	God will gather peoples and kingdoms to worship Him.

vv. 23-24	Forever God, lengthen my days on earth.
vv. 25-28	Eternal God, always the same

Chapter 103 — **Thanksgiving for Recovery from Illness**

vv. 1-5	Bless the Lord for meeting physical need.
vv. 6-14	Mighty God pities children.
vv. 15-18	God loves those keeping covenant
vv. 19-222	Heavenly hosts bless the Lord.

Chapter 104 — **Hymn to God of Creation**

vv. 1-4	Bless God, forever great.
vv. 5-9	God created whole earth.
vv. 10-13	God provides for birds and animals.
vv. 14-23	Animals and man provided for by God.
vv. 24-26	All creatures get life from God.
vv. 27-30	All creatures get life from God.
vv. 31-35	Thank God for being great.

Chapter 105 — **Wonderful Works of God**

vv. 1-6	Summoning Israel to praise and give thanksgiving.
vv. 7-11	God's faithfulness to His covenant with Israel's ancestors
vv. 12-15	Story of patriarchs protected by God
vv. 16-22	Story of Joseph as slave and prime minister
vv. 23-25	Story of Jacob and later, exodus from Egypt
vv. 26-36	Ten plagues are mentioned by Moses and Aaron on Egyptians and their gods.
vv. 37-42	God provides for Israelites going through wilderness from Egypt.
vv. 43-45	God keeps covenant by giving Canaan. Israel must keep covenant, too.

Chapter 106 — **God's Deeds and Israel's Rebellions**

vv. 1-3	Call to worship and need for righteousness
vv. 4-5	Psalmist prays he may share blessings as God prospers Israel.
vv. 6-7	Israel's unfaithfulness at Red Sea

vv. 8-12	Great God delivers Israel and drowns their foes.
vv. 13-15	God destroys Israelites when they craved quails.
vv. 16-18	God destroys those rebelling against Moses.
vv. 19-23	Moses pleads and God stops destroying rebellious.
vv. 24-27	Due to disbelief and rebellion God scatters Israelites among nations of world.
vv. 28-31	Phinehas stops plague sent to destroy Israelites.
vv. 32-39	Israelites accept religion and culture of Gentiles, sacrificing their babies.
vv. 40-46	God remembers covenant even though Israel forgets.
vv. 47-48	Save us, O Lord! Blessed be the Lord.
Chapter 107	**Group Thanksgiving for Pilgrims**
vv. 1-3	Call for everyone to give thanks
vv. 4-9	Description of wandering people who call on God for help
vv. 10-16	In distress they call on God and He delivers them.
vv. 17-22	They were sick; they cried to God; He sent His, healing them; be thankful.
vv. 23-32	They almost drowned, but God rescued them. Worship Almighty God!
vv. 33-38	God blesses labor, fields and cattle.
vv. 39-43	God rescues the suffering. Bless God!
Chapter 108	**Prayer for Victory over National Enemies**
vv. 1-4	David praises God for steadfast love.
vv. 5-6	Help and deliver, Oh Exalted God.
vv. 7-9	God is over all of David's enemies.
vv. 10-13	Help us, Oh God; vain is man's help.
Chapter 109	**Prayer for Deliverance from Personal Enemies**
vv. 1-5	David cries for God's help. Enemies return curses for love.
vv. 6-19	David counter-curses black magic of enemy.
vv. 20-25	David's prayer for deliverance
vv. 26-31	David praises God's care of needy and oppressed.

Chapter 110	**God Promises Victory to His King.**
v. 1	David prophesies God telling him Messiah will sit at His right hand.
vv. 2-4	God swears that Christ is priest forever like Melchizedek.
vv. 5-7	Christ, Priest and King, will rule the whole earth.
Chapter 111	**Hymn of Praise to God for Great Deeds**
vv. 1-10	Psalmist praises God for faithfulness in keeping covenant.
Chapter 112	**Rewards of Righteous Expounded**
vv. 1-10	God blesses generous and righteous. Desires of wicked are unfulfilled.
Chapter 113	**God Helps Humble**
v. 1	Praise the Lord His servants!
vv. 2-4	God's glory above heavens is exalted forevermore.
vv. 5-9	God helps poor and blesses barren women.
Chapter 114	**Praise God for Creating a Nation (A Hymn).**
vv. 1-2	Recalling of great Exodus
vv. 3-6	Miracle of crossing Red Sea and Jordan River
vv. 7-8	Physical world worships God who rules.
Chapter 115	**God's Power Contrasted with Idols**
vv. 1-2	Israel's sarcasm against heathen nations
vv. 3-8	Worshippers idols become like them.
vv. 9-11	Israel trust in the Lord; only God can help you.
vv. 12-13	God will bless Israel.
vv. 14-15	God, Who made everything, will bless you.
vv. 16-18	We, who are alive, bless God.
Chapter 116	**Thanksgiving for Healing**
vv. 1-4	Psalmist calls on God to save him.
vv. 5-7	The Lord deals bountifully with psalmist.
vv. 8-11	God delivers psalmist from death.
vv. 12-19	Psalmist pays his vows with gratitude for healing.

Chapter 117	**Doxology of Praise to God**
vv. 1-2	God's faithfulness endures forever.
Chapter 118	**Thanksgiving for Deliverance in Battle**
v. 1	Give thanks to God for steadfast love.
vv. 2-4	Let everyone proclaim God's steadfast, enduring love.
vv. 5-9	Who can harm \ me when I trust in God?
vv. 10-14	The Lord, Who helped me in battle, is my Salvation.
vv. 15-18	The Lord chastens but protects from death.
v. 19	Help me to be righteous and thankful.
v. 20	I shall be righteous!
vv. 21-25	Save, O Lord, and give success in battle.
vv. 26-27	Blessed be all who come in name of God.
v. 28	I thank and extol my Lord.
v. 29	Give thanks to God, for goodness and steadfast love.
Chapter 119	**Meditation on Law of God**
vv. 1-8	Prayer for help in keeping law
vv. 9-16	Prayer for help in observing law
vv. 17-24	Prayer for deliverance of enemies
vv. 25-32	Declaration of fidelity to law
vv. 33-40	Prayer to understand law
vv. 41-48	Prayer for help against scoffers
vv. 49-56	Confidence in keeping law in persecution
vv. 57-64	Declaring devotion to God
vv. 65-72	Recognizing value of discipline by God
vv. 73-80	God's ways are just; He is our Helper.
vv. 81-88	Prayer for deliverance from enemies
vv. 89-96	Confidence in God's word
vv. 97-104	Law is sweet and perfect.
vv. 105-112	Continuing prayer for God's help
vv. 113-120	Confidence in God's deliverance
vv. 121-128	Statement of loyalty to God's law
vv. 129-136	Prayer for deliverance and praise for law

vv. 137-144	Acknowledging God's justice
vv. 145-152	Cry for help from persecutors
vv. 153-160	Praying for deliverance from evildoers
vv. 161-168	He shows; persecutors show disgust for him.
vv. 169-176	He sings praises to Lord when rescued from enemies.

Chapter 120 — Prayer of Exile for Deliverance

vv. 1-2	Keep me, O Lord, from deceivers.
vv. 3-4	Tongue is like arrows from a tree.
vv. 5-7	Far from homeland, he yearns for peace.

Chapter 121 — Hymn of Blessing

vv. 1-2	Help comes from Creator.
vv. 3-4	God, always protects Israel.
vv. 5-6	God protects His people.
vv. 7-8	He watches Israel's ways.

Chapter 122 — Prayer for Israel's Prosperity

vv. 1-2	Humble submissiveness to God
vv. 3-5	Prayer for God's help
vv. 6-9	Blessings on those loving Jerusalem

Chapter 123 — Prayer for Deliverance from Enemies

vv. 1-2	We look to You for help.
vv. 3-4	Deliver us, God, from scornful pride.

Chapter 124 — Thanksgiving for National Deliverance

vv. 1-5	Since God delivered us, we are not destroyed.
vv. 6-9	Help is in God, rescuing us from enemy.

Chapter 125 — Prayer for Deliverance from Enemies

vv. 1-3	Expression of confidence in God
vv. 4-5	Prayer for help when Israel obeys God.

Chapter 126 — Prayer for Help against National Foes

vv. 1-3	Joy coms from God's aid in past
vv. 4-6	Prayer for God's help again

Chapter 127	**Good Home Is God's Gift**	
vv. 1-2	Anxiety has no place among God's faithful.	
vv. 3-5	Sons add security to a home.	
Chapter 128	**Large Prosperous Family Is Reward from God.**	
vv. 1-2	Blessed are those who reverence God.	
vv. 3-4	Good family is reward to God-fearers.	
vv. 5-6	Grandparents are added blessing.	
Chapter 129	**Prayer for Deliverance from Enemies**	
vv. 1-4	God preserved Israel despite sufferings.	
vv. 5-8	May Israel's enemies be defeated.	
Chapter 130	**Prayer for Deliverance from Personal Trouble**	
vv. 1-2	Hear me, Oh LORD!	
vv. 3-6	Psalmist awaits God's merciful, present help.	
vv. 7-8	Israel needs God's help personally and nationally.	
Chapter 131	**Act of Submission to God's Will**	
vv. 1-2	I am calm knowing God is there for me.	
v. 3	Israel, put trust in God.	
Chapter 132	**Commemorative of God's Choosing Zion**	
vv. 1-5	God reminded of David's desire to build sanctuary.	
vv. 6-10	Re-enacting of Ark's coming into sanctuary.	
vv. 11-18	Priest recites God's promise of David's sons' reigning and dynasty of Jerusalem.	
Chapter 133	**Joyful Song of Brotherly Harmony**	
vv. 1-3	God blesses brotherly harmony with joy of Holy Spirit.	
Chapter 134	**Priestly Blessing on Congregation**	
vv. 1-2	Priests are summoned to praise God.	
v. 3	Priests bless God's people.	
Chapter 135	**God's Deeds Are Praised.**	
vv. 1-4	A call to worship mighty God	
vv. 5-7	God controls nature.	

vv. 8-12	God removed Israel from Egypt and conquered Palestine for them.
vv. 13-14	God protects His people.
vv. 15-18	Idols can do nothing for people.
vv. 19-21	Priests and people bless and praise God!

Chapter 136 — God's Steadfast Love

vv. 1-3	Give thanks to God for steadfast love (Steadfast love is congregational response).
vv. 4-9	Praise for God's rule over creation
vv. 10-22	Praise for exodus and journey through territories overthrown by God.
vv. 23-25	Gratitude for God's protective love from foes
v. 26	Concluding summons thanking God.

Chapter 137 — Prayer for Vengeance on Babylon

vv. 1-3	Exiles required to sing songs of Zion.
vv. 4-6	Pledge of exiles to never forget Jerusalem
vv. 7-9	Prayers to abolish Edom and Babylon for destroying Jerusalem

Chapter 138 — Thanksgiving of David for Deliverance

vv. 1-3	David's praise to God in temple court
vv. 4-6	God blesses lowly but resists proud.
vv. 7-8	God protects beloved from harm.

Chapter 139 — Prayer for Help against Enemies

vv. 1-6	God knows everything about us!
vv. 7-12	Darkness and light are same to God. He is everywhere!
vv. 13-18	God formed us in our mother.
vv. 19-24	David's enemies are God's enemies.

Chapter 140 — Prayer for Safety from Evil Men

vv. 1-3	Evil men have sharp tongues like serpents.
vv. 4-5	Help me, God, from tongues of evil men.
vv. 6-8	Don't aid evil men against me, O Lord!
vv. 9-11	David prays for retribution against evil men.

vv. 12-13	Expressions of confidence in God's grace

Chapter 141 — **Prayer for Help against Enemies**

vv. 1-2	Prayer offered as evening sacrifice
vv. 3-4	Keep thoughts and mouth guarded, God.
vv. 5-7	Let good men anoint me, never evil.
vv. 8-10	Let wicked fall into their snares.

Chapter 142 — **God, Help Me When I Am Weak.**

vv. 1-3	God, I share needs with You.
v. 4	No man cares for my safety.
vv. 5-6	Lord, help me; You are my Refuge.
v. 7	Help me God; You deal well with me.

Chapter 143 — **Prayers for Protection and Deliverance**

vv. 1-2	Cry for vindication! No one is righteous!
vv. 3-4	Psalmist is weary before enemies.
vv. 5-6	I reach O Lord, for Your help.
vv. 7-8	God, I trust You to hear and help me.
vv. 9-10	Lead me, O Lord, on straight path.
vv. 11-12	As your servant, O Lord, defeat my foes.

Chapter 144 — **Prayer of David for Help from Foes**

vv. 1-2	Blessed by God for subduing all people.
vv. 3-4	Man is inadequate as a vapor.
vv. 5-8	Almighty God defeat my enemies.
vv. 9-11	Deliver David from alien foes.
vv. 12-15	Blessed are people whose God is Lord.

Chapter 145 — **David's Praise: "God Is Gracious"**

vv. 1-3	David's expression of praise to God
vv. 4-7	David lauds God's deeds.
vv. 8-9	God's love is for all creation.
vv. 10-13	God's kingship is everlasting.
vv. 14-20	God's care for His creatures
v. 21	We will bless His Holy Name.

Chapter 146	Blessedness of Trusting God
vv. 1-2	Last five praise psalms begin and end with "Hallelujah."
vv. 3-4	Don't trust in princes.
vv. 5-7	Blessed is just and merciful God.
vv. 8-9	The Lord watches over needy ones (Luke 4:18).
v. 10	God reigns forever, "Hallelujah."
Chapter 147	**Creation to Praise God**
vv. 1-6	Heavenlies called to praise God for doing good to all.
vv. 7-8	Let fish of sea praise God.
vv. 9-10	Let hills, trees, animals and birds praise God.
vv. 11-12	Let kings, rulers and all men praise Him.
vv. 13-14	Praise God Whose glory is above heaven and earth.
Chapter 148	**Angels and Nature Praise the Lord.**
vv. 1-6	Angels praise the Lord.
vv. 7-10	Nature praises the Lord.
vv. 11-14	Kings, judges and all people praise the Lord.
Chapter 149	**God Takes Pleasure in His People.**
vv. 1-5	Festive dancing with timbrel and lyre
vv. 6-9	This was a war-like dance in character.
Chapter 150	**Doxology to Book of Psalms**
vv. 1-2	Praise God for His Greatness.
vv. 3-6	Praise Him with instruments; everything with life, "Praise the Lord".

PROVERBS

Chapter 1	**Invitation to Wisdom**
V.1-6	Purpose of teacher is to train youth and give instruction to mature.
v. 7	Verse seven is theme for chapters 1-9, an attitude of obedience toward God.
vv. 8-19	Home- training is moral safety; it will protect youth from criminals.
vv. 20-33	Wisdom, personified as prophetess, denounces youth from despising instruction.
Chapter 2	**Reward of Pursuit of Wisdom**
vv. 1-22	Wisdom brings understanding and is safeguard against evil.
Chapter 3	**Good Religion Leads to Physical and Spiritual Life.**
vv. 1-12	Misfortune can be discipline of a loving Father. Reverence is essential to man.
vv. 13-18	Wealth is not measured in possessions but in overcoming life which wisdom brings.
vv. 19-20	World declares wisdom, knowledge and understanding of its Creator.
vv. 21-35	Wisdom is peace of mind from God Who blesses good and condemns evil.
Chapter 4	**Paternal Exhortation**
vv. 1-9	Teacher, instructed by parents, teaches his child to reverence God.
vv. 10-19	Pupils (sons) admonished to profit by these lessons.
vv. 20-27	Wisdom is life, health and integrity to those who embrace it.

Chapter 5	**Warnings against Immoral Women**
vv. 1-6	Be on guard concerning loose women.
vv. 7-14	Don't go near house of immoral woman.
vv. 15-23	God watches ways of man and judges his paths for good or evil.
Chapter 6	**Warnings against Surety and Idleness**
vv. 1-5	Don't co-sign. If you have money, make a loan, but don't co-sign.
vv. 6-11	Sluggard to learn from ants to prepare for future.
vv. 12-15	Evil man with suggestive gestures will be broken.
vv. 16-19	Seven abominations are listed.
vv. 20-35	Adulterer is dishonored; no compensation atones for wrong he has done.
Chapter 7	**Wisdom Is Safeguard against Adultery.**
vv. 1-5	Keep commandments given to your father, and live a good life.
vv. 6-9	A lustful youth to be taken by an adulteress.
vv. 10-20	Adulteress persuades foolish youth into her home.
vv. 21-23	Youth does not know this affair will cost his life.
vv. 24-27	House of adulteress leads to death.
Chapter 8	**Wisdom Speaks as a Prophetess.**
vv. 1-31	Wisdom was with God before creation.
vv. 32-36	All who hate wisdom love death.
Chapter 9	**Invitation of Wisdom and Foolish Woman**
vv. 1-6	Wisdom invites simple to banquet to learn from her knowledge.
vv. 7-12	Instruct wise, he becomes wiser. A fool abhors instruction.
vv. 13-18	A simpleton does not know end of an adulteress' trap leading to death.

Book Two -
Maxims Known as Proverbs of King Solomon

Chapter 10   **Righteous and Wicked**
vv. 1-32   Better to say little than much. God's blessings bring wealth.

Chapter 11   **Righteous and Wicked Continued**
vv. 1-31   God blesses giver and punishes withholder of finances.

Chapter 12   **Righteous and Wicked**
vv. 1-28   Hardworking man is blessed but lazy goes hungry.

Chapter 13   **Righteous and Wicked**
vv. 1-25   Money and discipline are a measure of man's relationship with God.

Chapter 14   **Righteous Versus Wicked**
vv. 1-35   Knowledge brings life, but foolishness of scoffer brings shame.

Chapter 15   **Righteous Versus Wicked**
vv. 1-33   Wise man rejoices in correction, but foolish man scorns discipline.

Chapter 16   **Life and Conduct**
vv. 1-33   If man pleases the Lord God directs his life.

Chapter 17   **Life and Conduct**
vv. 1-28   A friend covers mistakes of friends, but a foolish person doesn't.

Chapter 18   **Life and Conduct**
vv. 1-24   Wise man controls thoughts and words, but a foolish man does not.

Chapter 19   **Life and Conduct**
vv. 1-29   Kind man considers poor, but a foolish man considers himself.

Chapter 20   **Life and Conduct**
vv. 1-30   King sees claims of evil men and punishes them.

Chapter 21	**Life and Conduct**
vv. 1-31	Wise man controls his speech, but a scoffer is arrogant.
Chapter 22	**Life and Conduct**
vv. 1-16	Good name and rearing helps when adversity comes.
vv. 17-21	Thirty quotes written for pupil's admonition and knowledge.
vv. 22-29	Consider poor; do not co-sign; good worker is appreciated.
Chapter 23	**Precepts and Warnings**
vv. 1-18	Eat what is necessary, but never from a stingy host.
vv. 19-21	Don't be glutton or drunkard.
vv. 22-25	Honor father and mother.
vv. 26-28	Beware of wayward women.
vv. 29-35	Don't waste life with wine or liquor.
Chapter 24	**Precepts and Warnings**
vv. 1-2	Watch out for envious men.
vv. 3-7	Wise man is mightier than strong man.
vv. 8-9	A sinner devises evil.
vv. 10-12	Save innocent; God watches our response to others' needs.
vv. 13-14	Wisdom like honey, is good for body and soul.
vv. 15-16	Righteous man won't quit like wicked man.
vv. 17-18	Rejoice not when your enemy falls; God is watching!
vv. 19-20	Don't fret over evil men; they have no future.
vv. 21-22	Reverence both God and King.
vv. 23-25	Rebuke wicked and God will bless you.
vv. 26-27	True friends give right answers! Prepare field before your house!
vv. 28-29	Don't repay evil for evil.
vv. 30-34	Poverty overcomes lazy man.
Chapter 25	**Comparisons and Moral Instructions**
v. 1	Proverbs copied by Hezekiah's men.
vv. 2-7	Don't seek advancement or you might be demoted.
vv. 8-10	Do not settle disputes in court and don't reveal secrets.

vv. 11-14	Wise, faithful messengers refresh those sending them.
vv. 15-28	Be kind to enemies so God will take your cause against them.
Chapter 26	**Comparisons and Moral Lessons**
vv. 1-28	Drunkards, fools and sluggards cause their ruin.
Chapter 27	**Comparisons, Warnings and Instructions**
vv. 1-22	Close friend more helpful in trouble than faraway brother
vv. 23-27	Care for flocks and they will provide livelihood.
Chapter 28	**Comparisons, Warnings and Instructions**
vv. 1-28	Righteous man sees needs of the poor. He rebukes man instead of flattering him.
Chapter 29	**Life and Conduct**
vv. 1-27	Keeper of law is blessed and reverences Lord God not fearing man.
Chapter 30	**Words of Agur, Son of Jakeh of Massa**

Appendix II, Dialogue of Skeptic and Believer

vv. 1-4	Questions asked skeptic or seeker.
vv. 5-6	Answer of believer's rebuke to skeptic.
vv. 7-9	Agur asks for truth and daily food.
v. 10	Don't slander servant to master.

Numerical Proverbs
Appendix III: Chapter 30:10-33

vv.11-14	Four evil generations:
(1)	v. 11, those not honoring parents
(2)	v. 12, the self-righteous
(3)	v. 13, the proud and arrogant
(4)	v. 14, the cruel and oppressive
vv. 15-17	Grave, childless woman, desert ground and uncontrolled fire never satisfied.
vv. 18-19	Four things are mysterious; one cannot trace their paths.

v. 20	Adulteress does not acknowledge wrong.
vv. 21-23	Four people who can destroy society: slave, fool, unloved woman and maid.
vv. 24-28	Four insignificant things are very wise: ants, badgers, locusts and lizards.
vv. 29-31	Four stately things: lions, strutting cocks, male goats, and kings.
vv. 32-33	Don't be foolish by exalting yourself.
Chapter 31	**Words King Lemuel's Mother Taught**
vv. 1-9	Appendix IV; a queen mother's counsel
vv. 1-7	Warning against adultery and drink
vv. 8-9	Judge righteously and help needy.
vv. 10-13;	Appendix V; an acrostic on wife, using 22 letters in Hebrew alphabet
vv. 10-31	Good wife has honor: trusted, wise, industrious, considers poor and praised by family.

ECCLESIASTES
or The Preacher

Chapter 1	**Preacher's First Sermon**
vv. 1-3	Title and thesis: Experience as fleeting and insubstantial as vanity to "a breath".
vv. 4-11	Evidence for thesis: Generations pass; everything in motion, but no new results.
vv. 12-18	Fruitless search: (a) change world, (b) reach understanding, (c) possess happiness.
Chapter 2	**All Is Vanity.**
vv. 1-3	Pleasure is vain.
vv. 4-11	Works are vain.
vv. 12-23	Wisdom's fruits robbed by death.
vv. 24-26	Joy in one's labor.
Chapter 3	**Time for Everything**
vv. 1-15	Man cannot change pattern of his life. He repeats happenings of past.
vv. 16-22	God judges righteous and wicked. Difference of destinies in man and animal.
Chapter 4	**Injustice and Life's Hopelessness**
vv. 1-3	Oppression increases vanity.
vv. 4-6	Laziness is folding of hands in resignation. Forgetting wisdom is one's downfall.
vv. 7-12	Miser's wealth is not like human love.
vv. 13-16	Fame is temporary; here today, gone tomorrow.
Chapter 5	**Hasty Vows and Vanity of Life**
vv. 1-7	Caution against hasty vows; fear God.

vv. 8-20	Life is vanity unless a man's focus is God.

Chapter 6 — **Hopelessness of Life**
vv. 1-12	Life is vanity unless man enjoys his life day-by-day.

Chapter 7 — **Wisdom and Goodness Upheld**
vv. 1-10	One's reputation never established until death.
vv. 11-12	A wise heir lives to enjoy inheritance.
vv. 13-22	Moderation of wise better than piety of foolish.
vv. 23-29	Mankind has wandered from uprightness.

Chapter 8 — **Inequalities of Life**
vv. 1-5	Wise man respects leaders.
vv. 6-9	Wise l make allowances for inequities and hardships.
vv. 10-13	Men do wickedly not foreseeing speedy judgment for sins.
vv. 14-15	Enjoy life that God gives mankind.
vv. 16-17	Man knows not all God's work in short lifetime.

Chapter 9 — **Life Is Enjoyed as God Permits.**
vv. 1-12	Enjoy wife, food and work as God gives to you.
vv. 13-17	Wise men mightier than foolish rulers.

Chapter 10 — **Wisdom and Folly in Maxims**
vv. 1-3	Fool's folly follows him.
vv. 4-7	Angry rulers pacified if you do not react.
vv. 8-11	You can be hurt by your work.
vv. 12-15	Foolish talking is waste to people.
vv. 16-20	Don't curse rulers and work hard.

Chapter 11 — **Be Willing to Venture with Life**
vv. 1-8	Be generous and diligent; keep faith in God who plans everything.
vv. 9-10	Youth relish vitality because old age and death will come.

Chapter 12 — **Fear God and Do Right.**
vv. 1-8	Metaphors of old age and man's spirit returning to Creator
vv. 9-12	Biograph by a disciple of preacher or teacher
vv. 13-14	Fear God and keep commandments. God is final authority who judges mankind.

SONG OF SOLOMON
Song of Songs like Holy of Holies

Chapter 1	**Written in Jerusalem by Solomon**
vv. 1-8	Admiration of two lovers, Shulamite woman and King Solomon
vv. 9-17	Bride and bridegroom love talking to each other.
Chapter 2	**The Bride**
vv. 1-7	Maiden's longing for love when time is ripe.
vv. 8-15	Lover comes in springtime to summon bride.
vv. 16-17	Maiden delights in lover's presence.
Chapter 3	**Bride's Revelry**
vv. 1-5	Maiden dreams of searching for lover.
vv. 6-11	Wedding procession of bridegroom
Chapter 4	**Praises and Considerations**
vv. 1-7	Bridegroom describes charms of maiden.
vv. 8-16	Lover asks maiden to go with him, praising her love.
Chapter 5	**Maiden Seeks Lover.**
vv. 1-8	Maiden's fruitless search for lover
vv. 9-16	Bride praises bridegroom; he is lovely.
Chapter 6	**King Tells of Bride's Beauty.**
vv. 1-3	Appreciation and pleasure expressed between two lovers
vv. 4-13	King appeals to Shulamite bride.
Chapter 7	**King Continues to Admire Bride**
vv. 1-9	Solomon enjoys her beauty as she dances before him.
vv. 10-13	Maiden invites lover to come into fields to love him.

Chapter 8	**Lovers Speak To Each Other.**
vv. 1-4	Maiden desires to marry lover.
vv. 5-7	Maiden implores lover to be faithful.
vv. 8-12	Maiden tells Solomon to protect her and give her brothers 20% for past protection.
vv. 13-14	Lover calls and maiden responds to call.

ISAIAH

Chapter 1	**Background for Isaiah's Prophecy**
vv. 1-9	Sinful condition of Judah's rebellion against God
vv. 10-31	Isaiah's call for repentance: justice, helping oppressed, orphans and widows.
Chapter 2	**Day of the Lord is Judgment.**
vv. 1-4	Coming kingdom of Lord, Jesus Christ
vv. 5-22	God's end-time judgment on proud and vain.
Chapter 3	**Judgment on Judah and Daughters of Zion**
vv. 1-15	God's judgment on Judah's sin of Sodomy.
vv. 16-26	God's judgment on proud, vain women and death of men by enemies' swords
Chapter 4	**Jerusalem's Future Restoration**
v. 1	After men fall in battle, women outnumber men; husbands will be scarce.
vv. 2-6	God will send " Messiah" bringing restoration to land and redemption to people.
Chapter 5	**Parable of Vineyard or Judgment**
vv. 1-2	Allegory composed for celebration of Feast of Tabernacles during Jotham's reign.
vv. 3-4	Vineyard yields wild grapes, not choice grapes.
vv. 5-7	Because of wild grapes (disobedient people), God destroys vineyard (Jerusalem).
vv. 8-10	Beginning of six woes: first woe is judgment against covetousness; (Isaiah 10:1-4).
vv. 11-12	Woe number two is judgment against carousing.

vv. 13-19	Woe number three is a just God enlarging Sheol to accept proud, arrogant Hebrews.
v. 20	Woe number four is judgment against moral depravity.
v. 21	Woe number five is judgment against conceit.
vv. 22-23	Woe number six is judgment against bravado and bribery.
vv. 24-25	Though Hebrew slaves refuse to obey, God extends love to them.
vv. 26-30	Judah refuses to repent; God sends Assyrians to execute judgment on Jerusalem.
Chapter 6	**Isaiah's Vision and Calling**
vv. 1-13	Isaiah cleansed and called to land to be judged. God later sends Jesus as Deliverer.
Chapter 7	**The Emmanuel Sign**
vv. 1-9	Sign of remnant returning: Ahaz not to fear judgment; enemies to be destroyed.
vv. 10-17	Isaiah prophesies birth of Jesus as deliverer of land.
vv. 18-25	Four threats amplified of devastation by Assyrians to land of Judah.
Chapter 8	**Sign of "Maher-shalal-hash-baz" (The spoil speeds, the prey hastens).**
vv. 1-4	Isaiah's son is sign for end of Damascus and Samaria; Assyrians take their wealth.
vv. 5-8	Assyrians sweep over Judah.
vv. 9-10	God is with His people to deliver them.
vv. 11-15	Man proposes a thing but God disposes it.
vv. 16-22	God punishes those who look to demons in land of Israel.
Chapter 9	**Messianic Prince of Peace**
v. 1	Probably route of Assyrians invading Israel
vv. 2-7	King represents best qualities of Israel's heroes.
vv. 8-17	God's anger over sins of Israel does not overshadow compassion for His people.
vv. 18-21	Moral decay burns as a fire across land of Israel.

Chapter 10	**Proud Assyria to be Destroyed**
vv. 1-4	God's anger is against Israel.
vv. 5-11	Assyria thinks she is a mighty warrior, not realizing God uses her as a pawn.
vv. 12-19	God will one day judge proud, arrogant Assyria.
vv. 20-27	God will judge Assyria same as He judged Egypt.
vv. 28-34	The Lord of Hosts will move to cut down boastful Assyrians.
Chapter 11	**Messianic Rule and Restoration of Israel as a Nation**
vv. 1-2	Septuagint adds "piety" to six characteristics of coming Messiah.
vv. 3-5	Messiah to judge righteously
vv. 6-9	Messianic Kingdom on earth will be peaceful for animals and peoples.
vv. 10-16	Israel and Judah will be gloriously restored and repopulated.
Chapter 12	**Two Songs Conclude Section I:**
v. 1	Israel will be comforted.
v. 2	God will be Israel's salvation.
vv. 3-4	Israel will one day exalt God.
vv. 5-6	Rejoice, Holy One of Israel will be amidst His people.
Chapter 13	**Oracle against Babylon**
vv. 1-5	Babylon's doom predicted as God musters Medes for battle.
vv. 6-16	Before Exile, "day of the Lord" meant punishment; afterward, refers to oppressors.
vv. 17-19	Medes, a ruthless people, will destroy Babylon.
vv. 20-22	Industrial Babylon will be wasted and inhabited by wild animals.
Chapter 14	**Israel to be Preserved**
vv. 1-2	Return from Exile
vv. 3-11	Taunts against king of Babylon
vv. 12-20	Taunts against Satan, Babylon's power
vv. 21	Ignominy and hatred are fate and heritage.
vv. 22-23	God will rise against Babylon.

vv. 24-27	God's hand is against Assyria.
vv. 28-31	God's judgment is against Philistia.
v. 32	God will restore Israel.

Chapter 15 — Oracle Against Moab

vv. 1-9	Licentious Moab will be wasted.

Chapter 16 — Prophecy of Moab's Downfall

vv. 1-4	Moabites seek sanctuary in Judah.
v. 5	This is a reference to Messiah.
vv. 6-7	Let people wail for Moab's fate.
vv. 8-14	Proud Moab will soon be no more.

Chapter 17 — Downfall of Damascus and Ephraim

vv. 1-3	Doom of Damascus and Ephraim
vv. 4-6	Glory of Israel refers to Samaria.
vv. 7-9	Eventually man returns to God.
vv. 10-11	Those forsaking God will be displaced as Hivites and Amorites of Palestine.
vv. 12-14	Only God can defend His people.

Chapter 18 — Oracle against Ethiopia

vv. 1-2	Shabaka, of Ethiopia expects invasion from Assyria c. 714 B.C.
vv. 3-6	Assyria will waste Ethiopia and animals will feast on bodies.
v. 7	God will one day be blessed by Gentiles.

Chapter 19 — Oracle against Egypt

vv. 1-4	God will cause civil war in Egypt.
vv. 5-10	Agriculture along Nile will dry up.
vv. 11-15	Egypt will be confused as a drunkard.
vv. 16-25	At end Assyrians, Egyptians and Israelites worship together.

Chapter 20 — Assyria to Conquer Egypt and Ethiopia

vv. 1-6	Isaiah prophesies folly of trusting Egypt to conquer God's enemies.

Chapter 21	**Oracle against Babylon, Edom and Arabia**
vv. 1-10	Media aids Persia against Babylon.
vv. 11-12	Prophesy against Edom
vv. 13-17	Prophesy against Arabia
Chapter 22	**Warning to Jerusalem**
vv. 1-4	"Daughter of My People" refers to Jerusalem.
vv. 5-8a	Elam and Kir are eastern provinces of Arabia.
vv. 8b-11	City of David was oldest section of Jerusalem.
vv. 12-14	Party-goers not forgiven until death
vv. 15-25	Judgment of Shebna was thorough. His priesthood given to Eliakim, son of Hilki'ah.
Chapter 23	**Oracle against Tyre and Sidon**
vv. 1-12	Tyre and Sidon become barren.
vv. 13-18	After 70 years Tyre becomes city of shipping and commerce.
Chapter 24	**Universal Judgment (Chapters 24-27 are similar to Revelation).**
vv. 1-3	End-time destruction of earth predicted.
vv. 4-9	Bitterness is due to God's judgment and destruction.
vv. 10-13	Outcome of God's judgment
vv. 14-16	Triumph of Jews, but sadness in Isaiah, because of treachery among leadership.
vv. 17-20	During coming judgment people will be distraught.
vv. 21-23	God judges world leaders and manifests His glory.
Chapter 25	**God Will Swallow Death Forever.**
vv. 1-5	Psalm of thanksgiving similar to Psalm 145.
vv. 6-12	God's final triumph over His enemies.
Chapter 26	**Song of Victory**
vv. 1-6	Processional psalm sung entering Jerusalem
vv. 7-9	God's chastisement is a benefit to those whom He loves.
vv. 10-15	In good or bad times wicked do not acknowledge God.
vv. 16-19	Without God people are helpless before enemies.
vv. 20-21	People must await God's final victory.

Chapter 27	**Deliverance of Israel**
v. 1	God will punish Israel's enemies.
vv. 2-5	God's vineyard is Israel's people.
v. 6	In the coming days Israel will prosper.
vv. 7-11	Israel will be cleansed of idols, be blessed and enemies vanquished.
vv. 12-13	Israel will extend from Nile to Euphrates and Israelites re-gathered in Israel.
Chapter 28	**Judgment against Religious and Civil Leaders in Jerusalem and Israel**
vv. 1-4	Judgment pronounced against rulers in Ephraim.
vv. 5-6	One day God will bless His people.
vv. 7-8	Judgment pronounced on prophets and priests
vv. 9-10	Learning comes by "precept upon precept".
vv. 11-13	If people reject Isaiah, Assyrians will exile Israelites.
vv. 14-22	Isaiah prophecies judgment on Israel for trusting in false gods.
vv. 23-26	God conducts affairs according to His plans.
vv. 27-29	Whatever God does, it is right.
Chapter 29	**Judah's Eventual Restoration**
vv. 1-4	Prophesy concerning Jerusalem's degradation
vv. 5-8	God will restore and avenge Jerusalem.
vv. 9-12	God closes prophets' eyes as His judgment comes on insensitive Israelites.
vv. 13-14	God further explains His judgment on Israel due to insensitivity.
vv. 15-16	Further prophecy comes on Israel's dullness to things of God.
vv. 17-21	Israel's suffering shall soon be completed.
vv. 22-24	Israel and Judah will rejoice in the Lord their God.
Chapter 30	**Hope for Afflicted**
vv. 1-7	Concerning embassy sent to Egypt for help against Assyria
vv. 8-17	Isaiah writes scroll showing Judah will not get aid against Assyria.

vv. 18-26	Hope for afflicted from loving, almighty, eternal Father
vv. 27-33	Oracle against Assyria as the Lord delivers His people.
Chapter 31	**Woes against Egypt and Assyria**
vv. 1-3	God destroys those who seek help from nations, but not from Him.
vv. 4-5	The Lord protects those trusting in Him.
vv. 6-9	God's sword protects Jerusalem.
Chapter 32	**Women of Jerusalem Warned.**
vv. 1-8	King of righteousness will rule land of Israel.
vv. 9-14	Complacent Jewish women bemoan Jerusalem because it will be desolate.
vv. 15-20	When God pours out His Spirit, mankind will rejoice.
Chapter 33	**Prayers are Prophetic Oracles**
v. 1	Oracle against Babylon's destruction
vv. 2-6	Prayer for restoration of Israel
vv. 7-9	Israel's corruption lamented
vv. 10-13	God commands Israel to recognize His power.
vv. 14-16	Character and promises of God's overcomers
vv. 17-20	In Messianic kingdom Israel will forget unpleasant memories.
vv. 21-24	Land will be amply watered for all needs.
Chapter 34	**Terrible Ending of God's Enemies**
vv. 1-4	God's enemies will be slain and cast out.
vv. 5-7	God will dispose His enemy nations as He does Edom.
vv. 8-12	When God finishes with enemies, they shall be nothing.
vv. 13-14	Edom shall be a wasteland.
vv. 15-17	Animals and birds shall inhabit ruins of cities opposing God.
Chapter 35	**Zion Shall be Restored.**
vv. 1-2	All creation will see God's glory.
vv. 3-4	God will deliver Israel.
vv. 5-7	Downtrodden will receive hope.
vv. 8-10	People shall come to Zion singing praises to God.

Chapter 36		**Sennacherib's Coming Invasion**
vv. 1-3		Chief Steward Rabshakeh tells Hezekiah to surrender to Sennacherib.
vv. 4-10		Rabshakeh insults leaders on Jerusalem's wall for Judah's weakness.
vv. 11-12		Rabshakeh insults Hezekiah's leaders in Hebrew language.
vv. 13-20		Rabshakeh boasts of Assyria's might and Judah's weakness in Hebrew.
vv. 21-22		Leaders tell Hezekiah everything Rabshakeh spoke against Judah.
Chapter 37		**Hezekiah's Prayer, Isaiah's Prophecy**
vv. 1-4		Hezekiah sends message to Isaiah concerning Rabshakeh's mockery of God.
vv. 5-7		Prophet Isaiah tells Hezekiah's men not to fear because God will intervene.
vv. 8-13		Rabshakeh leaves for Assyria and again threatens Judah.
vv. 14-20		Hezekiah prays for God's deliverance from Sennacherib's Assyrian forces.
vv. 21-29		Isaiah sends message to Hezekiah explaining God will intervene for Judah.
vv. 30-35		God will defend Jerusalem for His and David's sake.
vv. 36-38		Sennacherib's two sons kill him after Angel of God slays 185,000 Assyrian soldiers.
Chapter 38		**Hezekiah's Illness and Recovery**
vv. 1-6		Hezekiah prays, God heals, and delivers from enemy, adding 15 years to his life.
vv. 7-8		God gives Hezekiah sign He has heard him by turning sundial back 10 degrees.
vv. 9-13		Hezekiah's lamentation before God promises to heal him
vv. 14-19		A "thank offering" is sung for deliverance.
vv. 20-22		Figs are applied to Hezekiah's boils for recovery.
Chapter 39		**Hezekiah Reveals All His Wealth.**
vv. 1-4		Hezekiah shows Babylon his wealth.

vv. 5-8   Isaiah prophesies Judah's captivity.

Book of Israel's Consolation, Chapters 40-55

Chapte 40	**Prophet Called to Announce God's Coming**
vv. 1-2	Words of comfort and pardon for Israel
vv. 3-5	Prophetic words of the Lord's coming
vv. 6-8	People fade but God's Word stands forever.
vv. 9-11	God takes care of His people.
vv. 12-17	God is great and nations are as dust.
vv. 18-20	Nothing can compare to God.
v. 21-23	He humbles rulers of earth.
v. 24	He blows on kings and they become dust.
vv. 25-26	No one can be compared to God.
vv. 27-31	Those who trust in God will be strong.
Chapter 41	**Israel's Assurance**
v. 1	Background scenes in courtroom
vv. 2-4	God protects as only He can.
vv. 5-10	God gives Israel assurance of His care.
vv. 11-13	"Fear not" God will help Israel.
vv. 14-16	Israel shall glory in God.
vv. 17-20	God's hand will bless Israel greatly.
vv. 21-24	Pagan nations' gods are nothing.
vv. 25-29	Pagan nations are nothing to God.
Chapter 42	**God's Servant, Israel**
vv. 1-4	Jesus is God's Chosen to bring peace.
vv. 5-9	Israel is to bring light to nations.
vv. 10-13	Israel's song of praise to God for victory
vv. 14-17	Recalling how God has protected Israel
vv. 18-25	God judges Israel for sins.
Chapter 43	**The Lord's Redemption of Israel**
vv. 1-7	God will gather Israelites from four corners of earth.
vv. 8-13	Israel is the Lord's witness to nations.

vv. 14-21	God will return Israel to land of Palestine.
vv. 22-24	Israel ignored and offended God.
vv. 25-28	God is gracious but just.
Chapter 44	**Futility of False Gods**
vv. 1-5	Nations will one day identify with Israel and her God!
vv. 6-8	No one can be compared to God.
vv. 9-20	Trees for fuel also make idols or images.
vv. 21-23	Israel will be forgiven and redeemed.
vv. 24-28	Israel will be restored.
Chapter 45	**Sovereignty of Creator God**
vv. 1-7	God is over everything!
vv. 9-17	God promises to prosper and bless Israel.
vv. 18-21	Only God brings deliverance to Israel and nations.
vv. 22-25	Nations will bow before Almighty God.
Chapter 46	**God Supports Israel.**
vv. 1-4	God will rescue Israel.
vv. 5-7	Who is comparable to God?
vv. 8-13	God promises to bring deliverance to Israel.
Chapter 47	**Downfall of Babylon**
vv. 1-4	Babylon will be cast down to dust.
vv. 5-9	Babylon will be filled with widows and poverty.
vv. 10-15	Nothing Babylon has trusted can save from God's judgment.
Chapter 48	**Stubborn Israel is Rebuked.**
vv. 1-5	God explains Israel's hardness.
vv. 6-13	God explains His Creatorship to Israel.
vv. 14-22	God challenges Israel to leave Babylon and return to Jerusalem.
Chapter 49	**Restoration of Israel**
vv. 1-6	Israel chosen to bring Gentiles into God's kingdom.
vv. 7-13	Praise God, O Israel, for the Lord brings deliverance.
vv. 14-21	Israel's children were born during exile.

vv. 22-26	All earth will acknowledge Israel's One True God.
Chapter 50	**Obedient Servant of God**
vv. 1-6	Isaiah refers to himself and prophecies about Messiah.
vv. 7-11	God will vindicate His servant.
Chapter 51	**The Lord Will Comfort Zion.**
vv. 1-6	Past revelation and future salvation
vv. 7-16	Deliverance draws near speedily.
vv. 17-23	Jerusalem's oppressors will know God's wrath.
Chapter 52	**God's Kingship**
vv. 1-2	Jerusalem is challenged to be free.
vv. 3-5	Israel will know their God.
vv. 7-10	Israel soon to be redeemed.
vv. 11-15	Israel, like Messiah, will astonish nations.
Chapter 53	**Suffering Servant**
vv. 1-3	Prophesy concerning Jesus' suffering.
vv. 4-6	Details of Jesus' suffering for Israel.
vv. 7-9	Innocent Jesus was buried with wicked
vv. 10-12	As He died, He prayed for enemies.
Chapter 54	**Zion Reconciled and Restored**
vv. 1-3	Israel's assurance of deliverance
vv. 4-8	God will remember Israel.
vv. 9-10	God will remember His covenant with Israel.
vv. 11-17	God's heritage for us is His protection.
Chapter 55	**Hymn of Joy and Triumph**
vv. 1-5	God's grace cannot be purchased only given.
vv. 6-11	Call for repentance
vv. 12-13	Future Exodus back into Eden
Chapter 56	**House of Prayer for all People**
vv. 1-5	God keeps covenant with outsiders who covenant with Him.
vv. 6-8	God's house shall be house of prayer for everyone He gathers.

vv. 9-12	God's word against corrupt leaders

Chapter 57 — **Grace and Consolation**

vv. 1-13	Prophecy against idolatry and encouragement for those trusting God
vv. 14-21	God's wrath will not last forever.

Chapter 58 — **Service God Requires.**

vv. 1-9	God hears when we fast by helping poor and oppressed.
vv. 10-14	God blesses those who honor Him and Sabbath. He gives them desired heritage.

Chapter 59 — **Call to National Repentance**

vv. 1-8	List of transgressions, even killing innocent babies.
vv. 9-15	Sins testify against them.
vv. 16-19	God, in vengeance, punishes evildoers for sins.
vv. 20-21	God blesses generations who turn from transgressions.

Chapter 60 — **Future Glory of Zion**

vv. 1-3	God's glory will come on Israel.
vv. 4-7	Wealth will come to Jerusalem one day.
vv. 8-14	Nations shall bow to Jerusalem, even those who had despised her.
vv. 15-18	Israel will be saved as people come to know Savior.
vv. 19-22	New Jerusalem spoken of here and in Revelation 21:22-25.

Chapter 61 — **Year of the Lord's Favor**

vv. 1-4	Prophets' encouragement to exiles
vv. 5-9	In Judah, nations will see God's blessings and eternal covenant.
vv. 10-11	Isaiah identifies with Zion and rejoices in Israel's salvation.

Chapter 62 — **Glory of God's People**

vv. 1-5	Israel's new name means new status with God.
vv. 6-9	Watchmen remind Jerusalem of coming salvation.
vv. 10-12	This is summary of Israel's hopes.

Chapter 63	**Prayer of Restoration**
vv. 1-6	Israel's deliverance from Egypt and God's calling and protection.
vv. 7-14	God is steadfast though Israel was faithless.
vv. 15-19	Isaiah begs God to deliver Israel from sins and restore people.
Chapter 64	**Continued Prayer for Restoration**
vv. 1-7	Prayer God would come in power as in former times.
vv. 8-12	Isaiah pleads God to have compassion on Jerusalem and destroyed temple.
Chapter 65	**God's Answer to Isaiah's Prayer**
vv. 1-7	God hates Israel's sins which defile His Name.
vv. 8-12	God separates good from bad Israelites.
vv. 13-16	God blesses faithful but destroys wicked.
vv. 17-25	In new Jerusalem all people will live in peace.
Chapter 66	**True Worship Endures Forever.**
vv. 1-6	God vindicates true worshippers.
vv. 7-11	Jerusalem's rebirth is miracle of God.
vv. 12-17	God destroys enemies but prospers Jerusalem.
vv. 18-21	God reveals His glory to nations. Some Gentiles become priests.
vv. 22-24	God's people endure forever but rebellious shall be punished.

JEREMIAH

Chapter 1		**Jeremiah's Call and Related Visions**
vv. 1-3		Introduction to Jeremiah; his name means "The Lord God Exalts."
vv. 4-10		At 20 years old, Jeremiah is commissioned by God to speak to nations and kingdoms.
vv. 11-12		Jeremiah's second vision shows he speaks and God performs spoken words.
vv. 13-19		Jeremiah's third vision shows God's provision to stand and overcome adversaries.
Chapter 2		**Apostasy of Israel**
vv. 1-3		Jeremiah's fourth vision tells of Israel's virgin and holy youthfulness as nation.
vv. 4-8		Jeremiah's first denunciation of priests and leaders for not following God.
vv. 9-13		Israel forsakes God and commits to depending on themselves, not God.
vv. 14-19		Israel forsakes God to make alliances with Egypt and Assyria.
vv. 20-22		Israel's apostasy is ever before the Lord.
vv. 23-25		Israel's lust drives her to seek foreign relationships, not God's.
vv. 26-28		Judah puts trust in many idols instead of God.
vv. 29-32		Israel has forgotten her God.
vv. 33-37		Israel is ravaged by Assyria and deceived by Egypt.
Chapter 3		**Israel Invited to Repent and Return.**
vv. 1-5		God withholds rain because Israel will not repent.

vv. 6-10	Israel returned to God in pretense.
vv. 11-14	Return O Israel and God will pardon you.
vv. 15-20	Israel has been faithless to God.
vv. 21-15	Israel by not obeying God, has lost God's blessings.
Chapter 4	**God Brings Foe from North.**
vv. 1-4	Return to God, Israel, or suffer wrath.
vv. 5-10	Prepare for disaster from north.
vv. 11-17	Besiegers are coming from afar.
vv. 18-22	Israel does not know to do good.
vv. 23-31	Israel will be as woman in travail.
Chapter 5	**Apostasy Brings Punishment.**
vv. 1-3	Seek man who wants truth if you can find one.
vv. 4-5	Neither poor nor rich seek God.
v. 6	God sends animals to destroy apostates.
vv. 7-9	God punishes apostates.
vv. 10-13	People think they can ignore God and prophets and do wrongly.
vv. 14-17	God brings foreigners to punish Israel's idolatry.
vv. 18-19	Israel has served idols. She will serve false idols in another country.
vv. 20-29	God will avenge Himself on Israel's idolatry and wickedness.
vv. 30-31	False prophets and priests bring Israel's downfall.
Chapter 6	**Prepare for Defeat from North.**
vv. 1-5	Jeremiah predicts coming doom.
vv. 6-8	Jerusalem must be punished, says God.
vv. 9-12	All taken and houses given to strangers.
vv. 13-21	God will not accept burnt offerings but will punish Israel.
vv. 22-26	Destruction will come on Israel because of idolatry.
vv. 27-30	The Lord rejects disobedient Israelites.
Chapter 7	**Apostasy and Impending Judgment**
vv. 1-7	If Israel repents, she remains in land.

vv. 8-15	The Lord will cast Israel out because of wickedness.
vv. 16-20	Because of idolatry, God will not spare man or beast.
vv. 21-26	Stiff-necked Israelites have done worse than forefathers.
vv. 27-34	Israel will become wasteland because of abuses in worship.
Chapter 8	**Israel Forgot God's Laws.**
vv. 1-3	The Lord will punish idolatrous kings.
vv. 8-12	God's judgment will come.
vv. 13-15	They want peace but judgment comes.
vv. 16-17	God's judgments are like serpent's bites.
vv. 18-21	Jeremiah hurts for coming judgment.
v. 22	No help in Israel's medicines
Chapter 9	**Lamentation over Zion (Israel)**
vv. 1-3	God's people know not wicked Israelites.
vv. 4-6	Israelites refuse to know God.
vv. 7-9	God will avenge Himself on wayward people.
vv. 10-11	Israel will be without people.
vv. 12-16	God will scatter Israel worldwide.
vv. 17-19	Israel will be ruined.
vv. 20-22	Bodies will be scattered everywhere.
vv. 23-26	God will punish Israelites and surrounding nations.
Chapter 10	**Prepare for Exile.**
vv. 1-5	House of Israel cannot do good, only evil.
vv. 6-10	No nation endures God's indignation.
vv. 11-16	Only God provides needs.
vv. 17-18	Israel will feel God's pressures.
vv. 19-21	Israel will be unprepared.
vv. 22-24	Invading nation comes from north.
v. 25	Punish Godless nations!
Chapter 11	**Jeremiah and Broken Covenant**
vv. 1-5	Cursed are those forgetting His covenant.
vv. 6-8	God will bring on godless words of His covenant.
vv. 9-13	Judah's gods cannot save.

vv. 14-17	Baal worship provoked God's anger.
vv. 18-23	God will bring evil on those trying to kill Jeremiah.
Chapter 12	**Jeremiah's Personal lament**
vv. 1-4	Why do wicked prosper?
vv. 5-6	Don't believe false prophets.
vv. 7-13	God's anger will consume Judah.
vv. 14-17	God will destroy nations not listening to Him.
Chapter 13	**Waistcloth, Wine Jar and Last Opportunity**
vv. 1-7	God told Jeremiah to see spoiled waistcloth which is no good.
vv. 8-11	Israel would not praise God; they are like spoiled waistcloths, worthless.
vv. 12-14	God will not have compassion for Judah.
vv. 15-19	Jeremiah weeps realizing Jerusalem's soon destruction.
vv. 20-27	God sees Jerusalem's wickedness and will put her shame.
Chapter 14	**Lament of Catastrophic Drought**
vv. 1-6	Judah languishes due to God's judgment of drought.
vv. 7-9	Jeremiah implores the Lord not to forsake Judah.
v. 10	God remembers Judah's transgressions and punishes her.
vv. 11-12	Not accepting Judah's sacrifices, God punishes with sword, famine and pestilence.
vv. 13-16	God destroys false prophets who proclaim peace to Judah.
vv. 17-18	Priests and prophets have no insight of God's coming judgments.
vv. 19-22	Only God of heavens can forgive, restore and bring rain on Judah.
Chapter 15	**Jeremiah's Further Lamentation**
vv. 1-4	God prepares to destroy Israelites in Judah.
vv. 5-9	God announces what He will do to inhabitants of Jerusalem.
vv. 10-18	Jeremiah's second lament comes from his rejection and persecution.
vv. 19-21	God promises support to Jeremiah, but no help to protesters.

Chapter 16	**Jeremiah not to Marry**
vv. 1-4	Due to God's judgment of Judah's sin, it is best to be single.
vv. 5-9	God causes Jews to die by enemies and not to be buried.
vv. 10-13	Israel, as forefathers who sinned, will be lonely in another nation.
vv. 14-15	Afterwards, God will produce exodus and return Israel to land.
vv. 16-18	Babylonians will not allow Jews to escape.
vv. 19-20	Here is vanity of idol worship.
v. 21	All nations will one day worship God.
Chapter 17	**Blessed Those Trusting in the Lord**
vv. 1-4	God's fire kindled against His people.
vv. 5-6	Cursed are they who trust in men.
vv. 7-8	Blessed is man trusting in God; he shall be blessed in drought.
vv. 9-10	God rewards man by his actions.
v. 11	Cursed is he who gets riches unrighteously.
vv. 12-13	All who forsake God will be put to shame.
vv. 14-18	"Put to shame and destruction," cries Jeremiah, "those who try to destroy me."
vv. 19-23	Jews refuse to listen to Jeremiah's teaching on Sabbath-keeping.
vv. 24-27	Angry God warns Judah and Jerusalem about Sabbath-breaking.
Chapter 18	**Allegory of Potter**
vv. 1-11	God warns through example of potter that people are as clay.
vv. 12-17	In Judah's calamity people will be shown "God's backside."
v. 18	People plot to silence Jeremiah.
vv. 19-23	Jeremiah pleads with God to deal with persecutors according to His anger.
Chapter 19	**Sign of Broken Flask**
vv. 1-9	God makes siege so strong these murdering people will eat own sons.

vv. 10-13	As Topheth is defiled so shall be people sacrificing to pagan gods.	
vv. 14-15	What prophesied against Topheth will come on its inhabitants.	
Chapter 20	**Jeremiah's Fifth and Sixth Personal Laments**	
vv. 1-6	Priest Pashhur, who beat and put Jeremiah in stocks will die in Babylon.	
vv. 7-12	Jeremiah cries to God for vengeance on his persecutors.	
v. 13	A praise to God for deliverance	
vv. 14-18	Jeremiah's lament for being born and persecuted	
Chapter 21	**God Will Fight against Judah.**	
vv. 1-2	King seeks help from Jeremiah.	
vv. 3-7	Jeremiah warns Zedekiah of Nebuchadnezzar's victory over Judah.	
vv. 8-10	Those surrendering will not be killed.	
vv. 11-12	Do right or expect God's wrath.	
vv. 13-14	God is against royal palace and will destroy it.	
Chapter 22	**Fate of Jehoiakim and Coniah**	
vv. 1-9	God will preserve Jerusalem if it repents, if not, He will destroy city due to idolatry.	
vv. 10-12	King Josiah's son, King Shallum, will not see Jerusalem again.	
vv. 13-23	Josiah and sons have to endure shameful fates for not heeding Jeremiah's counsel.	
vv. 24-30	Due to King's wickedness, no sons will ever rule in Jerusalem, land of Judah.	
Chapter 23	**Rule of Righteous Branch**	
vv. 1-4	God warns rulers who scatter His sheep.	
vv. 5-6	Messiah will rule righteously and save His people.	
vv. 7-8	God will deliver Jews from Babylon.	
vv. 9-15	Samaria's and Judah's prophets captured by Assyrians for spiritual adultery.	

vv. 16-17	False prophets who reject Jeremiah prophesy peace to Judah.
vv. 18-20	God's wrath will not be appeased.
vv. 21-22	God did not send false prophets.
vv. 23-32	God is against false prophets who lead His people astray.
vv. 33-40	God hates prophesy that is not God's word.
Chapter 24	**Vision of Two Baskets of Fire**
vv. 1-3	Jeremiah sees good and bad figs.
vv. 4-7	Good figs are those the Lord will return from exile.
vv. 8-10	Bad figs are King Zedekiah and all who remain in Judah.
Chapter 25	**Seventy Years of Exile**
vv. 1-7	Jeremiah warns inhabitants of Judah not to worship idols.
vv. 8-14	After 70 years God will return Judah and punish Babylon.
vv. 15-16	God sends His sword upon nations.
vv. 17-26	Nations shall drink wine of God's wrath and so will Babylon.
v. 27	God will strike with sword of other nations.
vv. 28-29	God's sword will be against all nations.
vv. 30-32	God will put wicked to His sword.
vv. 33-38	Land shall be wasted by God Almighty.
Chapter 26	**Jeremiah Brought to Trial.**
vv. 1-6	Sermon proclaims repentance or Judah becomes cursed nation.
vv. 7-9	No one accepted Jeremiah's sermon.
vv. 10-11	Leaders demand Jeremiah's death for prophesying against Jerusalem.
vv. 12-15	Repent and God will spare you from destruction.
vv. 16-19	Some leaders speak for Jeremiah to save his life.
vv. 20-23	Some examples of men who spoke truth and were killed.
v. 24	Ahikam keeps Jeremiah alive.
Chapter 27	**Sign of Yoke for Jeremiah**
vv. 1-7	Babylon will control Judah's people for approximately 70 years.

vv. 8-11	Submit to Babylon's rule or die.
vv. 12-15	King and prophets will die if not submitting to King Nebuchadnezzar.
vv. 16-22	Temple treasures remain in Babylon until God returns them to Jerusalem.
Chapter 28	**Jeremiah and Hananiah**
vv. 1-4	Hananiah prophesies peace to Jerusalem whereas Jeremiah prophesies destruction.
vv. 5-9	Jeremiah says Hananiah speaks falsely.
vv. 10-11	Hananiah prophesies release from Babylon in two years.
vv. 12-16	Jeremiah rebukes Hananiah's false prophesy, condemning him to death.
v. 17	That year Hananiah died.
Chapter 29	**Jeremiah and Shemaiah**
vv. 1-9	Jeremiah writes exiles in Babylon to obey king, live godly and don't believe lies.
vv. 10-14	After 70 years God will bring you home.
vv. 15-23	Jeremiah prophesies deaths of false prophets living in Babylon.
vv. 24-28	Shemaiah, friend of Hananiah, tries to get Jeremiah jailed.
vv. 29-32	God judges Shemaiah that he nor his people will see God's restoration of Judah.
Chapter 30	**Return and Restoration of Israel**
vv. 1-3	Prophesy concerning Judah's restoration
vv. 4-9	In future strangers no longer will rule Judah; the Lord, will be Judah's God.
vv. 10-11	God will punish and restore Israel and Judah.
vv. 12-17	Those devouring Israel and Judah will be destroyed but they shall be restored.
vv. 18-21	God will raise ruler from Jews who will reverence Him.
v. 22	All Israel shall reverence God.
vv. 23-24	God's wrath will punish wicked.

Chapter 31	**New Covenant**
vv. 1-6	Again God's people will plant vineyards in Samaria and Jerusalem and worship God.
vv. 7-9	God will gather scattered Israel and return her to land.
vv. 10-14	God will again bless priests and people.
v. 15	Rachel weeps for Israelites in exile.
vv. 16-20	God's mercy will remember exiled people and return them to their land.
vv. 21-22	God says return to your land and be faithful.
vv. 23-34	God will make new covenant with Israel and put covenantal laws in them.
vv. 35-37	God's promises to Israel are sure.
vv. 38-40	Boundaries of Jerusalem are defined.
Chapter 32	**Jeremiah's Land in Anathoth**
vv. 1-5	Jeremiah prophesies Zedekiah's imprisonment, causing Jeremiah's imprisonment.
vv. 6-8	Hanamel offers to sell property in Anathoth to Jeremiah who is in prison.
vv. 9-15	After purchase of land Jeremiah tells Baruch to put deeds in secure place.
vv. 16-25	Jeremiah is to buy land before witnesses as Chaldeans are preparing for war.
vv. 26-35	God's anger against leaders of Jerusalem because of disobedience against Him.
vv. 36-41	God drives them out in wrath but He will bring them back in love.
vv. 42-44	God will restore fortunes of people in Israel.
Chapter 33	**Righteous Branch**
vv. 1-9	God will punish Judah by Chaldeans but will return her to prosperity.
vv. 10-11	God promises to restore joy to Judah.
vv. 12-13	Jeremiah is encouraging Judah.
vv. 14-16	Jesus will come bringing His righteousness.

vv. 17-18	God will always have Jesus on throne.
vv. 19-22	God's covenant with His people will never be broken.
vv. 23-26	God will always keep covenant with Abraham, Isaac, Jacob and David.
Chapter 34	**Breach of Faith Concerning Slavery**
vv. 1-5	Jeremiah prophesies King Zedekiah's captivity and death in Babylon.
vv. 6-7	Lackish and Azekah remain undefeated.
vv. 8-22	Judah refuses to liberate Hebrew slaves; God will destroy Jerusalem.
Chapter 35	**Sign of Rechabites**
vv. 1-11	Rechabites are offered wine but due to a promise, they refuse.
vv. 12-17	God will bring judgment on Jerusalem since people do not obey commands.
vv. 18-19	Rechabites obeyed their father; God honors them.
Chapter 36	**King Jehoiakim Burns Jeremiah's Scroll.**
vv. 1-3	God commands Jeremiah to write on scroll.
vv. 4-8	Jeremiah dictates to Baruch who writes and reads to men who enter temple.
vv. 9-10	Baruch reads scroll to Jews.
vv. 11-19	After hearing Baruch read, princes tell Baruch and Jeremiah to hide.
vv. 20-26	Jehoiakim, king of Judah destroys scroll as it is read.
vv. 27-31	God tells Jeremiah to rewrite scroll pronouncing judgment on Jehoiakim.
v. 32	Baruch writes on second scroll.
Chapter 37	**Jeremiah Arrested and Imprisoned.**
vv. 1-2	Zedekiah does not listen to Jeremiah.
vv. 3-5	When Chaldeans learn of Egypt's helping Jerusalem, Chaldeans withdraw.
vv. 6-10	Jeremiah warns Jerusalem Chaldeans will return and destroy city.

vv. 11-15	Irijah thought Jeremiah was defecting, he placed him in prison.
vv. 16-21	Zedekiah removes Jeremiah from dungeon and places him in court of guard.

Chapter 38	**Jeremiah Rescued by Ebed-melech.**
vv. 1-6	Jeremiah put in pit for warning people to surrender to Babylon.
vv. 7-13	Ethiopian eunuch, Ebed-melech, gets permission to rescue Jeremiah.
vv. 14-16	Zedekiah seeks counsel from Jeremiah.
vv. 17-23	If Zedekiah surrenders, Jerusalem will not be destroyed by fire.
vv. 24-28	Jeremiah spared from returning to dungeon.

Chapter 39	**Jeremiah and Fall of Jerusalem**
vv. 1-10	Nebuchadnezzar enters city; captures Zedekiah; leaving poor in Jerusalem.
vv. 11-14	Jeremiah is left in Jerusalem.
vv. 15-18	Ebed-melech spared because he trusted in the Lord God of Israel.

Chapter 40	**Jeremiah Remains in Judah.**
vv. 1-6	Jeremiah dwells with new Governor Gedaliah of Judah,
vv. 7-12	Jews living in other lands return to Judah under Gedaliah.
vv. 13-18	Johanan tells Gedaliah of Ismael's plot to murder him. Gedaliah won't believe it.

Chapter 41	**Ishmael Slays Governor Gedaliah.**
vv. 1-3	Ismael and 10 men kill Gedaliah at Mizpeh.
vv. 4-8	Ishmael kills 70 men from Shechem and Shiloh but spares 10 of these 80 men.
vv. 9-10	Ishmael takes captives and goes to Ammon.
vv. 11-18	Johanan rescues captives from Ishmael. Ishmael and eight of his men escape.

Chapter 42	**Jeremiah Warns against Flight to Egypt.**
vv. 1-6	Jeremiah asked directions from God.

vv. 7-17	God tells Jeremiah not to flee to Egypt but stay in Judah.
vv. 18-22	Jeremiah warns remnant if they flee to Egypt they will die.
Chapter 43	**Jeremiah in Land of Egypt**
vv. 1-7	Johanan refusing Jeremiah's instructions from God led remnant to Egypt.
vv. 8-13	God tells Jeremiah Nebuchadnezzar will come to Egypt and destroy people.
Chapter 44	**Oracles against Refugees in Egypt**
vv. 1-10	God warns that people who fled to Egypt will not be protected.
vv. 11-14	A few fugitives will return to Judah.
vv. 15-19	Israelite women returned to pagan practices.
vv. 20-23	God punished forefathers for pagan practices.
vv. 24-30	God will punish those worshiping "queen of heaven."
Chapter 45	**Baruch's Concluding Memoirs**
vv. 1-5	God promises evil for remnant in Egypt but He will spare Baruch.
Chapter 46	**Oracles against Egypt**
vv. 1-6	Nebuchadnezzar defeats Pharaoh Necho II.
vv. 7-12	Egypt defeated by the Babylonians under Nebuchadnezzar.
vv. 13-17	Pharaoh Necho II and Nebuchadnezzar fight to stalemate in Egypt.
vv. 18-21	Prepare O Egypt, for exile to Babylon.
vv. 22-24	Queen of Egypt exiled to Babylon.
vv. 25-26	After exile in Babylon, Egypt will be re-inhabited.
vv. 27-28	Israel will be chastised by God but not destroyed as other nations.
Chapter 47	**Oracles against Philistines**
vv. 1-7	God uses Egypt to destroy Philistines.
Chapter 48	**Oracles against Moab**
vv. 1-2	Nebuchadnezzar advances on Moab.
vv. 3-8	Cities, peoples and Chemosh (chief God of Moab) will be destroyed.

v. 9	Moab will be without inhabitants.
v. 10	Cursed are those who serve God lazily.
vv. 11-13	Moab will be ashamed of Chemosh, its god.
vv. 14-17	Moab will have same fate as Judah.
vv. 18-20	Moab will be laid waste.
vv. 21-27	As Moab derided Israel so shall Moab be derided.
vv. 28-33	Proud Moab is humiliated before its conqueror.
vv. 34-36	Moab's riches now perish.
vv. 37-43	Moab shall no longer be a people.
v. 44	No one shall escape from Moab.
vv. 45-47	Moab now destroyed; God promises to restore her.
Chapter 49	**Oracles against Ammon**
vv. 1-6	God destroys Milcom, god of Ammon and its priests; He will restore Ammon.
vv. 7-11	God will strip Esau (Edom) of inhabitants.
vv. 12-16	God will bring Edom down as He punishes her.
vv. 17-22	Edom's punishment is like pains in childbirth.
vv. 23-33	God proclaims demise of Damascus and city of Hazor.
vv. 34-39	God promises to destroy Elam and later to restore her.
Chapter 50	**Judgment on Babylon**
vv. 1-3	Nation from north will defeat Babylon.
vv. 4-5	Israel will return to God's covenant.
vv. 6-7	Israel's enemies don't take blame for her suffering.
vv. 8-10	Northern nations will punish Chaldeans.
vv. 11-16	Babylon will become desolate and despicable.
vv. 17-20	God will punish Babylon and restore Israel.
vv. 21-27	Babylon's time of punishment has come.
v. 28	God will avenge destruction of temple.
vv. 29-30	Babylonian soldiers will be destroyed.
vv. 31-32	Babylonian cities will be burned.
vv. 33-34	God will give rest to Israel and unrest to Babylon.
vv. 35-38	Idolatrous Babylon will be destroyed.

vv. 39-40	Babylon will become desolate as Sodom.
vv. 41-42	Northern nations will destroy Babylon.
v. 43	King of Babylon will be in anguish.
vv. 44-46	Cry of Babylonians will be heard among nations.
Chapter 51	**God's Judgment against Babylon**
vv. 1-5	Chaldeans guilty against Holy God of Israel.
vv. 6-10	Babylon's wickedness is noticed and time of judgment has come.
vv. 11-14	God sends Medes to destroy Babylon.
vv. 15-19	Israel is God's inheritance.
vv. 20-23	God's hammer has been Babylon.
vv. 24-26	Babylon shall be a waste.
vv. 27-33	Babylon's destruction will surely come.
vv. 34-37	Babylon will be without inhabitants.
vv. 33-44	God will destroy Bel of Babylon and no nations serve this idol.
vv. 45-46	Flee Babylon; judgment is coming.
vv. 47-51	Cities of Babylon will be destroyed!
vv. 52-53	God will destroy the images of Babylon.
vv. 54-57	God will make the rulers of Babylon drunk with perpetual sleep.
v. 58	Walls of Babylon will fall.
vv. 59-64	Babylon will sink like a stone thrown into Euphrates.
Chapter 52	**Nebuchadnezzar Destroys Jerusalem.**
vv. 1-3	God casts out evil Zedekiah from His presence.
vv. 4-11	Zedekiah captured and blinded; sons and rulers, killed.
vv. 12-16	Nebuzaradan destroys Jerusalem's cities and carries people to Babylon.
vv. 17-23	Articles from temple and court are taken to Babylon.
vv. 24-27	Nebuchadnezzar kills leaders in Jerusalem.
vv. 28-30	Three deportations total 4,600 Jews.

LAMENTATIONS

Chapter 1	**Jerusalem Calls on God and Men for Pity.**
vv. 1-2	Jerusalem weeps in desolation.
vv. 3-5	God brings Judah into sufferings.
vv. 6-7	Jerusalem remembers afflictions.
vv. 8-9	Jerusalem did not foresee judgment from God.
vv. 10-11	Jerusalem cries for God's mercy.
vv. 12-13	God is He who judges and changes us.
vv. 14-15	God thoroughly judged Judah.
vv. 16-17	Judah gets no help besides God.
vv. 18-19	Judah learns to trust God.
vv. 20-21	Judah prays enemies to be as she is.
vv. 22	Grieving Judah, weary from God's chastisement.
Chapter 2	**Jerusalem's Agony and Cry for Mercy**
v. 1	God deals strongly with Israel.
vv. 2-3	God's wrath consumes Israel.
vv. 4-5	God multiplied Israel's mourning.
vv. 6-7	God destroyed Israel's religious systems.
vv. 8-9	Israel no longer receives visions from God.
vv. 10-11	Youth faint in streets of Zion.
vv. 12-13	Who can restore Jerusalem?
vv. 14-15	Is Jerusalem now beauty and joy of earth?
vv. 16-17	Jerusalem's enemies rejoice over her ruin.
vv. 18-19	Cry out in presence of God!
vv. 20-21	Starving mothers eat young.
v. 22	No one escapes from siege of Chaldeans' brutality.

Chapter 3	**Personal Distress and Trust in God**
vv. 1-3	Jerusalem is as a man afflicted by God.
vv. 4-6	God made me dwell in darkness like the dead.
vv. 7-12	God is like an animal lying in wait to destroy Jerusalem.
vv. 13-18	Jerusalem cannot expect good from God.
vv. 19-21	Remember me, O God; I hope in You!
vv. 22-24	God's mercies are new every morning.
vv. 25-27	God blesses men who learn to wait on Him.
vv. 28-30	Let afflicted wait in silence.
vv. 31-33	God doesn't willingly afflict people.
vv. 34-36	God doesn't approve of injustice.
vv. 37-39	Why complain about punishment for sins?
vv. 40-42	Repent to be forgiven.
vv. 43-45	God has made us as refuse.
vv. 46-48	Weeping due to destruction of people.
vv. 49-51	I weep for death of maidens.
vv. 52-54	In despair I cried saying, "I'm lost."
vv. 55-60	O Lord, judge my enemies.
vv. 61-63	My enemies sing taunting songs.
vv. 64-66	Destroy my adversaries, O Lord.
Chapter 4	**Horrors of Siege of Jerusalem**
vv. 1-2	Men are scattered over grounds.
vv. 3-4	Children die for lack of food.
vv. 5-6	Jerusalem's judgment greater than Sodom's
vv. 7-8	Mighty diminished to nothing
vv. 9-10	Women eat their young.
vv. 11-12	Foes could not believe this in Jerusalem.
vv. 13-14	God's wrath is against priests and prophets.
vv. 15-16	Priests and elders, defiled and scattered
vv. 17-18	No nation helps Jerusalem; end has come.
vv. 19-20	Enemies chased and killed us.
vv. 21-22	Edom to be punished as Jerusalem

Chapter 5   **Judah's Lament and Petition for Restoration**
vv. 1-6   Now Judah buys drinking water and wood for fuel.
vv. 7-18   Jerusalem and Judah, torn asunder; have no joy.
vv. 19-22   Restore us, O Lord. Why have You forsaken Jerusalem?

EZEKIEL

Chapter 1	**Call of Ezekiel; Throne Chariot Vision**
vv. 1-3	Ezekiel hears God's word on July 31, 593 B.C.
vv. 4-14	Ezekiel sees four creatures come from fire. Each has four faces and four wings.
vv. 15-21	Spirits of four creatures look human, lion, ox and eagle and are in four wheels.
vv. 22-25	Sound of cherubim's four wings was like sound of many waters.
vv. 26-28(a)	Above heads sat the Lord upon throne.
vv. 28(b)	Ezekiel prostrates before Almighty God.
Chapter 2	**First Commission of Five**
vv. 1-7	God commissions Ezekiel to speak to rebellious Israel without fear.
vv. 8-10	Ezekiel is to eat what God gives him.
Chapter 3	**Second Commission of Five**
vv. 1-3	Ezekiel eats scroll with lamentations; it was sweet in his mouth.
vv. 4-11	Ezekiel is sent to Israelites who have hard, stubborn countenance.
vv. 12-15	Ezekiel spends seven days at Tel-abib with Jewish exiles.
vv. 16-21	Ezekiel warns wicked and righteous or their blood will be on him.
vv. 22-27	Ezekiel is to speak to rebellious Israelites when God opens his mouth.
Chapter 4	**Coming Siege of Jerusalem**
vv. 1-3	Ezekiel portrays on brick coming siege of Jerusalem.

vv. 4-8	Israel will be punished 390 years and Judah 40 years.
vv. 9-17	God gives Ezekiel a ration of cake cooked over cows' dung; water is rationed.

Chapter 5 — Fate of Jerusalemites

vv. 1-12	God pronounces judgment on Israel. They will eat their families in siege.
vv. 13-17	God will send famine, pestilence and sword.

Chapter 6 — Oracle against Mountains

vv. 1-7	By judgments they will know the Lord is God.
vv. 8-10	After judgments survivors acknowledge God.
vv. 11-14	Survivors seeing dead Israelites will know the Lord is God.

Chapter 7 — Oracles on Coming Judgment

vv. 1-4	God will punish Israel's sins.
vv. 5-9	Israel will know God smites them.
vv. 10-13	No one maintains livelihood.
vv. 14-23(a)	Israel's enemies will profane God's Temple.
vv. 23(b)-27	God judges His people by their wicked standards and judgments.

Chapter 8 — Vision of Idolatry

vv. 1-4	God takes Ezekiel in a vision to Jerusalem.
vv. 5-6	Ezekiel sees evil Jews are doing.
vv. 7-13	Ezekiel sees evil practiced in dark by 70 elders of Israel.
vv. 14-15	Ezekiel sees women weeping for Tammuz, vegetation god.
vv. 16-18	Ezekiel sees 25 men, backs to God's temple, worshipping sun.

Chapter 9 — Punishment of Guilty

vv. 1-2	Six men, one in linen came to bronze altar.
vv. 3-8	These men marked those groaning due to unrighteousness and destroyed wicked.
vv. 9-10	God requites deeds upon their heads.
v. 11	Man in linen said, "I have done as You have commanded."

Chapter 10 — Glory of the Lord Leaves Temple.

vv. 1-2	Burning coals to be scattered over Jerusalem

vv. 3-5	Sound of cherubim like voice of God
vv. 6-8	Cherub gave man in linen coals of fire.
vv. 9-14	Four faces on whirling wheels have all-seeing eyes of God.
vv. 15-17	Spirit of cherubim is in wheels.
vv. 18-19	The Lord's glory (19 times in Ezekiel) stands over cherubim and wheels.
vv. 20-22	Each cherub has four faces, four wings with human hands.
Chapter 11	**Judgment and Promise**
vv. 1-4	Ezekiel commanded to prophesy against two evil princes.
vv. 5-12	God commands Ezekiel to pronounce judgment on Jerusalem. Walls won't protect.
v. 13	While Ezekiel prophesied, Benaiah, son of Pelatiah, is judged and dies.
vv. 14-21	God, scattered Israel among nations. He will bring them again to their land.
vv. 22-25	Vision of cherubim and wheels brought Ezekiel to Chaldea where he shares vision.
Chapter 12	**Symbols of Exile**
vv. 1-6	Ezekiel has been made a sign of an exile to rebellious Israel.
v. 7	He dug through wall with baggage to escape.
vv. 8-16	God will scatter exiles. Their ruler will be caught and die in Babylon.
vv. 17-20	Israel shall be desolate and laid waste by Chaldeans.
vv. 21-25	God is going to fulfill judgment on Israel without delay.
vv. 26-28	Ezekiel prophesies God's judgment is imminent.
Chapter 13	**Oracles against False Prophets**
vv. 1-7	Ezekiel pronounces judgment on false prophets.
vv. 8-16	God is going to destroy walls of Jerusalem and false prophets.
vv. 17-19	Prophesy against women sorceresses
vv. 20-23	God will deliver His people from sorceresses.

Chapter 14	**Righteous Save Themselves.**
vv. 1-5	God will punish those guilty of idolatry.
vv. 6-11	God will punish false prophets with inquirers seeking prophecy.
vv. 12-20	Noah, Daniel and Job delivered; all others, destroyed.
vv. 21-22	God justified in all He does!
Chapter 15	**Allegory of Vine**
vv. 1-8	Like wood, for fuel, God consumes and destroys Jerusalem.
Chapter 16	**Allegory of Unfaithful Wife**
vv. 1-5	Jerusalem abhorred, entering Canaan.
vv. 6-7	God helps Israelites grow and mature.
vv. 8-14	God married Israel by covenant; she became His queen.
vv. 15-22	Jerusalem castigated by God for unfaithfulness and prostitution.
vv. 23-29	Israel played unfaithful wife with Egypt, Assyria and Chaldea.
vv. 30-34	Israel bribed nations to be unfaithful with her.
vv. 35-52	Judah's sins exceeded Samaria and Sodom.
vv. 53-58	Judah, one day restored, now bears reproach for her sins.
vv. 59-63	God will establish everlasting covenant with Judah and forgive her sins.
Chapter 17	**Allegories of Eagles and Cedars**
vv. 1-6	Nebuchadnezzar is eagle who takes Jerusalem, (Cedar).
vv. 7-10	Zedekiah resisted Nebuchadnezzar, (East Wind) for 19 months.
vv. 11-21	Zedekiah left Nebuchadnezzar asking Egypt's aid to resist Babylon.
vv. 22-24	Jesus is Branch and Mt. Zion, lofty mountain.
Chapter 18	**Principle of Individual Responsibility**
vv. 1-4	Only soul that sins shall die.
vv. 5-9	"The righteous who obey Me shall live," says God.
vv. 10-13	Unrighteous who disobey God shall die.

vv. 14-18	Son is responsible as father for actions.
vv. 19-20	No generation shall be responsible for another's acts.
vv. 21-24	If wicked repents, he shall live.
vv. 25-29	God is just. Are Israel's ways just?
vv. 30-32	God has no pleasure in anyone's death. So, Israel, repent and live.
Chapter 19	**Allegories of Lioness and Vine**
vv. 1-9	Lioness is Judah. First whelp (Johoahaz) to Egypt; second (Jehoiachin) to Babylon.
vv. 10-14	Judah (Vine); Zedekiah (stem) taken by Nebuchadnezzar (East wind) to Babylon.
Chapter 20	**Fall and Rise of Israel**
vv. 1-8a	Ezekiel told elders of Israel every man must forsake idols of Egypt.
vv. 8b - 13a	God gave Sabbaths; Israel rejected them.
vv. 13b - 17	God did not completely destroy Israel in wilderness.
vv. 18 - 21a	Israel continued rebelling in wilderness against God.
vv. 21b - 26	God horrified Israel that she might know Him.
vv. 27-31	God will not be inquired by rebels.
v. 32	Israel desired to worship idols.
vv. 33-38	God will purge rebels from Israel. Rebels will not enter Israel.
v. 39	Israel serve idols if you will but you will not profane My Name.
vv. 40-44	God will re-gather Israelites returning them to their land.
vv. 45-49	Judah will be consumed by Babylon.
Chapter 21	**Sword of King of Babylon**
vv. 1-7	Judah's day of reckoning will come.
vv. 8-13	Judah will mourn when taken by sword.
vv. 14-17	Sword of Babylon will satisfy God's fury.
vv. 18-23	Babylon consults magic to see whom she destroys first.
vv. 24-27	Sword will cut down Zedekiah, Judah's king.

vv. 28-32	Ammonites will succumb to sword of God's wrath.
Chapter 22	**Indictment against Jerusalem's Sins**
vv. 1-5	Judah's time of being purged draws near.
vv. 6-12	Wicked Israel has forgotten God.
vv. 13-16	God will be profaned for punishing Israel.
vv. 17-22	Israel will know God's wrath.
vv. 23-31	God could not find a man to stand for Him.
Chapter 23	**Samaria and Jerusalem, Unfaithful Wives**
vv. 1-4	Oholah is Samaria and Oholibah is Jerusalem.
vv. 5-10	Oholah destroyed by Assyrian's lovers.
vv. 11-21	God turns from Oholibah because of lewdness with Egypt, Assyria and Babylon.
vv. 22-35	Because Jerusalem is worse than Israel she'll be destroyed by God.
vv. 36-42	Jerusalem's idolatry will be punished.
vv. 43-45	Blood is upon Jerusalem's adulteress hands.
vv. 46-49	Jerusalem (Oholibah) will be punished for lewdness.
Chapter 24	**Death of Ezekiel's Wife**
vv. 1-14	"I will judge you (Jerusalem)," says Lord God, " for sins."
vv. 15-18	Ezekiel's wife died but he did not mourn.
vv. 19-24	When God strikes Jerusalem, they are also not to mourn aloud.
vv. 25-27	Ezekiel, sign to Jerusalem for God's judgment; they'll know He is God.
Chapter 25	**Oracles against Ammon, Moab, Edom and Philistia**
vv. 1-7	God will destroy Ammon; she'll know He is God.
vv. 8-11	God will judge Moab; she'll know He is God.
vv. 12-14	Edom shall know God's vengeance.
vv. 15-17	Philistia will be judged; she'll know He is God.
Chapter 26	**Tyre to Be Destroyed by Nebuchadnezzar**
vv. 1-6	Tyre will be judged, becoming a wasteland.
vv. 7-14	Tyre will be broken and never rebuilt.

vv. 15-18	Nations appalled at Tyre's destruction
vv. 19-21	Tyre will be cast to (pit) nether world.

Chapter 27 — Lamentation over Tyre

vv. 1-9	Previously craftsmen, sailors and merchants dwelt in Tyre.
vv. 10-11	Tyre had warriors on walls from Persia, Lud, Phut, Arvad, and Gammadims.
vv. 12-36	Tyre to be despised by nations as they see destruction.

Chapter 28 — Fate of Prince of Tyre

vv. 1-10	Tyre will die by foreigners.
vv. 11-19	God cast out King of Eden for iniquity.
vv. 20-23	Sidon, Jerusalem's ally, will be destroyed.
v. 24	Israel will be free of enemies.
vv. 25-26	Israel shall dwell in her land.

Chapter 29 — Oracle against Egypt

vv. 1-5	Egypt will be food to beasts and birds.
vv. 6-12	Egypt will be laid waste 40 years.
vv. 13-16	Egypt will never be great nation.
vv. 17-20	Egypt's wealth to be wages for Nebuchadnezzar's men for plundering Tyre and Egypt.
v. 21	"Horn" refers to Israel's power being restored as when David was king.

Chapter 30 — Nebuchadnezzar Will Destroy Egypt.

vv. 1-5	"Day of the Lord" is "Day of Judgment."
vv. 6-8	Egypt and mercenaries will be destroyed.
v. 9	God will send messengers to terrify Ethiopia.
vv. 10-12	Egypt's wealth to be destroyed by Nebuchadnezzar
vv. 13-19	When God executes judgment on Egypt, they will know God is Lord.
vv. 20-26	God uses Nebuchadnezzar to scatter Egyptians so they'll know He is God.

Chapter 31 — Fall of Egypt (Great Cedar)

vv. 1-9	Egypt was as a beautiful cedar, beautiful as in God's garden.

vv. 10-14	Egyptians will go to pit as dishonored.
vv. 15-18	Egypt is to be brought down to nether world as were trees of Eden. |//

Chapter 32 — **Lamentation over Egypt**

vv. 1-8	God reveals what HE will do to proud Pharaoh and Egypt bring them low.
vv. 9-16	People will chant over Egypt what God has done.
vv. 17-21	Egypt's dead will join Tyre in underworld.
vv. 22-23	Assyria to be dishonored in underworld.
vv. 24-25	Elam is among uncircumcised dead.
vv. 26-28	Meshech and Tubal are with pagan dead.
v. 29	Edom is with dishonored dead.
v. 30	Sidon is among uncircumcised dead.
vv. 31-32	Pharaoh and Egyptians will be with dishonored dead.

Chapter 33 — **Responsibility and Retribution**

vv. 1-6	Watchman (prophet) has responsibility.
vv. 7-9	Wicked warned to repent.
vv. 10-16	If wicked repents, none of his deeds shall be remembered by God.
vv. 17-20	God judges each by his ways.
vv. 21-22	Ezekiel's tongue is loosed to speak.
vv. 23-29	God shows why each land will be desolate and wasted.
vv. 30-33	A prophet has been among people!

Chapter 34 — **Lord's Care for His People**

vv. 1-6	Shepherds (pastors) don't care for people.
vv. 7-10	God will rescue uncared for sheep.
vv. 11-16	God will be Shepherd over Israel.
vv. 17-19	God will separate good from bad.
vv. 20-24	David's throne will be re-established.
vv. 25-31	God will restore Israel to safety, prosperity and loyalty to Him.

Chapter 35	**Oracle against Edom**
vv. 1-9	Edom helped to destroy Israel. Therefore, Edom is destroyed.
vv. 10-15	Edom rejoiced over Israel's captivity and desolation. Edom will be laid desolate.
Chapter 36	**A New Israel**
vv. 1-7	God will make nations around Israel a reproach.
vv. 8-15	God will take away Israel's reproach.
vv. 16-21	God will restore Israel for sake of His Name.
vv. 22-32	God will put a new spirit in Israel. He will again bless Israel.
vv. 33-36	God will make Israel like Eden.
vv. 37-38	God will increase men's numbers.
Chapter 37	**Valley of Dry Bones**
vv. 1-6	God will cause exiles to resuscitate Israel.
vv. 7-10	God's breath will bring life to Israel.
vv. 11-14	God's people will inhabit Israel.
vv. 15-23	God will bind Judah and Israel into one nation.
vv. 24-28	Davidic king shall rule over all Israel. Peace shall be seen in land.
Chapter 38	**Restoration of United Israel**
vv. 1-6	Prophecy against nations of north and east
vv. 7-9	Israel will be restored and completed.
vv. 10-13	God will rescue Israelites.
vv. 14-16	God will cause northern nations to fight Israel.
vv. 17-23	Nations will know the Lord is God.
Chapter 39	**Defeat of Gog and Magog**
vv. 1-6	God will cause Gog's and allies' defeat.
vv. 7-8	Defeated nations will know God.
vv. 9-10	Israel will plunder nations who plundered them.
vv. 11-16	Seven months needed for Israel to bury invaders from north and east.
vv. 17-20	Birds and animals will feast on dead.

vv. 21-24	God dealt with Israel's disobedience.
vv. 25-29	God will bless and restore Israel among nations.

Chapter 40 — Vision of Temple

vv. 1-4	Ezekiel to declare visions to Israel
vv. 5-16	Ezekiel sees chambers, passageways and gates and palm trees.
vv. 17-19	He measures outer court.
vv. 20-23	North gates and steps are measured.
vv. 24-27	South gates of outer court are measured.
vv. 28-31	South gates of inner court are measured.
vv. 32-34	Description of inner court on east side.
vv. 35-37	North gate is measured.
vv. 38-43	Facilities for sacrifices
vv. 44-47	Zadokite priests minister in this area.
vv. 48-49	Instead of seven or eight are ten steps.

Chapter 41 — Temple's Inner House

vv. 1-4	Measurement of most Holy Place.
vv. 5-11	Areas for storing equipment.
v. 12	Area served as stable for horses?
vv. 13-14	Temple measures 100 cubits long.
v. 15	Auxiliary building is 100 cubits long.
vv. 16-20	Temple has wooden paneling with cherubim, palm trees, and lions carved on walls.
vv. 21-26	Holy Place has table perhaps for Bread of His Presence.

Chapter 42 — Priest's Rooms and Outer Place

vv. 1-10	Chambers described that lead to outer court.
vv. 11-12	As on north, are chambers on south.
vv. 13-14	Priests eat holy offerings here and change robes.
vv. 15-20	Temple's sides are 500 cubits long and 500 cubits wide.

Chapter 43 — God's Glory Enters Temple.

vv. 1-9	Ezekiel sees glory of the Lord coming from east and filling temple.

vv. 10-12	Area, as well as temple, is holy.
vv. 13-17	Altar is 12 cubits high.
vv. 18-27	Zadokite priests from Levites dedicate altar.

Chapter 44 — **Ordinances of Temple**

vv. 1-3	Outer gate facing east shall remain shut.
vv. 4-8	The Lord rebukes Israel for abominations.
vv. 9-14	Levites cannot touch sacred things; only do temple work because of sin.
vv. 15-27	Levitical priests, sons of Zadok, minister in Holy Place due to faithfulness.
vv. 28-31	Levitical priests have no possessions, except God.

Chapter 45 — **Land Distribution and Regulations**

vv. 1-5	Priests and Levites apportioned land for ministry
v. 6	Section apportioned for entire house of Israel
vv. 7-8	Prince of Israel apportioned land
v. 9	Exhortation for princes to be righteous
vv. 10-12	Exhortation for just weights
vv. 13-17	Exhortation for just measurements
vv. 18-20	Offerings for sins by error or ignorance
vv. 21-25	Celebration of Passover for seven days

Chapter 46 — **Regulations Regarding Prince**

vv. 1-8	Entrances by prince are regulated.
vv. 9-10	Prince enters and exits with his people.
vv. 11-12	After prince leaves, temple gate is shut.
vv. 13-15	Prince provides for daily sacrifices.
vv. 16-18	Prince must not dispossess his people of property.
vv. 19-20	Place designated for priests to prepare offerings
vv. 21-24	Places where those ministering in temple boil people's sacrifices.

Chapter 47 — **River Flowing from Temple**

vv. 1-2	Sacred water flows from south side.
vv. 3-6a	Ezekiel sees man measuring rising river.

vv. 6b - 12	River causes Dead Sea to be alive. Fruit and leaves, for food and healing of people.
vv. 13-14	Land divided; Joseph's people get two portions.
vv. 15-17	North side boundaries are defined.
v. 18	East side boundaries are defined.
v. 19	South side boundaries are defined.
v. 20	West side boundaries are defined.
vv. 21-23	Aliens residing with Israelites, apportioned land as Israelites
Chapter 48	**Boundaries and Land Divisions**
vv. 1-7	Seven tribes are apportioned land.
vv. 8-14	Land given to priests and Levites.
vv. 15-22	Prince's land lies between Judah and Benjamin.
vv. 23-29	Remaining five tribes are allotted inheritance.
vv. 30-35	Lord-Shammah (The Lord is there) is name of new city with 12 gates.

DANIEL

Chapter 1	**Daniel and Friends from Judah**
vv. 1-7	Daniel, Hananiah, Mishael and Azariah of Judah given new names
vv. 8-16	Daniel and three friends eat vegetables, not king's rich food and wine.
vv. 17-21	Daniel and friends wiser than counselors. Daniel ministers 70 years in Babylon.
Chapter 2	**Nebuchadnezzar's Dreams**
vv. 1-11	King demands both dream and interpretation from wise men.
vv. 12-16	Daniel goes before Nebuchadnezzar.
vv. 17-23	God reveals dream to Daniel.
v. 24	Daniel asks Arioch not to destroy wise men.
vv. 25-30	Daniel tells king that God in heaven revealed dreams.
vv. 31-35	God's kingdom will last forever.
vv. 36-45	God's kingdom breaks Babylonian, Medo-Persian, Greek, Roman and Mohammedan.
vv. 46-49	Daniel and three friends made rulers over all other counselors.
Chapter 3	**Three Hebrews in Fiery Furnace**
vv. 1-7	Everyone commanded to worship golden image
vv. 8-12	Hebrew youth accused of not worshipping golden image
vv. 13-15	King's threat to Hebrews
vv. 16-18	Three Hebrews won't worship golden image.
vv. 19-23	Hebrews are cast into over-heated furnace.
vv. 24-25	Four men in furnace; One like Son of God
vv. 26-30	Hebrews promoted in Babylon by King Nebuchadnezzar

Chapter 4	King's Dream of Great Tree
vv. 1-12	Nebuchadnezzar tells Daniel about tree.
vv. 13-18	Nebuchadnezzar explains about watchers (holy ones) to Daniel.
vv. 19-27	Daniel tells Nebuchadnezzar tree to be cut down is king's downfall.
vv. 28-33	Nebuchadnezzar like an ox eats grass next seven years.
vv. 34-37	Nebuchadnezzar's reason returns: he extols Great God of Heaven.
Chapter 5	**Handwriting on Wall**
v. 1	Belshazzar makes feast for 1,000 lords.
vv. 2-4	They drink from golden and silver vessels plundered from temple in Jerusalem.
vv. 5-9	Belshazzar becomes "dumbfounded."
vv. 10-12	Queen (probably Nitocris) says, " Look for Daniel."
vv. 13-16	Daniel asked to interpret writing on wall.
vv. 17-23	You and your lords have not glorified true God.
vv. 24-28	Daniel interprets this judgment from God.
v. 29	Daniel is rewarded for interpretation.
vv. 30-31	The Median, Darius 62 years of age, slays Belshazzar and takes kingdom.
Chapter 6	**Daniel in Lion's Den**
vv. 1-5	Daniel is positioned to be destroyed by envy.
vv. 6-9	King Darius signs a decree that ensnares Daniel.
vv. 10-13	Daniel discovered praying to God
vv. 14-15	Darius seeks a way to save Daniel.
vv. 16-18	Darius worries over Daniel in lion's den
vv. 19-24	Daniel's angel from God saves him. His accusers and families eaten by lions.
vv. 25-27	Darius praises God of Daniel.
v. 28	Daniel prospers during reigns of Darius and Cyrus.

Chapter 7	**Daniel's Vision of Four Beasts**
vv. 1-14	Lion, (Babylon), bear (Medes), four-headed leopard (Persia), dragon-like (Greece)
vv. 15-18	Last kingdom will be God's eternal one.
vv. 19-22	Antiochus Epiphanes persecutes believers.
vv. 23-27	After 3 ½ years Antiochus Epiphanes' reign ends; messianic kingdom is established.
v. 28	Daniel, alarmed but keeps the matter in mind.
Chapter 8	**Daniel's Vision of Ram and He-Goat**
vv. 1-4	Two-horned ram is Medo-Persian empire.
vv. 5-8	He-Goat, Alexander; four leaders: Cassander, Lysimachus, Seleucus and Ptolemy
vv. 9-14	Antiochus violated temple 3-1/2 years until restored, December 14, 164 B.C.
vv. 15-17	Gabriel tells Daniel vision is for end of time.
vv. 18-26	Evil Antiochus defiles himself and persecutes Jews until God destroys him.
v. 27	Daniel was sick and appalled by vision.
Chapter 9	**Daniel's Prayer and 70 Weeks**
vv. 1-2	These 70 years are referred to in Jeremiah 25:11, 12 and Jeremiah 29:10.
vv. 3-19	Prayer for Israel bringing violations by Antiochus against Israel and temple
vv. 20-23	Gabriel comes to give understanding to Daniel.
vv. 24-27	Jeremiah's 490 years; 7 weeks is 49 years; 62 weeks is 434 years; 1 week is 7 years; 1/2 week is 3 1/2 years; then messianic kingdom comes.
Chapter 10	**Daniel's Vision by Euphrates River**
v. 1	Word and vision are understood by Daniel.
vv. 2-9	Supernatural Gabriel speaks to Daniel.
vv. 10-14	Gabriel leaves Michael to fight Satan; he tells Daniel vision is for future days.

vv. 15-17	Daniel is helped by angel because vision has weakened him.
vv. 18-21	Michael fights Persia and Greece, who do not want future of Jews explained.

Chapter 11 — Conflicts and Contemptible Person

v. 1	Gabriel strengthens Darius the Mede.
vv. 2-4	Alexander the great is the "mighty king."
vv. 5-6	South kings are the Ptolemies; the North, the Seleucids.
vv. 7-9	Seleucus II loses war against Egypt in 242 B.C.
vv. 10-13	Ptolemy IV defeats Antiochus and Antiochus defeats Egypt.
vv. 14-19	Antiochus is stopped in coastlands by Roman commander and dies in Elymais.
vv. 20-28	Antiochus IV Epiphanes, evil king plunders Palestine's and Jerusalem's treasury.
vv. 29-35	Antiochus enraged when stopped; he profanes temple; puts pagan altar in Jerusalem.
vv. 36-39	Antiochus changes Tammuzadonis cult for Zeus Olympus cult.
vv. 40-45	Predictions Ptolemy will lose to Antiochus who will conquer Libya and Ethiopia.

Chapter 12 — The Time of the End

vv. 1-4	Resurrection will come for life or for shame.
vv. 5-13	End will be in 1,335 days (or years?). Daniel will have place in that ending.

HOSEA
First of minor prophets... due to the brevity of the books

Chapter 1	**God's Word to Hosea**
v. 1	Kings listed in Judea and Israel to whom Hosea prophesied.
vv. 2-3	Hosea commanded by God to marry harlot exposing Israel's and Judah's harlotry.
vv. 4-5	Hosea's and Gomer's son is named Jezreel, "God sows."
vv. 6-7	Second child, a girl, is named Lo-ruhamah, "not be pitied."
vv. 8-9	Third child, a son, is named Lo-ammi, "Not My People."
vv. 10-11	In years to come Israel and Judah are united.
Chapter 2	**Israel Will Suffer Shame as Harlot.**
v. 1	Israel's punishment is temporary.
vv. 2-13	God will punish Israel and take back His blessings.
vv. 14-23	The Lord will lure Israel back to Himself.
Chapter 3	**Restoration of Gomer to Hosea**
vv. 1-5	As Gomer is restored, so in future, Israel will be restored to God.
Chapter 4	**God's Controversy with Israel**
vv. 1-3	Violence covers land of Israel.
vv. 4-6	People have forgotten God. He will forget their children.
vv. 7-10	God will change Israel's glory to shame since people have forsaken Him.
vv. 11-13a	They have left God for idolatry (harlotry).
vv. 13b-14	A people without understanding come to ruin.
vv. 15-16	Though Israel plays harlot, there is hope for Judah.
vv. 17-19	Ephraim shall be ashamed because of idolatry.

Chapter 5		**Israel's Apostasy**
vv. 1-2		God will chastise Israel's leaders.
vv. 3-4		Spirit of harlotry is in Ephraim and Israel.
vv. 5-7		When Israel, Ephraim and Judah seek God, they will not find Him.
vv. 8-12		God will judge Ephraim and Judah completely.
vv. 13-14		Assyria will not be able to help Ephraim and Judah.
v. 15		God will hide until they acknowledge guilt and seek Him.
Chapter 6		**Israel's Love Is as a Faithless Harlot.**
vv. 1-3		Return to God and He will heal us.
vv. 4-6		God desires love and not sacrifice.
vv. 7-10		They transgressed God's covenant
v. 11		Judah will surely be judged by God.
Chapter 7		**Israel's Deeds Bring Chastisement.**
vv. 1-7		Due to wickedness none call on God.
vv. 8-10		Israel is decadent but doesn't realize it.
vv. 11-13		God would redeem Israelites but they speak lies against Him.
vv. 14-16		They turned to Baal, not to God.
Chapter 8		**Sow Wind and Reap Whirlwind**
vv. 1-3		Israel spurned God; Assyria shall pursue Israel.
vv. 4-6		God spurned Samaria's sacrifices.
vv. 7-10		Israel's alliance will not deliver her.
vv. 11-14		Israel and Judah's fortifications won't help.
Chapter 9		**Israel's Day of Punishment Has Arrived.**
vv. 1-3		People will be deported from Israel.
vv. 4-6		Israel governed badly without God.
vv. 7-10		Israel shall cease as a productive nation for some time.
vv. 11-14		Israel and Judah have fortified their cities; God will devour them.
v. 15		God will drive them out of His house.
vv. 16-17		Israelites shall be wanderers among nations.

Chapter 10	**Punishment of Israel**
vv. 1-2	Israel increased in prosperity and sin.
vv. 3-6	Israel sinned by rejecting God and seeking a king.
vv. 7-8	Samaria shall perish and cry out.
vv. 9-12	Repentance by acts of kindness and righteousness brings salvation.
vv. 13-15	Rebellious Israel hears tumult of war chariots.
Chapter 11	**Punishment and Restoration**
vv. 1-4	More God loved Israel, more she turned away.
vv. 5-7	Israel rejected Me and more is her yoke.
vv. 8-9	God doesn't want to destroy Israel; He loves her.
vv. 10-12	Israel filled with deceit but Judah faithful to Lord God
Chapter 12	**Rebellion and Punishment**
v. 1	Israel does everything to make false alliances.
vv. 2-6	Israel shall prevail with God as did Jacob.
vv. 7-9	As punishment Israel will dwell in tents.
vv. 10-14	Israel spurned counsel of prophets; she shall be accountable.
Chapter 13	**Rebellion and Restoration**
vv. 1-3	Because of worship of false idols, Israelites shall be removed.
vv. 4-8	Because of Israel's deceitful prosperity, God will bring her down.
vv. 9-11	Israel's kings cannot defend as God can.
vv. 12-14	Iniquity of Ephraim is stored for judgment.
vv. 15-16	Samaria shall bear her guilt.
Chapter 14	**Israel Entreated to Return to the Lord.**
vv. 1-3	Assyria cannot save Samaria.
vv. 4-7	If Israel returns, God will pardon.
vv. 8-9	Upright walk in God's ways!

JOEL

Chapter 1	**Locust Plague**
vv. 1-3	Give prophecy from generation to generation.
v. 4	Locusts (nations) have overpowered the land.
vv. 5-7	This nation fighting Israel has lion's teeth.
vv. 8-10	Israel's sins causing everything in field to become waste, the priests mourn.
vv. 11-12	Because of barrenness gladness fails.
v. 13	Mourn because God's blessings are withheld.
v. 14	Elders, sanctify a fast to God.
vv. 15-16	Food is no longer in God's house.
vv. 17-18	Cattle and sheep have no food.
vv. 19-20	Fires dried all water brooks.
Chapter 2	**Call to Repentance and Fasting**
vv. 1-2	This is worst Israel ever faced.
v. 3	Nothing is left in this devastation.
vv. 4-9	Locusts, describing powerful army, devour everything in the way.
vv. 10-11	Who can endure day of the Lord's wrath?
vv. 12-14	Repent, Israel, and God will pardon.
vv. 15-16	Return and God will forgive.
v. 17	Why should heathen scorn God's people?
vv. 18-19	After repentance, God will restore .
v. 20	Repent and God will drive away enemy.
vv. 21-22	Animals and trees will bear fruit.
v. 23	Former and latter rains will return.

vv. 24-25	God will restore what was destroyed by locusts He sent to Israel.
vv. 26-27	God's people shall never again be shamed.
vv. 28-29	God will pour Spirit upon all flesh.
vv. 30-32	Whoever calls upon the Lord shall be delivered when He judges.
Chapter 3	**Judgment on Nations**
vv. 1-3	God promises to judge Israel's enemies.
vv. 4-8	What nations do to Israel, Israel will do to them.
vv. 9-10	Preparations made for war.
vv. 11-12	God will judge nations in Valley of Jehoshaphat.
v. 13	Time to judge for wickedness overflows.
vv. 14-15	People are awaiting Day of the Lord's judgment.
v. 16	The Lord is Refuge to people of Israel.
vv. 17-18	Jerusalem shall be God's holy tabernacle.
vv. 19-21	God will judge Judah's oppressors.

AMOS

Chapter 1	**Judgment on Nations**
vv. 1-2	Repetition of Joel 3:16; two years prior to earthquake
vv. 3-5	Four transgressions bring judgment up Syria
vv. 6-8	Four transgressions because Hebrew slaves taken to Edom by Philistia
vv. 9-10	Four transgressions bring judgment against Tyre.
vv. 11-12	Judgment comes on Edom for four transgressions.
vv. 13-15	Four transgressions bring judgment on Ammonites.
Chapter 2	**Judgment on Israel and Moab**
vv. 1-3	For four transgressions destruction comes to Moab.
vv. 4-5	For four transgressions judgment comes to Judah.
vv. 6-8	For four transgressions judgment comes to Israel.
vv. 9-11	God tells what He does for Israel in giving prophets and Nazirites.
vv. 12-16	Israel made Nazirites drink wine and prophets not to prophesy judgment.
Chapter 3	**Israel to Be Punished**
vv. 1-2	Israel punished for her iniquities.
vv. 3-8	Before God judges, He tells prophets.
vv. 9-11	God sends adversaries to surround Israel.
v. 12	God's punishment on Israel is thorough.
vv. 13-15	Significant ivory houses of Israel to be destroyed.
Chapter 4	**God's Warnings Repeated.**
vv. 1-3	Wealthy women, too, will be punished.
vv. 4-5	Israel's rituals scorned.
v. 6	God tried previously to humble Israel
vv. 7-8	God chastised some of Israel but she did not repent.
v. 9	Israel's farmlands, destroyed
v. 10	Israel's armies, destroyed

v. 11	Some of Israel, destroyed with Sodom and Gomorrah
v. 12	Prepare, O Israel, to meet the Lord your God.
v. 13	God, who does all things, is the Lord of Hosts.
Chapter 5	**Day of the Lord**
vv. 1-2	When Israel falls none revive her.
v. 3	Only a tenth will remain in Israel.
vv. 4-5	O Israel, seek the Lord and live!
vv. 6-7	Seek God or see Him destroy cities.
vv. 8-9	God made heavens and will destroy Israel.
vv. 10-13	God knows how Israel disdained poor and needy.
vv. 14-15	Seek good, not evil, that you may live.
vv. 16-17	There shall be great wailing in Israel.
vv. 18-20	Day of the Lord is a time of judgment on house of Israel.
vv. 21-24	Justice and righteousness are called for.
vv. 25-27	Because of idolatry, Israel is exiled.
Chapter 6	**Israel Will Be Punished.**
vv. 1-3	Woe to Israelites secure in Samaria
vv. 4-7	Woe to Israelites living in luxury.
v. 8	God hates pride of Israel.
vv. 9-10	Many shall die in a siege.
vv. 11-14	God will raise a nation to oppress Israel.
Chapter 7	**Visions of Amos**
vv. 1-3	Judgment by locusts, but God repents …
vv. 4-6	Judgment by fire, but God repents …
vv. 7-9	Judgment by sword, from plumb line
vv. 10-13	Jeroboam told of Amos' prophetic words.
vv. 14-17	Amos prophesies Amaziah the priest's punishments.
Chapter 8	**Amos versus Amaziah, the Priest**
vv. 1-3	Summer fruit foretells of Israel's finality.
vv. 4-6	Israel's sins pointed out by Amos.
vv. 7-8	God will never forget Israel's sins.

vv. 9-10	Mourning will cover land of Israel.
vv. 11-12	A famine of God's Word
vv. 13-14	Idols of Dan and Beersheba will be of no help.
Chapter 9	**Restoration of David's House**
v. 1	None shall escape God's judgments.
vv. 2-4	God will judge everyone completely.
vv. 5-6	The Lord Who does all judgments is God.
vv. 7-8	He will not utterly destroy house of Jacob.
vv. 9-10	He will shake house of Israel thoroughly.
vv. 11-12	He will restore house of David.
vv. 13-15	Israel shall be replanted in own land and prosper.

OBADIAH

Chapter 1	**Downfall and Future Consummation of Edom**
v. 1	Vision of Obadiah concerning Edom is war!
vv. 2-4	God will humble proud Edom.
vv. 5-7	Edom's allies shall betray her.
vv. 8-11	Portrayal seen of Edom's destruction
vv. 12-14	Edom's judgment for failure to help Jerusalem against Babylonians.
vv. 15-18	Judgment will come especially on Edom at day of the Lord.
vv. 19-21	Israel shall dominate Edom; God will reign over all nations.

JONAH

Chapter 1	**Jonah's First Call to Preach to Nineveh**
vv. 1-3	Jonah tries to flee presence of God.
vv. 4-6	Captain rebukes Jonah for sleeping during storm.
vv. 7-10	Jonah tells crew he is fleeing from presence of the Lord.
vv. 11-16	Jonah is thrown overboard and storm ceases.
v. 17	God prepares fish to swallow Jonah for three days and three nights.
Chapter 2	**Jonah prays and is delivered.**
vv. 1-10	Jonah prays to God inside fish and is delivered on land.
Chapter 3	**Jonah's Second Call to Preach Is Obeyed.**
vv. 1-5	People proclaim fast during Jonah's preaching.
vv. 6-9	King of Nineveh calls on everyone to repent.
v. 10	God does not destroy Nineveh!
Chapter 4	**The Lord Has Pity Upon Nineveh.**
vv. 1-5	Jonah watches to see what happens to Nineveh.
vv. 6-11	God explains why He saved Nineveh.

MICAH

Chapter 1	**Lament of Micah Against Israel and Judah**
v. 1	God's word proclaimed in reigns of Jotham, Ahaz and Hezekiah, kings of Judah.
vv. 2-7	Prophesy against sins of Israel
vv. 8-9	Sins have reached Judah.
vv. 10-16	Peoples of Israel shall go into exile.
Chapter 2	**Israel Responsible for Moral Abuses.**
vv. 1-5	Woes to Israelites who do evil to others.
vv. 6-11	Micah quotes preaching of false prophets.
vv. 12-13	God will re-gather Israel's remnant.
Chapter 3	**Threats against Israel's and Judah's Sins**
vv. 1-3	Prophesy against rulers in Israel and Judah
v. 4	God will not respond to their evils.
vv. 5-8	Micah prophesies against false prophets who only care about themselves.
vv. 9-12	Evil rulers and false prophets will bring Israel and Judah to ruin.
Chapter 4	**Prophecies of Israel's Glorious Future**
vv. 1-4	Swords shall be turned into plowshares.
v. 5	Israel will walk in Name of God forever.
vv. 6-7	God will redeem and rule Israel and Judah.
v. 8	Judah's dominion is to be restored.
vv. 9-10	In Babylon, Israel will be redeemed by God.
vv. 11-13	Israel shall be exalted.

Chapter 5	**Shepherd King Comes from Bethlehem.**
v. 1	Israel, is besieged by Assyrians.
vv. 2-4	Shepherd King shall protect flock.
vv. 5-6	Security of people depends on His strength. Aggressors encounter Shepherd.
vv. 7-9	Remnant, a blessing to nations receiving them and curse to those rejecting them.
vv. 10-15	Day of the Lord He will abolish war in Israel and punish disobedient nations.
Chapter 6	**Series of Laments against Israelites**
vv. 1-2	God has controversy with Israel.
vv. 3-5	Israel has forgotten God's saving acts.
vv. 6-8	God requires: "do justice, love kindness, and walk humbly with your God."
vv. 9-16	Jerusalem, as Samaria, must be destroyed.
Chapter 7	**Israel's Sins and Moral Restoration**
vv. 1-7	Micah laments of sins of his nation.
vv. 8-10	Chastisement comes before restoration.
vv. 11-13	One day Israel's boundaries will be restored.
v. 14	Micah prays for Transjordan to be restored to Israel.
v. 15	God will show marvelous things to Israel.
vv. 16-18	Nations shall fear because of Israel.
vv. 19-20	Israel praises God for His compassion.

NAHUM

Chapter 1	**God's Judgments Foretold; God's Majesty in Mercy and Judgment.**
v. 1	Nahum's oracle on Nineveh
vv. 2-3	God's attributes are stated here.
vv. 4-5	God's power is revealed here.
vv. 6-11	God's general wrath against Nineveh
vv. 12-13	God's particular wrath against Nineveh
v. 14	The Lord promises Nineveh's end.
v. 15	God promises "good news" for Israel.
Chapter 2	**Overthrow of Nineveh**
v. 1	Siege has come against Nineveh.
v. 2	God is restoring majesty of Israel.
vv. 3-9	Nahum envisions ruin of Nineveh.
vv. 10-12	Lion symbolizes destroyer who comes against Nineveh.
v. 13	God will completely destroy Nineveh.
Chapter 3	**Nineveh and Her Destruction**
vv. 1-7	None will sympathize with Nineveh's fall.
vv. 8-9	Nineveh captured Thebes; now Nineveh is captured, too.
vv. 10-13	Nahum's comparisons of Thebes and Nineveh
vv. 14-15	Nineveh's futility foretold
vv. 16-17	Locusts refer to swarms of attackers.
vv. 18-19	Nineveh lacks all hope of victory.

HABAKKUK
Embracer

Chapter 1	**Why God Allows Injustice.**
vv. 1-4	Wicked compass the righteous.
vv. 5-11	God plans to use Chaldeans (Babylonians) to subdue Assyrians.
vv. 12-17	Why should God use wicked Chaldeans to conquer Assyria and Judah?
Chapter 2	**Righteous Shall Live by Faith.**
vv. 1-4	"The Just shall live by his faith," says Habakkuk.
vv. 5-20	God is He Who will use and judge unrighteous.
Chapter 3	**Psalm (Prayer) Of Habakkuk**
vv. 1-3	Habakkuk recounts mercies as God appears from South Sinai, Teman and Mt. Paran.
vv. 4-9	Habakkuk rehearses God's victories in Sinai, the desert and Canaan.
vv. 10-15	Habakkuk continues with solar miracle in Gibeon and victories at Jordan.
vv. 17-19	Rejoice, God is in charge. "Selah" used 71 times in psalms and three in Habakkuk.

ZEPHANIAH

Chapter 1	**Proclamation of Doom on Judah**
v. 1	Zephaniah, from Hezekiah's family, prophesied in reign of Josiah, 640- 609 B.C.
vv. 2-6	Promise to destroy all in Judah who do not seek or inquire of the Lord.
vv. 7-9	The Lord's Day will be destruction to those engaged in violence and fraud.
vv. 10-13	A great wailing in Jerusalem as God punishes wicked peoples.
vv. 14-16	The day of the Lord is a day of tremendous pain.
vv. 17-18	God will make a sudden end to all inhabitants of earth.
Chapter 2	**Judgment on Nations**
vv. 1-4	Humble seeking God, spared from God's anger.
vv. 5-7	Philistia shall be destroyed.
vv. 8-11	Moab and Ammon shall be like Sodom and Gomorrah in destruction.
v. 12	Ethiopians shall be slain by sword.
vv. 13-15	Nineveh and Assyria shall be destroyed.
Chapter 3	**Destruction but Also Resurrection of Israel**
vv. 1-2	Woe to Jerusalem for being rebellious
vv. 3-5	Unjust in Jerusalem have no shame.
vv. 6-7	More God blesses more they disobey.
v. 8	By fire of God's wrath all nations to be consumed
vv. 9-10	God will give pure speech to (Acts. 2:4) people to call and serve Him.

vv. 11-13	Nations will be converted and righteous remnant left in Israel.
vv. 14-20	By making Israel renowned, God fulfills promise to Abraham, Isaac and Jacob.

HAGGAI

Chapter 1	**Haggai Prophesies to Governor Zerubbabel and to Joshua, High Priest.**
vv. 1-6	It is time to rebuild temple in Jerusalem!
vv. 7-11	God will not bless people until His temple rebuilt.
vv. 12-15	The Lord stirred remnants to rebuild temple in Jerusalem.
Chapter 2	**Splendor of Latter Temple**
vv. 1-9	God will shake nations to donate in rebuilding latter temple.
vv. 10-19	Previously God withheld blessings; now He will prosper Israel.
vv. 20-23	God has chosen His servant Zerubbabel, as coming ruler.

ZECHARIAH

Chapter 1	**Call to Repentance plus Two Visions**
vv. 1-6	Return to God and He will return to you.
vv. 7-17	Vision of red horse and comforting words that Jerusalem shall be restored.
vv. 18-21	"Four horns" and "four carpenters" are nations scattering Israel and Judah.
Chapter 2	**Vision of Man and Measuring Line**
vv. 1-5	God, not walls, is Jerusalem's guard and glory.
vv. 6-12	God appeals to exiles in Babylon.
v. 13	God is ready to act from heaven.
Chapter 3	**High Priest, Joshua, Vindicated. (The Fourth Vision)**
vv. 1-5	Joshua puts off dirty clothes and clothed with clean garments and turban.
vv. 6-10	Joshua, now cleansed, has access in prayers to God.
Chapter 4	**Golden Lampstand and Two Olive Trees (The Fifth Vision)**
vv. 1-10a	Lampstand represents God and Jewish community. Olive trees represent fuel.
vv. 10b-14	Seven lamps represent eyes of God and two olive trees are two anointed ones.
Chapter 5	**Flying Scroll and Woman in Ephah of Iniquity**
vv. 1-4	Flying scroll is God's curse on all who steal and falsely swear; it consumes them.
vv. 5-11	Judah will be purified of its sins; carried to Babylon and worship the woman (idol).

Chapter 6	**Four Chariots and Crowning of Priest and King**
vv. 1-8	Four horses with chariots are sent in four different directions to patrol whole earth.
vv. 9-14	Joshua and Zechariah will make new office for Messiah, King and Priest.
v. 15	Future age will see return of Jew, conversion of Gentiles and completion of Temple.
Chapter 7	**Not Fasting Required but Kindness and Mercy.**
vv. 1-7	Jews fast due to Temple destroyed and Governor Gedaliah murdered.
vv. 8-14	Land of Judah laid waste by Babylonians was because of disobedience to God.
Chapter 8	**Future Restoration of Judah and Israel**
vv. 1-8	Jerusalem shall be restored to former joy and peace.
vv. 9-13	House of Judah, and house of Israel, will be a blessing to nations and not a curse.
vv. 14-17	God demands righteousness and moral living.
vv. 18-19	Fasts shall be celebrations of joy, love, truth and peace.
vv. 20-23	One day all peoples of other nations will go with Jews to serve the Lord.
Chapter 9	**Judgment on Gentiles and Messianic Kingdom**
vv. 1-4	Surrounding nations will be punished.
vv. 5-8	Philistia will observe Jewish dietary laws with other nations.
vv. 9-10	Messianic King shall come to Jerusalem and command peace to all nations.
vv. 11-13	Re-gathering of dispersed Israelites will come to pass.
vv. 14-15	Israel shall become valiant in victory.
vv. 16-17	Israel shall again be prosperous.
Chapter 10	**God's Control over Nature and History**
vv. 1-2	Ask God for rain because He controls it.
vv. 3-5	More than Maccabean victories; it is a Messianic prophecy.
vv. 6-12	God will raise Israel among all surrounding nations.

Chapter 11	**Two Staffs; Grace and Union**
vv. 1-3	Cedars, oaks and lions refer to fallen rulers.
vv. 4-6	Because of their rejection, God causes Israelites to be abused by their rulers.
vv. 7-14	Zechariah breaks staves, God's covenant with Israel; brotherhood of Judah & Israel.
vv. 15-17	God pronounces judgment on worthless shepherd who cares not for people.
Chapter 12	**Future Deliverance of Jerusalem**
vv. 1-5	Coalition of nations come against Israel in last days.
v. 6	God will give unusual power to Judah.
vv. 7-9	God will destroy all nations that come against Jerusalem.
vv. 10-14	Jews will mourn bitterly for Messiah whom they pierced.
Chapter 13	**Cleansing of Jerusalem**
v. 1	People willing to be purged from sin
vv. 2-6	In last days God's revelation will be complete; no need for prophets?
vv. 7-9	God's Shepherd is smitten and sheep are scattered; a remnant is saved.
Chapter 14	**Jerusalem and Nations**
vv. 1-5	Jerusalem goes through disaster before God comes with His holy ones.
vv. 6-7	Drastic changes in nature will occur.
v. 9	Jesus will become king of all earth.
vv. 10-11	No more curses, for Jerusalem is safe.
vv. 12-15	Plagues shall come upon all who fight against Jerusalem.
vv. 16-19	God punishes not going to Jerusalem to worship Him during Feast of Tabernacles.
vv. 20-21	No longer will people "buy or sell" in God's holy house of worship.

MALACHI

Chapter 1	**God's Love for Israel is Reaffirmed.**
v. 1	Malachi (My Messenger) is the priestly prophet declaring oracle of God.
vv. 2-5	God tells Israelites of His love for them.
vv. 6-14	God rebukes Israel for dishonoring Him with blemished animal sacrifices.
Chapter 2	**God Hates Divorce and Demands Faithfulness.**
vv. 1-9	God rebukes Levite priests for failure to give Godly instructions to His people.
vv. 10-12	Jews are not to marry heathens (Gentiles).
vv. 13-16	God wants Jewish couples to produce Godly children.
v. 17	Jews have wearied God by evil ways.
Chapter 3	**Tithes and Offerings versus Curses and Blessings**
vv. 1-4	God will send His messenger to prepare for coming Day of Judgment.
v. 5	God will judge the evil who oppress poor, widows and strangers.
vv. 6-12	If you are fair with tithes and offerings, God will bless you; if not, God will curse you.
vv. 13-15	Israel's words have been against God.
vv. 16-17	God will preserve righteous when He judges the land.
Chapter 4	**Coming Day of The Lord**
vv. 1-3	God burns wicked and spares righteous on Day of Judgment.

v. 4	Remember God's "Ten Commandments" and Prophet Moses.
v. 5	Remember Prophet Elijah who turns hearts of families to each other.
CONCLUSION:	**God's two witnesses reveal "Word and the Spirit."**

The New Testament

MATTHEW

Chapter 1	**Jesus' Royal Descent and Birth**
vv. 1-6a	Genealogy from Abraham to King David
v. 6b-11	Genealogy from David to Jechoniah at deportation to Babylon
vv. 12-16	Genealogy, Jechoniah to Joseph and Mary, to whom Jesus was physically born.
v.17	By 14 generations: Abraham to David; David to Jechoniah; Jechoniah to Christ.
vv. 18-25	Joseph told in dream by Gabriel not to divorce Mary; birth was by Holy Spirit.
Chapter 2	**Jesus' Birth; Wise Men; Escape to Egypt.**
vv. 1-6	Isaiah's prophecy, Savior would be born in Bethlehem in Judah.
vv. 7-12	Wise men present gold, frankincense and myrrh to Jesus and return home.
vv. 13-15	Joseph is warned by angel to flee to Egypt since Herod will try to destroy Jesus.
vv. 16-18	Herod destroys all male children in Bethlehem from birth through 2 years of age.
vv. 19-23	Joseph returns from Egypt to live in Nazareth of Galilee with Mary and Jesus.
Chapter 3	**Activity of John the Baptizer**
vv. 1-6	John begins his ministry of preaching repentance.
vv. 7-10	John preaches "Bear good fruit that befits repentance."
vv. 11-12	"… the chaff He will burn with unquenchable fire."
vv. 13-17	John baptizes Jesus to fulfill all righteousness.

Chapter 4	**Jesus' Temptation and First Part of Ministry**
vv. 1-11	Satan tempts Jesus Who quotes Scripture and commands Satan to leave Him.
vv. 12-17	"Kingdom of heaven is at hand." God's dealings with creation coming to climax
vv. 18-22	Jesus calls Peter, Andrew, James and John who leave nets and follow Him.
vv. 23-25	Jesus heals; fame spreads in Syria, Galilee, Decapolis, Jerusalem, Judea, etc.
Chapter 5	**Jesus Teaches Beatitudes.**
vv. 1-10	Teachings proclaim God's favor to those who desire to live under Him.
vv. 11-12	Eternal rewards come from being falsely accused.
v. 13	We are to be usable as good salt for His rule.
vv. 14-16	We are to let the light of God shine through us.
vv. 17-20	We are to live and teach God's commandments.
vv. 21-26	We who insult others will not leave hell until we "have paid last penny."
vv. 27-30	It is better to be disciplined than be cast into hell.
vv. 31-32	Divorce and remarriage is serious with Christ Jesus.
vv. 33-37	We are not to amplify our "yes" or "no"; be simple.
vv. 38-42	We are not to strive with our oppressors.
vv. 43-48	We are only to be focused on our Heavenly Father.
Chapter 6	**Jesus Teaches Us How We Are to Pray.**
v. 1	To be rewarded in heaven we must serve anonymously.
vv. 2-4	God rewards those who give alms secretly.
vv. 5-6	God rewards those who pray in secret.
vv. 7-15	Glory to God; help us; lead us; deliver us from evil.
vv. 16-18	When we fast do it secretly only to our Father.
vv. 19-21	Lay up for yourselves treasures in heaven.
vv. 22-23	Keep your eyes full of God and you'll have light.
v. 24	We cannot serve God and the world.

vv. 25-33	If we put God and His kingdom first, He will meet all of our needs.
v. 34	Each day has enough to be concerned about.
Chapter 7	**Hearers and Doers of Jesus' Teachings**
vv. 1-5	We must judge ourselves, not our fellow man.
v. 6	Be careful not to share God's gifts with mockers.
vv. 7-12	God gives good gifts to those who ask Him. (1 Chronicles 4:9-10)
vv. 13-14	The door to eternal life (God's kingdom) is narrow.
vv. 15-20	We are known for good or bad fruits.
vv. 21-23	Not many know or are known by Christ Jesus.
vv. 24-27	Those who hear and do Jesus' words will be stable and solid in their faith.
vv. 28-29	Jesus taught with God's anointing and authority.
Chapter 8	**Healings and Deliverances in Galilee**
vv. 1-4	Jesus heals a leper by a command and a touch.
vv. 5-13	Centurion comes to Jesus; Jesus speaks, centurion believes; servant healed.
vv. 14-17	Jesus heals Peter's mother-in-law and all coming to Him at Peter's house.
vv. 18-22	Jesus implies obedience to call must take precedence over every other duty.
vv. 23-27	Disciples are amazed at Jesus' authority over wind and waves.
vv. 28-34	Gentiles beg Jesus to leave after sending demons into swine that drowned.
Chapter 9	**Healing and Forgiving Sins by Jesus**
vv. 1-8	Jesus heals and forgives a paralytic.
v. 9	Jesus calls Matthew and he follows Jesus.
vv. 10-13	Jesus eats with tax collectors and sinners.
vv. 14-17	Jesus insists John the Baptizer's ways do not fit into Kingdom of Heaven's ways.

vv. 18-26	Jesus' robe is touched by a woman who is healed enroute to ruler's house.
vv. 27-31	Jesus heals two blind men who have faith.
vv. 32-34	Jesus delivers from mute spirit causing Pharisees to harden their hearts.
vv. 35-38	Jesus heals and tells disciples to pray God will send out more laborers.
Chapter 10	**Jesus Gives Authority over Demons to Apostles.**
vv. 1-4	Twelve are named individually here.
vv. 5-15	Jesus commissions and sends twelve to do all He has been doing.
vv. 16-23	Jesus warns twelve to be bold and not fear man but acknowledge Jesus as Lord.
vv. 24-39	We are to put no one before Jesus - ever!
vv. 40-42	We receive eternal rewards by receiving those whom Jesus sends to us.
Chapter 11	**Jesus and John the Baptizer**
v. 1	Jesus teaches in disciples' home cities; (good evangelism strategy).
vv. 2-6	John's disciples come to Jesus to verify that Jesus is the Messiah.
vv. 7-15	John was great prophet but anyone in kingdom of God is greater than John.
vv. 16-19	People called John a demoniac and Jesus a glutton and drunkard.
vv. 20-24	Jesus rebukes Chorazin, Bethsaida and Capernaum.
vv. 25-30	Jesus thanks Father for revealing wisdom and knowledge to His disciples.
Chapter 12	**Jesus and Sabbath Laws**
vv. 1-8	Jesus is Lord of the Sabbath, not reverse.
vv. 9-14	Jesus says it is always acceptable to do good on Sabbath or any day.
vv. 15-21	Jesus will bring salvation to Gentiles.

vv. 22-32	Unforgivable sin is utter rebellion against God, denying Him of His own deeds.
vv. 33-37	We are justified or condemned by what comes out of our hearts by our mouths.
vv. 38-42	Only sign given by Jesus is He will be in earth 3 days and be resurrected.
vv. 43-45	Person delivered from evil spirits must fill space with God or spirits will return.
vv. 46-50	Whoever does will of God is Jesus' family.
Chapter 13	**Parables of Jesus' Kingdom**
vv. 1-9	Spiritually open to God understand parables about 30, 60, and 100-fold.
vv. 10-17	Jesus explains parables to disciples so hostiles won't understand.
vv. 18-23	We won't yield fruit if bad soil. If good soil, we yield fruit, 30, 60 or 100-fold.
vv. 24-30	Good wheat will be harvested after weeds have been bundled and burned first.
vv. 31-32	Greatness comes from ordinary Christians (little seeds); Kingdom is manifested.
v. 33	Leaven will increase in flour. Kingdom will likewise increase slowly.
vv. 34-35	Jesus speaks in parables what has been hidden since beginning of world.
vv. 36-43	At end-time angels will throw evil ones into lake of fire and gather righteous.
v. 44	When man finds kingdom life he will sacrifice to enter God's kingdom life.
v. 45	Once person finds kingdom's true value "he will sacrifice all to enter into it."
vv. 46-50	At end-of-the-age angels throw evil into lake of fire (to be cleansed?).
vv. 51-52	Scribes in Mosiac law, now a disciple, can put past with new teachings.

Chapter 14	**John the Baptizer and Jesus' Miracles**
vv. 1-12	Herod Antipas has John the Baptizer beheaded.
vv. 13-21	Jesus uses 5 loaves and 2 fish to feed 5,000+ having 12 baskets left over.
vv. 22-27	Jesus walks on water arriving at storm-tossed boat with disciples at dawn.
vv. 28-33	Peter walks on water before falling. He calls on Jesus and is rescued.
vv. 34-36	Woman previously healed of an issue, arouses sick people to be healed.
Chapter 15	Conflict between Jesus and Elders' Traditions
vv. 1-9	Jesus rebukes Pharisees about dishonoring parents and washing of hands.
vv. 10-20	What defiles is not what enters his mouth, but what comes from unclean heart.
vv. 21-28	A Gentile woman pleads for her demonized daughter; Jesus delivers her child.
vv. 29-31	People glorify God when they see people oppressed by sickness being healed.
vv. 32-39	Jesus uses 7 loaves and few fish to feed 4000 + people; seven deacons?
Chapter 16	**Peter's Confession of Jesus as Messiah**
vv. 1-4	Only sign of Jonah will be given which was Jesus' 3 days and nights in grave.
vv. 5-12	Jesus warns disciples to beware of leaven of Pharisees and Sadducees.
vv. 13-20	Jesus is proclaimed by Peter as the Christ.
vv. 21-23	Jesus rebukes Peter for trying to hinder Jesus' sufferings and death on the cross.
vv. 24-28	To follow Jesus is to deny one's physical life to liberate one's spiritual life.

Chapter 17	**Transfiguration, Near Caesarea Philippi**
vv. 1-8	Jesus, Moses and Elijah are transfigured; God tells Peter to listen to Jesus.
vv. 9-13	Jesus explains to disciples they are not to share vision until His resurrection.
vv. 14-21	Jesus delivers youth from epileptic demon, chiding his disciples for lack of faith.
vv. 22-23	Jesus tells the 12 that He is to be killed and raised third day.
vv. 24-27	Jesus pays half-shekel tax for Peter and Himself not to offend tax collectors.
Chapter 18	**Lost Sheep and Unforgiving Servant**
vv. 1-4	Whoever is as a child (in spirit) will become greatest in kingdom of heaven.
vv. 5-6	There are severe consequences in causing new believers to stumble spiritually.
vv. 7-9	Better is affliction than to be tormented spiritually outside of God's kingdom.
vv. 10-14	God's will is that no little one (new believer) should be lost or separated from Him.
vv. 15-20	Unrepentant believer excludes himself from protective covering of Christ's church.
vv. 21-22	We must always at all times forgive others when they ask for forgiveness from us.
vv. 23-35	If we forgive others from our hearts, our Heavenly Father will also forgive us!
Chapter 19	**Marriage, Divorce and Obstacles of Riches**
vv. 1-2	Jesus heals all people who follow after him.
vv. 3-9	God made man and woman to be one; divorce is due to hardness of hearts.
vv. 10-12	Not everyone can be celibate; only those to whom this is given by God.
vv. 13-15	Jesus blesses little children because He truly loves them.

vv. 16-22	Rich ruler (Rabbi) could not give earthly treasures to get God's treasures.
vv. 23-30	Those who give all will be rewarded by Christ in kingdom of God (v.28).
Chapter 20	**Laborers and True Greatness**
vv. 1-16	The last receives what first receives because of Christ's graciousness.
vv. 17-19	This is third time Jesus foretells His death and resurrection.
vv. 20-28	We are to be servants and lay our lives down for the family of God.
vv. 29-34	Jesus gives sight to 2 blind men by the road.
Chapter 21	**Palm Sunday; Temple Cleansing; Vineyard Parable**
vv. 1-11	Jesus enters Jerusalem on a donkey with her colt.
vv. 12-13	Jesus cleanses Temple by putting out vendors with their birds and animals.
vv. 14-17	People's praises disturb rulers who rebuke Jesus for allowing this to happen.
vv. 18-22	Faith in God's power can wither figs or put mountain in sea if not doubting.
vv. 23-27	Priests won't tell Jesus of Baptizer's authority; He won't tell of His authority.
vv. 28-32	Worldly ones enter kingdom before religious because of faith in Baptizer.
vv. 33-41	Jesus shares parable of vineyard and killing of owner's servants and son.
vv. 42-44	Kingdom of God is given to nation that produces Godly fruit.
vv. 45-46	Pharisees resented Jesus' parables; due to fear they would not seize Him.
Chapter 22	**Marriage Feast; Taxes; Resurrection**
vv. 1-10	Invited people won't come to Jesus' wedding; He invites who are willing to come.
vv. 11-14	Those with wedding garments can attend wedding with Bridegroom Jesus.

vv. 15-22	Jesus says, "Give to Caesar what belongs to him and God what belongs to Him."
vv. 23-28	Sadducees try to trap Jesus concerning marriages in the resurrection.
vv. 29-33	Jesus proclaims to the Sadducees there are no marriages in heaven.
vv. 34-40	Pharisees test Jesus about commandments; "love God and neighbor."
vv. 41-46	Jesus asked Pharisees about David as Lord; they stopped asking questions.
Chapter 23	**Woe to Scribes and Pharisees**
vv. 1-12	Don't follow Pharisees and scribes; they are " actors" or "hypocrites".
vv. 13-15	Scribes and Pharisees won't enter kingdom but keep others from entering.
vv. 16-22	Temple and alter sanctify gifts and are therefore greater than gifts.
vv. 23-24	Leaders tithe to tiniest object but neglect justice, mercy and faith.
vv. 25-26	Leaders look clean outwardly but are unclean in their hearts.
vv. 27-28	Leaders appear outwardly righteous but inwardly are full of hypocrisy and iniquity.
vv. 29-36	Jesus denounces these false leaders to hell.
vv. 37-39	Jerusalem not to see Jesus until saying, Blessed He who comes in Name of Lord.
Chapter 24	**Signs Foretold of End of Age**
vv. 1-2	Jesus foretells destruction of Temple buildings.
vv. 3-8	Wars and rumors of wars are not final sign for end of this age.
vv. 9-14	After falling away with wickedness and kingdom preached, end will come.
vv. 15-28	After many things happen: tribulations, signs, wonders, etc. Christ returns.

vv. 29-31	After tribulations, Christ sends His angels to gather His people from all over.
vv. 32-35	This generation will not pass till all the above takes place.
vv. 36-44	Christ will return when no one is expecting Him.
vv. 45-51	Christ will honor faithful servants; He will punish wicked, unfaithful servants.
Chapter 25	**Teachings on Coming of Kingdom**
vv. 1-13	Christ knows wise virgins prepared to meet Him for marriage feast.
vv. 14-30	Worthy servants rewarded but unworthy cast into outer darkness.
vv. 31-46	Christ blesses who care for others; He punishes those who neglect others.
Chapter 26	**Last Supper and Jesus' Betrayal**
vv. 1-2	Jesus foretells His crucifixion.
vv. 3-5	The chief priests plot Jesus' death.
vv. 6-13	Mary's anointing Jesus' feet became known worldwide.
vv. 14-16	Judas Iscariot deals with priests to betray Jesus for 30 pieces of silver.
vv. 17-19	Jesus sends disciples to prepare Passover meal.
vv. 20-25	Jesus warns Judas it would have been better if he had not been born.
vv. 26-29	Jesus institutes the Lord's Memorial Supper.
vv. 30-35	Jesus explains all disciples will renounce Him after His last supper with them.
vv. 36-46	Jesus prays three times for God's will to be done.
vv. 47-56	Jesus is taken captive and His disciples flee.
vv. 57-68	Jesus is accused of blasphemy by High Priest.
vv. 69-75	Peter denies Christ three times and leaves weeping bitterly.
Chapter 27	**Jesus' Death and Burial**
vv. 1-2	Jesus is bound and delivered to Governor Pilate.
vv. 3-10	Judas Iscariot returns 30 coins and hangs himself.

vv. 11-14	Jesus is accused by chief priests before Pilate.
vv. 15-23	Crowd shouts for Jesus' crucifixion.
vv. 24-26	Barabbas is set free and Jesus is delivered to be crucified.
vv. 27-31	Roman soldiers mock and beat Jesus leading Him away to be crucified.
vv. 32-44	Various people at cross mock Jesus.
vv. 45-50	Jesus cries out to God and releases His Spirit.
vv. 51-54	Darkness fell; earthquake shook; dead bodies raised; guards believed Jesus.
vv. 55-61	Joseph of Arimathea, requests Jesus' body to be buried in his tomb.
vv. 62-66	Chief priests and Pharisees okayed by Pilate to post guards and seal tomb.
Chapter 28	**Resurrection and Great Commission**
vv. 1-8	Angel rolls stone away and tells 2 Marys to tell disciples to meet Jesus in Galilee.
vv. 9-10	Jesus meets 2 Marys and tells them to have His disciples meet Him in Galilee.
vv. 11-15	Soldiers bribed by priests rumoring, Jesus' body stolen while guards slept.
vv. 16-20	Jesus tells disciples to make disciples of all nations and baptize them.

MARK
Probably written before fall of Jerusalem in A.D. 70

Chapter 1	**Jesus Baptized by John; Jesus Calls His Disciples.**
vv. 1-8	Baptizer's water baptism for repentance; of Jesus' baptism with Holy Spirit.
vv. 9-11	God's blessing upon Jesus' baptism by John
vv. 12-13	Jesus tested 40 days in wilderness
vv. 14-15	Jesus preaches that God's kingdom is at hand.
vv. 16-20	Jesus calls His disciples to leave all and follow him.
vv. 21-28	Jesus casts out unclean spirit in synagogue of Galilee; Jesus' fame spreads.
vv. 29-31	Jesus heals Peter's mother-in-law. (Looks like Rome's first pope had a wife).
vv. 32-34	Jesus heals people and casts out demons.
vv. 35-39	Jesus goes through all Galilee healing and delivering.
vv. 40-45	Jesus heals leper; charges him not to tell; wanting spiritual message to Jews.
Chapter 2	**Healing a Paralytic; Calling of Levi**
vv. 1-12	Jesus wants people to know Him spiritually not just physically as healer.
vv. 13-14	Jesus calls Levi, and he follows Him.
vv. 15-17	Jesus justifies His calling and eating with tax collectors and sinners.
vv. 18-22	Jesus says be joyful while He (bridegroom) is with His Bride (disciples).

vv. 23-28	Jesus states He is Lord of Sabbath; Sabbath made to meet human needs.
Chapter 3	**Jesus Appoints Twelve Apostles.**
vv. 1-6	Jesus heals withered hand on Sabbath, causing Pharisees to hate Him.
vv. 7-12	Jesus' fame concerning healings continues to grow.
vv. 13-19(a)	Jesus appoints 12 to live and work with Him.
vv. 19(b)-27	Jesus explains why Satan doesn't cast out demons.
vv. 28-30	Jesus explains "unforgivable sin" against Holy Spirit is due to hardened hearts.
vv. 31-35	Jesus says "Whoever does will of God is my brother, sister, and mother."
Chapter 4	**Parables of Kingdom of God**
vv. 1-9	Jesus teaches the 30, 60 and 100-fold depending on soil (hearer).
vv. 10-20	Good soil (receptive) hear Jesus, producing fruit up to 30, 60 or 100-fold.
vv. 21-25	Jesus states more will be given to those who are receptive to His teachings.
vv. 26-29	God's kingdom appears almost unnoticeable.
vv. 30-32	God's kingdom begins small but grows to be great.
vv. 33-34	Jesus explains everything to His disciples.
vv. 35-41	Jesus rebukes wind and calms sea.
Chapter 5	**Deliverance of Gerasene Demoniac**
vv. 1-3	Jesus sends 6000 demons into 2000 pigs who drown in Sea of Galilee.
vv. 14-20	Jesus sends delivered Gerasene back to his people who later become believers.
vv. 21-24(a)	Jesus goes with Jairus to heal his daughter.
vv. 24(b)-34	Woman with bloody disease for 12 years touches Jesus' robe and is healed.
vv. 35-43	Jesus raises Jairus' daughter from death.

Chapter 6	**Death of John; Feeding of Five Thousand Men plus Families**
vv. 1-6	Jesus does no mighty works in Nazareth because of their unbelief.
vv. 7-13	Jesus tells disciples to stay in worthy houses, to minister and preach.
vv. 14-29	Recounting of Herod Antipas' beheading of John the Baptizer
vv. 30-44	Jesus feeds 5,000 men plus their families.
vv. 45-52	Jesus rescues disciples from drowning during storm.
vv. 53-56	In Genesaret people who touched Jesus' garments were healed.
Chapter 7	**Tradition of Elders Vs. Healing Faith**
vv. 1-8	Elders leave God's commandments to hold to rituals of men.
vv. 9-13	Elders ignore caring for their parents.
vv. 14-23	Not what enters man but what comes out of sinful heart defiles a person.
vv. 24-30	Syrophoenician's daughter delivered from demon due to mother's faith.
vv. 31-37	Jesus heals a deaf and mute man in Decapolis.
Chapter 8	**Four Thousand Men and Families Are Fed.**
vv. 1-10	Jesus feeds people and goes to Dalmanutha, (Magadan or Magdala).
vv. 11-13	Jesus is grieved because people want signs from heaven to test Him.
vv. 14-21	Jesus reasons with disciples about leaven of Pharisees and Herod.
vv. 22-26	Jesus heals a blind man in Bethsaida.
vv. 27-30	Peter declares Jesus is "the Christ."
vv. 31-33	Later, Jesus rebukes Peter for his carnal thinking.
vv. 34-38	Jesus commissions people to take up their crosses and follow Him.

Chapter 9	**Jesus' Transfiguration and Teaching**
v. 1	Jesus says God's kingdom and power will arrive soon.
vv. 2-8	Peter, James and John see Jesus, Moses and Elijah and hear God's voice.
vv. 9-13	Jesus explains that Elijah did come in personality of John the Baptizer.
vv. 14-29	Jesus tells disciples this kind of deaf and mute spirit comes out by prayer.
vv. 30-32	Jesus tells them about His resurrection after three days in grave.
vv. 33-37	Jesus tells them how to be great in His kingdom.
vv. 38-41	Jesus tells them not to forbid others to cast out demons.
vv. 42-50	Jesus warns about the consequences of sin and hell to follow.
Chapter 10	**Blind Bartimeus is Healed**.
v. 1	Jesus teaches in region of Judea.
vv. 2-9	Jesus teaches about marriage and divorce.
vv. 10-12	In Palestine women could not sue for divorce.
vv. 13-16	Jesus blesses children and says one must be child-like to enter God's kingdom.
vv. 17-22	Rich young ruler could not give up his possessions to follow Jesus.
vv. 23-31	To be saved means ability to see God's kingdom. (John 3:3).
vv. 32-34	Jesus again tells of His death, burial and resurrection.
vv. 35-45	Jesus explains a servant of others will be greatest in God's kingdom.
vv. 46-52	Bartimeus (son of Timeus) is healed of blindness and follows Jesus.
Chapter 11	**Palm Sunday and Cleansing Temple**
vv. 1-10	Disciples believe Jesus is going to set up His kingdom literally on earth.
v. 11	Jesus surveys Temple and goes to Bethany with 12 disciples.
vv. 12-14	Jesus curses fig tree enroute to Jerusalem.
vv. 15-19	Jesus drives out money changers from Temple.

vv. 20-26	Jesus uses withered fig tree as example for disciples' faith for miracles.
vv. 27-33	Jesus challenged by chief priests and scribes as to His authority for miracles.

Chapter 12 — Paying Taxes; Resurrection; Great Commandment

vv. 1-11	Jesus tells parable of vineyard and tenants who kill messengers and son.
v. 12	Priests and scribes know Jesus was referring to them and left Him.
vv. 13-17	Jesus tells Pharisees and Herodians to pay taxes to Caesar and serve God.
vv. 18-23	Sadducees try to trap Jesus about one widow belonging to 7 brothers.
vv. 24-27	Jesus tells Sadducees people in heaven will be like angels, without spouses.
vv. 28-34	Jesus tells scribe that loving God and neighbor are 1st and 2nd commands.
vv. 35-37	Christ is not David's son but God's Son.
vv. 38-40	Scribes who devour widows' finances will receive greater condemnation.
vv. 41-44	Jesus commends widow who gives to Temple treasury all she has, 2 coins.

Chapter 13 — Destruction of Jerusalem and End Times Foretold

vv. 1-2	Jesus foretells destruction of Jerusalem Temple.
vv. 3-8	Jesus explains wars and rumors of wars will take place before end comes.
vv. 9-13	Jesus tells disciples when persecuted, Holy Spirit will speak through them.
vv. 14-23	Jesus warns disciples to flee when Jerusalem is seized by conquerors.
vv. 24-27	After Jerusalem's fall to end-time, Jesus will return and set up His kingdom.

vv. 28-31	He returns to tell what will happen locally to Jerusalem during that generation.
vv. 32-37	Jesus warns disciples be on guard about destruction of Temple in 70 A.D.
Chapter 14	**Last Supper; Gethsemane; Jesus before Caiaphas**
vv. 1-2	Chief priests and scribes seek to destroy Jesus.
vv. 3-9	Pure nard this woman used to anoint Jesus' feet was costly, imported from India.
vv. 10-11	Judas Iscariot goes to the chief priests to betray Jesus for money.
vv. 12-16	Disciples prepare Passover meal in an upper room designated by Jesus.
vv. 17-21	Jesus tells 12 that one of them will betray Him as they eat Passover Supper.
vv. 22-25	Jesus tells them He will drink wine again with them in kingdom of God.
vv. 26-31	Jesus tells His disciples they all will fall away from Him this night.
vv. 32-42	Jesus prays in Gethsemane; finds disciples sleeping, not watching.
vv. 43-50	Jesus is arrested after Judas points Him out; afterward, disciples all flee.
vv. 51-52	John Mark flees naked from soldiers.
vv. 53-65	Jesus is accused of blasphemy by High Priest and is condemned to death.
vv. 66-72	Peter denies Jesus three times before cock crows.
Chapter 15	**Crucifixion of Jesus on Cross**
vv. 1-5	Jesus stands before Pilate for judgment.
vv. 6-15	Pilate releases Barabbas and delivers Jesus to be crucified.
vv. 16-20	Soldiers mock and strike Jesus before leading him away to be crucified.
vv. 21-32	Priests and scribes, one thief and others mock Jesus who is on cross.

vv. 33-39	Jesus cries out to God and physically dies.
vv. 40-41	Women who loved Jesus watch His crucifixion.
vv. 42-47	Joseph of Arimathea gets permission from Pilate to bury Jesus in his tomb.
Chapter 16	**Empty Tomb and Resurrection**
vv. 1-8	Women are told by angel to tell disciples Jesus would meet them in Galilee.
vv. 9-11	Mary Magdalene tells unbelieving disciples that Jesus is resurrected.
vv. 12-13	Two men enroute to Emaneus report Jesus' resurrection to disciples.
vv. 14-18	Jesus commissions 11 disciples to preach gospel and baptize believers.
vv. 19-20	Jesus goes into heaven and disciples preach and minister with anointing.

LUKE

Chapter 1	**Birth of John the Baptizer**
vv. 1-4	Theophilus (an official) knows about Jesus is informed by Luke's writings.
vv. 5-7	John's father, Zechariah a priest, married to Elizabeth, a descendant of Aaron.
vv. 8-23	Angel Gabriel tells Zechariah that elderly Elizabeth will bear a son named John.
vv. 24-25	Elizabeth conceives around 7-6 B.C. and hides for five months from public.
vv. 26-38	Angel, Gabriel, tells Mary God's Holy Spirit will conceive a Son in her womb.
vv. 39-56	When Mary visits cousin Elizabeth she blesses Mary who magnifies the Lord.
vv. 57-66	When John is named, Zechariah's tongue is loosened, verifying John's name.
vv. 67-80	Zechariah prophesies John will be forerunner to prepare way for the Messiah.
Chapter 2	**Jesus' Birth and Presentation in Temple**
vv. 1-7	Jesus is born in Bethlehem in a manger, wrapped in swaddling cloths.
vv. 8-14	Angel of Lord tells Jesus' birth to shepherds, (October, Feast of Tabernacles).
vv. 15-20	Shepherds share with Joseph and Mary what angels declared to them.
v. 21	Jesus is circumcised and given the Name which means salvation.

vv. 22-35	Simeon, by Holy Spirit prophecies over Jesus to Mary about future of Israel.
vv. 36-38	Prophetess Anna speaks of Him Who is to bring redemption to Jerusalem.
vv. 39-40	Returning to Nazareth from Egypt, God's favor rests on Jesus as He grows up.
vv. 41-51	Jesus at 12 is found in Temple by Joseph and Mary after Feast of Tabernacles.
v. 52	Next 18 years Jesus increases in wisdom, stature and favor with God and man.
Chapter 3	**Jesus is Baptized in Water and Spirit.**
vv. 1-6	John begins preaching baptism of repentance for forgiveness of sins.
vv. 7-9	He warns people God is ready to destroy evil people of Israel and burn them.
vv. 10-14	John tells people that true repentance is doing what is right to others.
vv. 15-17	John warns of Messiah's coming with judgment upon unrighteous.
vv. 18-20	Herod imprisons John due to John's preaching about Herod's evil lifestyle.
vv. 21-22	God approves of Jesus as He is water baptized by sending Holy Spirit on Him.
vv. 23-37	Jesus' ancestry goes back to Adam and God. Jesus at 30 starts preaching.
Chapter 4	**Jesus' Wilderness Temptation and Early Ministry**
vv. 1-13	Jesus defeats 3 major temptations Satan throws at Him in wilderness.
vv. 14-15	Jesus returns in power of Holy Spirit to Galilee, teaching in synagogues.
vv. 16-30	Jesus tells Jews God fed a Gentile widow and healed Gentile army officer.

vv. 31-37	Jesus' fame grows when He casts a demon out of a man in the synagogue.
vv. 38-39	Jesus heals Peter's mother-in-law of fever who then serves food to them.
vv. 40-41	Demons silenced when Jesus casts them out because they know He's the Christ.
vv. 42-44	Jesus preaches in synagogues in Judea because this is what He was sent to do.
Chapter 5	**Jesus Cleanses Leprosy and Forgives Sins.**
vv. 1-11	Jesus shows disciples where to catch fish; they left nets and followed Jesus.
vv. 12-16	Jesus heals a leper; His fame grows.
vv. 17-26	Jesus heals a paralyzed man and also forgives man's sins.
vv. 27-28	Levi (Matthew) tax collector, leaves his business to follow Jesus.
vv. 29-32	Jesus came not for self-righteous, but sinners, tax collectors and outcasts.
vv. 33-39	Jesus reveals kind of people (like disciples) who make up Kingdom's Bride.
Chapter 6	**Choosing Twelve and Beatitudes**
vv. 1-5	Jesus is Lord over Sabbath, not vice versa.
vv. 6-11	Pharisees seek to destroy Jesus for restoring man's withered hand on Sabbath.
vv. 12-16	Jesus names 12 disciples, "apostles!"
vv. 17-19	Jesus heals and later teaches multitude.
v. 20	God's kingdom is open to the poor (because they want to change and be blessed).
v. 21a	To the hungry-hearted will come God's satisfaction.
v. 21b	To those mourning over unrighteousness in land will one day come kingdom joy.
vv. 22-23	Blessed those rejected for loving Jesus. Reward will be great in God's kingdom.
v. 24	Woe to rich who want nothing from Jesus.

v. 25a	Woe to those who have no hunger for Jesus.
v. 25b	Woe to carefree, they 'll weep as Christ blesses others and punishes them.
v. 26	Woe to those who are accepted by society's standards.
vv. 27-31	Be generous, not hard, to everyone who asks of your goods.
v. 32-36	Give even to enemies who ask of you. Heavenly Father is merciful to all.
vv. 37-38	We will receive the measure we give to others.
vv. 39-42	Everyone, who is fully taught, will become like his teacher.
vv. 43-45	We produce good or bad fruit because we are good or we are bad.
vv. 46-49	If we do what Jesus taught, we'll have a good foundation against storms.
Chapter 7	**Centurion's Servant, Jesus and John the Baptizer**
vv. 1-10	Jesus marvels at Roman centurion's faith and heals his servant.
vv. 11-17	Jesus stops funeral procession and heals son of the widow of Nain.
vv. 18-23	Jesus tells John the Baptizer's disciples He is Whom John expected in Israel.
vv. 24-30	Jesus honors John, proclaiming least in God's kingdom is greater than John.
vv. 31-35	Jesus shows Pharisees people who are different aren't demon possessed.
vv. 36-50	Jesus tells Simon the Pharisee the woman loved Jesus more than did Simon.
Chapter 8	**Sower; Gerasene Demoniac; Jairus' Daughter**
vv. 1-3	Women who provided for Jesus' needs.
vv. 4-8	Jesus tells parables about different soils (people).
vv. 9-15	Jesus explains about good and bad soils.
vv. 16-18	God adds to good soil but takes away from bad soil (hearts of people).
vv. 19-21	Jesus' true family are people who hear and do God's Word.

vv. 22-25	Jesus calms wind and water and rebukes disciples' lack of faith.
vv. 26-33	Jesus delivers demon possessed man and demons are allowed to enter hogs.
vv. 34-39	The formerly demonized man proclaims Jesus.
vv. 40-42(a)	Jairus requests Jesus to heal his daughter.
vv. 42(b)-48	Jesus is touched by a woman of 12 years plague and healed and made whole.
vv. 49-56	Jesus commands Jairus' daughter's spirit to return and she's raised from death.
Chapter 9	**Feeding Five Thousand Men; Peter's Confession; Transfiguration**
vv. 1-6	Jesus commissions 12 disciples to preach kingdom of God and do what He did.
vv. 7-9	Herod the tetrarch is perplexed concerning Jesus.
vv. 10-17	Jesus multiplies 5 loaves and 2 fish feeding 5,000 men plus their families.
vv. 18-22	Jesus asks disciples who is He and tells them of death and resurrection.
vv. 23-27	Jesus told disciples not to be ashamed of Him but follow Him regardless of cost.
vv. 28-36	Jesus, Moses and Elijah are transfigured in presence of Peter, James and John.
vv. 37-43(a)	Jesus commands a demon to come out of a youth.
vv. 43(b)-45	Jesus tells disciples about His coming death but they understand it not.
vv. 46-48	Jesus tells disciples that humility is best way.
vv. 49-50	"Whoever is not against you is for you," says Jesus.
vv. 51-56	Samaritans won't receive Jesus since He is going only to Jerusalem.
vv. 57-62	Kingdom of God must always take first place.

Chapter 10	**Mission of Seventy; Good Samaritan**
vv. 1-12	Jesus commissions 70 other disciples to do what He earlier had told 12 to do.
vv. 13-15	Gentile cities receive less penalty on judgment day than some Jewish cities.
v. 16	"Whoever rejects you also rejects My Father and Me."
vv. 17-20	Rejoice, not that demons bow to you, but your names are written in heaven.
vv. 21-22	Open-hearted understand identity of God and Son of God.
vv. 23-24	The 70 disciples are blessed to see into God's kingdom.
vv. 25-28	To love God completely and to love others as yourself leads into eternal life.
vv. 29-37	Jesus tells "Good Samaritan" parable to Jewish lawyer who had tested Him.
vv. 38-42	Jesus tells Martha that Mary's listening to teachings has eternal value.
Chapter 11	**Concerning Prayer; Jonah's Sign; Woes to Pharisees**
vv. 1-4	Jesus teaches His disciples how to pray, known as "The Lord's Prayer."
vv. 5-13	We are challenged to boldly ask "Father of all mercy" for our needs.
vv. 14-23	Jesus tells Pharisees He casts out demons by finger of God, not by Satan.
vv. 24-26	After house is cleansed it must be filled with God's Spirit or demons return.
vv. 27-28	"Blessed ... who hear the word of God and keep it!"
vv. 29-32	Nineveh will judge those who reject Jesus.
vv. 33-36	When your eyes are full of light body is sound.
vv. 37-41	Jesus tells Pharisees what is within us is as important as what is outside of us.
vv. 42-44	Woe to Pharisees for not making spiritual changes within their hearts.

vv. 45-52	Woe to lawyers who keep people from entering into God's kingdom.
vv. 53-54	Scribes and Pharisees tried to say something that could be held against Jesus.
Chapter 12	**Don't Be Anxious; Be Watchful and Faithful**.
vv. 1-3	Jesus tells His disciples that all things will one day be revealed.
vv. 4-7	Don't fear anyone but Almighty God!
vv. 8-12	Only blasphemy against the Holy Spirit will not be forgiven.
vv. 13-21	"A man is a fool to lay up treasures for himself and not be rich toward God."
vv. 22-31	"Do not be anxious, but seek God's kingdom and He will meet the needs."
vv. 32-34	"Seek God's kingdom first of all!"
vv. 35-40	Be ready! The Son of God will return at an unexpected time.
vv. 41-48	God will judge everyone according to light of understanding each one has.
vv. 49-53	Jesus came to bring contrasts (divisions), not peace!
vv. 54-56	People can interpret weather but not the time of Jesus' presence with them.
vv. 57-59	No one gets out of judgment till he has paid the last cent for his crimes.
Chapter 13	**Repentance; Healing; End of Age; Weeping for Jerusalem**
vv. 1-5	Unless people repent, they will perish (soul and body). See Matt. 10:28.
vv. 6-9	Unless we bring forth good fruit we'll be replaced.
vv. 10-17	"Every day is a good day to be healed," says Jesus.
vv. 18-19	Faith starts small as a seed but grows to become a tree.
vv. 20-21	Leaven placed in flour causes it to expand as does faith in God's kingdom.
vv. 22-30	We enter God's kingdom only through knowing Jesus Christ.

vv. 31-35	Jerusalem will say one day, "Blessed is He who comes in the Name of the Lord!"
Chapter 14	**Humility; Banquet; Discipleship**
vv. 1-6	A person's well-being is important on any day.
vv. 7-11	God exalts the humble and rejects the proud.
vv. 12-14	If you minister to the needy, God will reward you.
vv. 15-24	God's banquet is open to all who will come to Him.
vv. 25-33	To be Christ's disciple, He must be preeminent.
vv. 34-35	If we lose our desire for Christ, we become worthless.
Chapter 15	**Lost Sheep and Coin; and Lost Son**
vv. 1-2	Pharisees murmur concerning Jesus' types of friends.
vv. 3-7	Heaven rejoices over one sinner who repents, i.e., lost sheep.
vv. 8-10	Heaven rejoices over one sinner who repents, i.e., lost coin.
vv. 11-24	When the proud prodigal humbly returns, God receives him.
vv. 25-32	Jesus shows God's forgiveness compared to man's unforgiving, judgmental nature.
Chapter 16	**Dishonest Steward; Rich Man and Lazarus**
vv. 1-9	Worldly people are shrewder than the sons of Light.
vv. 10-13	No one can serve both the world and God!
vv. 14-15	What the world exalts, God hates!
vv. 16-17	It is difficult for one to enter God's kingdom.
v. 18	Putting away one's mate and marrying another is a committal of adultery.
vv. 19-31	If we can't accept Jesus, we can't accept word of one returning from death.
Chapter 17	**Forgiveness and Faith; Ten Lepers Cleansed.**
vv. 1-4	When rebuked person repents, we must forgive him.
vv. 5-6	Faith as small as a mustard seed can move obstacles.
vv. 7-10	We as unworthy servants obey God because it's our duty.
vv. 11-19	A Samaritan, cleansed of leprosy, returns to worship Jesus.
vv. 20-21	God's kingdom, within Jesus, comes without signs.
vv. 22-37	Be prepared! The end-of-the-age comes unexpectedly.

Chapter 18	**Unjust Judge; Pharisee and Tax Collector; Rich Ruler**
vv. 1-8	Don't quit crying out to God; He will vindicate His own.
vv. 9-14	God rejects the proud but gives grace to the repentant.
vv. 15-17	Only the child-like, open-hearted enter God's kingdom.
vv. 18-30	Entering God's kingdom is true salvation (eternal life).
vv. 31-34	Jesus tells the 12 again of His death and resurrection.
vv. 35-43	A blind man cries out to Jesus and is healed.
Chapter 19	**Zacchaeus; Talents; Palm Sunday; Temple Cleansed.**
vv. 1-10	Jesus eats with tax collector, Zacchaeus, who's willing to restore fourfold to wronged.
vv. 11-27	Jesus returning with kingdom, rewards faithful and punishes unfaithful.
vv. 28-40	Jesus enters Jerusalem; disciples shout, "Blessed is He who comes in the name of the Lord."
vv. 41-44	Jesus weeps over Jerusalem; people did not know time of God's visitation.
vv. 45-46	Jesus cleanses Temple for second time.
vv. 47-48	Chief priests and scribes seek to destroy Jesus but fear people around Him.
Chapter 20	**Jesus' Authority; Vineyard; Resurrection**
vv. 1-8	Pharisees refuse about Baptizer's authority, He refuses about His authority.
vv. 9-18	Jesus explains Father's judgment will come for killing God's only begotten Son.
vv. 19-26	Pharisees try to trap Jesus by asking if Jews should pay taxes to Caesar.
vv. 27-33	Sadducees try to trap Jesus about His belief in resurrection and afterlife.
vv. 34-40	Jesus explains in resurrection sons of God are like angels, they do not marry.
vv. 41-44	Jesus proclaims He is David's Lord!
vv. 45-47	Jesus tells disciples beware of scribes of a greater condemnation.

Chapter 21	**Poor Widow; Signs Forecasting Kingdom of God**
vv. 1-4	Poor widow gives all of her money into treasury.
vv. 5-9	End of Jerusalem will not be immediate.
vv. 10-19	Faithfulness to Christ will give entrance to eternal life.
vv. 20-24	Jerusalem will be under Gentile rule until this period of time is fulfilled.
vv. 25-28	Redemption of Jerusalem comes when Jesus returns with power and glory.
vv. 29-33	When signs take place, you will know the kingdom of God is nearby.
vv. 34-36	Be praying that you will escape and stand before the Son of man.
vv. 37-38	Jesus taught during day in Temple but lodged at night on Mt. Olivet.
Chapter 22	**Last Supper; Judas' Betrayal and Peter's Denial**
vv. 1-2	As Passover drew near chief priests and scribes plan to put Jesus to death.
vv. 3-6	Satan enters Judas and he plots with chief priests and officers to betray Jesus.
vv. 7-13	Jesus directs Peter and John to prepare Passover meal in upper room.
vv. 14-23	Jesus eats Passover meal with disciples and explains one will betray Him.
vv. 24-27	Jesus teaches the one who serves is the greatest.
vv. 28-30	Jesus promises disciples will sit with Him in kingdom judging 12 tribes of Israel.
vv. 31-34	Jesus tells Simon Peter of Peter's denial.
vv. 35-38	Jesus explains that His disciples will need supplies and swords.
vv. 39-46	Jesus prays that He will do His Father's will.
vv. 47-53	Jesus is betrayed by Judas' kiss and tells crowd this darkness is their hour.
vv. 54-62	Peter weeps bitterly after denying his relationship with Jesus.

vv. 63-65	Jesus is reviled and beaten by guards who were holding Him.
vv. 66-71	Jesus condemned by Caiaphas, claiming, " Son of man will be seated with God." |//

Chapter 23 — Jesus before Pilate and Herod; Crucifixion

vv. 1-5	Jesus is accused before Pilate of stirring up people.
vv. 6-12	Jesus is accused before Herod and returned to Pilate.
vv. 13-17	Pilate says neither he nor Herod finds Jesus worthy of death.
vv. 18-25	Barabbas released to go free; Jesus sentenced to be crucified.
vv. 26-31	Jesus warns women to prepare for coming destruction of Jerusalem in 70 A.D.
vv. 32-38	Rulers and soldiers mock Jesus asking His "Father to forgive them."
vv. 39-43	One of criminals welcomed into Paradise for believing in Jesus.
vv. 44-49	Jesus commits His spirit to God.
vv. 50-56	Joseph of Arimathea takes Jesus' body and places it in his rock tomb.

Chapter 24 — Empty Tomb; Walk to Emmaus; Jesus' Commission

vv. 1-12	Women went to tomb to be told by 2 angels Jesus had risen from dead.
vv. 13-27	Jesus talks to 2 men enroute to Emmaus, 7 miles from Jerusalem.
vv. 28-35	Jesus reveals Himself as He breaks bread with these two men in Emmaus.
vv. 36-43	Jesus appears to His disciples and eats fish.
vv. 44-49	Jesus exhorts disciples to stay in Jerusalem until Holy Spirit empowers them.
vv. 50-53	Jesus is received up into heaven.

JOHN

Chapter 1	**Testimony of John the Baptizer**
vv. 1-5	Jesus, the Word, was in the beginning with God.
vv. 6-8	John the Baptizer came to bear witness to the Light (Jesus).
vv. 9-13	All who received this Light (Jesus) received right to become children of God.
vv. 14-18	Jesus has come to make the Father known.
vv. 19-23	John was sent to prepare people for coming of their Messiah, Jesus Christ.
vv. 24-28	John says he is not worthy to untie thongs of Jesus' sandals.
vv. 29-34	John sees Jesus as Son of God; as baptized, dove (Holy Spirit) lights on Jesus.
vv. 35-42	John the Baptizer proclaims Jesus as Messiah and 2 disciples follow Jesus.
vv. 43-51	Philip finds Nathaniel and they follow Jesus.
Chapter 2	**Wedding at Cana**
vv. 1-11	Jesus turns water into wine at marriage feast in Cana; Jesus' first miracle.
v. 12	Jesus goes to Capernaum with mother, brothers and disciples for a few days.
vv. 13-22	Jesus cleanses Temple of animals and money changers before Passover.
vv. 23-25	Jesus knows what is in every man and does not trust Himself to man.
Chapter 3	**Nicodemus Comes to Jesus by Night.**
vv. 1-15	Jesus explains to Nicodemus spiritual birth is belief by water and Holy Spirit.

vv. 16-21	People rejecting Jesus, condemned; those accepting Jesus as Lord, saved.
vv. 22-24	Jesus and disciples were baptizing near place where John was also baptizing.
vv. 25-30	John points to Jesus as Bridegroom and rejoices as a friend of Bridegroom.
vv. 31-36	Believing in Jesus brings eternal life; not believing brings God's wrath.
Chapter 4	**Jesus and Woman of Samaria**
vv. 1-6	Jesus' disciples baptize more than John the Baptizer; He waits at well.
vv. 7-15	Jesus offers Samaritan woman gift of God to be made eternally righteous.
vv. 16-26	Jesus reveals to woman at well He is Messiah, Savior of the world.
vv. 27-30	Woman leaves water jar at well and tells citizens she has met the Christ.
vv. 31-38	Jesus sows, disciples reap; harvest comes from death, burial and resurrection.
vv. 39-42	Samaritans believed woman's testimony; later believed after meeting Jesus.
vv. 43-45	Galileans welcome Jesus as the Messiah.
vv. 46-54	Jesus' 2nd miracle in Galilee, healing of Roman official's near-death son.
Chapter 5	**Lame Man Healed; Jesus' Relation to God.**
v. 1	Jesus goes up to Jerusalem for a feast of the Jews.
vv. 2-9	Jesus heals a man who had been paralyzed for 38 years.
vv. 10-18	Jesus angers Pharisees for Sabbath healing, making Himself one with God.
vv. 19-24	Jesus tells Pharisees He does what He sees His Father who sent Him is doing.
vv. 25-29	Jesus will raise dead to resurrection of life or resurrection of judgment.

vv. 30-47	Jesus rebukes Pharisees for disbelieving Moses' writing about coming Messiah.
Chapter 6	**Feeding Five Thousand Men; Jesus, Bread of Life**
vv. 1-14	Jesus takes 5 barley loaves and 2 fish, feeding 5000 men and families.
v. 15	Jesus leaves multitude, perceiving they were going to make Him their king.
vv. 16-21	Jesus walks on water to rescue disciples caught in storm on Sea of Galilee.
vv. 22-24	People whom Jesus fed entered their boats looking for Jesus.
vv. 25-34	Jesus tells crowd who find Him, He is God's true Bread of Life.
vv. 35-40	Everyone who believes in Jesus will be raised on last day into God's eternal life.
vv. 41-51	Jesus explains He will lay down His life, for people His father draws to be saved.
vv. 52-59	Jesus tells rulers eating His flesh and drinking His blood brings eternal life.
vv. 60-65	Jesus tells disciples His flesh is life and blood is spirit giving eternal life.
vv. 66-71	Peter declares Jesus the Holy One of Israel Who has words of eternal life.
Chapter 7	**Water of Life; Feast of Tabernacles (Booths)**
vv. 1-9	Jesus' half-brothers did not yet believe Jesus was actually God's Son.
vv. 10-13	Jesus goes privately to Feast of Booths.
vv. 14-24	Jesus challenges rulers to judge with righteous judgment.
vv. 25-31	Jesus' human origin known; but His real, spiritual origin comes from God.
vv. 32-36	Jesus tells Pharisees they will not be able to go where He will be going.
vv. 37-39	Jesus declares those who believe in Him will be filled with God's Holy Spirit.

vv. 40-44	Some believed in Jesus as Messiah while others wanted to destroy Jesus.
vv. 45-52	Pharisees wanted to kill Jesus; Nicodemus defends Jesus as the Messiah.

Chapter 8 — Woman Caught in Adultery; Jesus, Light of Life.

vv. 1-11	Jesus shows judgment to leaders, trapping Him with woman caught in adultery.
vv. 12-20	Jesus explains spiritual judgment; He is from above; Pharisees judge carnally.
vv. 21-30	Jesus judges according to what His Father reveals to Him through Spirit (Light).
vv. 31-33	Jesus proclaims, continuing in His words brings truth setting people free.
vv. 34-38	Jesus says belief in Him will set Jews free from "slavery of sinning!"
vv. 39-47	Jesus says Jews cannot believe He is Son of God because they are of the devil.
vv. 48-59	Jews judged Jesus by Old Testament; Jesus judged by Light (Spirit) in Himself.

Chapter 9 — Jesus Manifests Himself as Light of Life.

vv. 1-12	Jesus heals man who was born blind as he obediently washes in pool of Siloam.
vv. 13-17	Pharisees can't believe Jesus who does not keep Sabbath can heal blind man.
vv. 18-23	Blind man's parents fear being put out of synagogue due to son's healing.
vv. 24-34	Blind man healed by Jesus cast out of synagogue for sharing with Pharisees.
vv. 35-40	Former blind man worships Jesus when Jesus explains He is the Messiah.

Chapter 10 — Jesus, Good Shepherd Who Gives Life.

vv. 1-6	Jesus explains His sheep know Him and follow Him.
vv. 7-18	Jesus lays His life down for sheep which pleases the Father.

vv. 19-21	Jews argue whether Jesus has a demon or doesn't have a demon.
vv. 22-30	Jesus tells Jews He and His Father are One and Jesus guards His sheep.
vv. 31-39	Jews try to stone Jesus because He tells them He is Son of God.
vv. 40-42	Jesus returns to where John had baptized people; many believed on Jesus.
Chapter 11	**Jesus Raises Lazarus Back to Life.**
vv. 1-4	Lazarus is ill; Jesus explains his illness will reveal God's glory.
vv. 5-16	Jesus goes to Bethany to raise Lazarus.
vv. 17-27	Jesus explains to Martha He is resurrection and life of God for world.
vv. 28-37	Mary goes to Jesus Who is moved with compassion for people at tomb.
vv. 38-44	Jesus calls and Lazarus comes out of tomb.
vv. 45-53	Many Jews believed but Pharisees took counsel to kill Jesus.
v. 54	Jesus goes with His disciples to Ephraim.
vv. 55-57	Pharisees tell Jews to let them know of Jesus' whereabouts.
Chapter 12	**Jesus Concludes His Public Ministry.**
vv. 1-8	Jesus defends Mary at Bethany for anointing His feet with costly ointment.
vv. 9-11	Jews plan to kill Lazarus because his testimony caused many to believe in Jesus.
vv. 12-19	Pharisees feared when crowds proclaimed Jesus as "King of Israel."
vv. 20-26	Jesus tells Greeks whoever follows and serves Him, Father will honor him.
vv. 27-36	Father blesses Jesus from heaven; Jesus tells people to walk in Light (Jesus).
vv. 37-43	People believed in Jesus but fear of ex-communication silences them.

vv. 44-50	Jesus says whoever believes in Him, believes in the Father Who sent Him.

Chapter 13 — Last Supper and Feet Washing

vv. 1-11	Jesus washes disciples' feet in spirit of a humble servant.
vv. 12-20	Jesus tells disciples they need to wash feet of others as humble servants.
vv. 21-30	Satan enters Judas Iscariot "and it is night."
vv. 31-35	Jesus tells disciples as they love one another men know they are His disciples.
vv. 36-38	Jesus tells Peter before cock crows Peter will deny his Lord 3 times.

Chapter 14 — Jesus' Farewell and Believer's Relation to Christ

vv. 1-7	Jesus tells disciples they'll one day go where He goes, kingdom of heaven.
vv. 8-11	Jesus tells Philip Father is in Jesus and Jesus is in Father; they are One.
vv. 12-14	Jesus says whatever we ask in His Name, He will do it for us.
vv. 15-17	Jesus promises those keeping His commands, He will send Holy Spirit to them.
vv. 18-24	Whoever loves Jesus will keep His commands and He and Father will live in him.
vv. 25-31	Jesus' death and resurrection will soon break Satan's power over world.

Chapter 15 — Pattern of Believer's Life

vv. 1-11	Believer's relation to Christ is to abide in Him.
vv. 12-17	Relationship of believers to one another is brotherly love.
vv. 18-27	Believer's relation to worldliness is separation; world hates Jesus' judgment.

Chapter 16 — Believer's Relation to World

vv. 1-4(a)	Jesus warns disciples, persecutors will kill them thinking they are serving God.

vv. 4(b)-11	Jesus must go to Father for Counselor (Comforter) to be with them.
vv. 12-15	Comforter will declare to disciples things that are to come.
vv. 16-24	Jesus tells disciples they will be sorrowful for 3 days but later will rejoice.
vv. 25-28	Jesus is soon to leave world and return forever to the Father.
vv. 29-33	Jesus tells disciples to be of good cheer for He has overcome world.
Chapter 17	**Jesus' High Priestly Prayer**
vv. 1-5	Jesus' prayer for Himself to His Father.
vv. 6-19	Jesus prays for disciples: unity, joy, overcomes and show Christ to world.
vv. 20-26	Jesus prays for church universal to show Father's and Son's love to world.
Chapter 18	**Jesus' Arrest and Trial**
vv. 1-11	Jesus arrested by soldiers; Peter cuts off Malchus' right ear with a sword.
vv. 12-14	Soldiers bind Jesus and take Him to Annas, father-in-law of Priest Caiaphas.
vv. 15-18	John and Peter enter court of High Priest.
vv. 19-24	Annas sends Jesus bound to Caiaphas.
vv. 25-27	Peter denies Jesus for 3rd time before rooster crowed twice.
vv. 28-32	Jewish and Roman soldiers take Jesus from Caiaphas' place to Pilate's residence.
vv. 33-37	Jesus tells Pilate everyone who is of the truth hears Jesus' voice.
vv. 38-40	Jews want Barabbas released and Jesus crucified.
Chapter 19	**Jesus' Death, Burial and Resurrection**
vv. 1-11	Jews' reason for crucifying Jesus was He made Himself the Son of God.
vv. 12-16	Pilate reluctantly hands Jesus over to be crucified.
vv. 17-22	Pilate wrote on Jesus' cross "Jesus of Nazareth, the king of the Jews."

vv. 23-24	Soldiers divide Jesus' clothing into 4 parts and cast lots for His tunic.
vv. 25-27	Jesus gives His mother into John's care.
vv. 28-30	Jesus says, "I thirst;" "it is finished;" releases His Spirit and lays down His life.
vv. 31-37	Soldiers pierce Jesus' side; blood and water pour out, signifying He was dead.
vv. 38-42	Jesus is laid in Joseph of Arimathea's hewn-out rock tomb.
Chapter 20	**Jesus' Resurrection and Appearances**
vv. 1-10	Peter, John and Mary Magdalene see empty tomb where Jesus had laid.
vv. 11-18	Jesus reveals Himself to weeping Mary Magdalene.
vv. 19-23	Jesus imparts Holy Spirit's life into some of His disciples.
vv. 24-25	Thomas demands physical proof before he will believe in Jesus' resurrection.
vv. 26-29	Jesus rebukes Thomas for not believing in resurrection without evidence.
vv. 30-31	Jesus did many other signs that are not recorded in John's gospel.
Chapter 21	**Jesus' Post-Resurrection Appearances**
vv. 1-3	Peter and 6 other disciples go fishing.
vv. 4-8	Jesus told these fishermen disciples to cast net on boats' right and catch fish.
vv. 9-14	Jesus feeds these disciples bread and fish.
vv. 15-19	Jesus questions Peter's love and commands Peter to feed and tend His sheep.
vv. 20-23	Jesus emphasizes again for Peter to follow Him.
v. 24	John states that His writing is true.
v. 25	Only a few signs are recorded here about Jesus during His earthly life.

ACTS

Christianity spreads from Jerusalem to Samaria (8:5), seacoast (8:40), Asia Minor (13:13), Europe (16:11), and Rome (28:16).

Chapters 1-13 deal with traditions of Jerusalem church and Antioch church. Chapters 16-28 deal with Luke's eyewitness reports.

Chapter 1	**Resurrection and Ascension of Christ**
vv. 1-5	Luke relates Jesus' command to tarry in Jerusalem until Holy Spirit comes.
vv. 6-11	Two angels tell disciples Jesus will return in same manner as He ascended.
vv. 12-14	Apostles, Mary and children with others wait and pray in one accord.
vv. 15-26	Matthias is elected to replace Judas Iscariot who committed suicide.
Chapter 2	**Peter's Sermon on Day of Pentecost**
vv. 1-4	Fifty days after crucifixion, 120 baptized in Holy Spirit with "tongues of fire."
vv. 5-13	Jews from many nations heard "tongues of fire" in each one's own language.
vv. 14-21	Day of Pentecost Peter preaches Joel's prophesy, the coming of Holy Spirit.
vv. 22-28	Peter quotes from King David Jesus would not taste corruption in His flesh.
vv. 29-36	God has made Jesus both Lord and Christ whom Jews crucified.
vv. 37-42	3000 people added to church through repentance, faith and water baptism.

vv. 43-47	Disciples believed, were together, Lord adding to early Jerusalem church.
Chapter 3	**Lame Man Healed, and Peter's Preaching.**
vv. 1-10	Lame man healed, praising God he could enter temple and not be an outcast.
vv. 11-16	Peter tells crowd it was power of Jesus Christ that healed lame man.
vv. 17-26	Peter says Jews killed Jesus; forgiven when they repent and turn to Jesus.
Chapter 4	**Peter's and John's Boldness When Arrested.**
vv. 1-4	Five thousand believed in Jesus through Peter's preaching and boldness at arrest.
vv. 5-12	Peter tells Sadducees and elders the cripple was healed through Jesus' Name.
vv. 13-22	After hearing Peter's defense, the two apostles were threatened and released.
vv. 23-31	Apostles ask for boldness in Jesus' Name, and they were filled with Holy Spirit.
vv. 32-37	People sold properties and laid money at apostles' feet; no one had needs.
Chapter 5	**Ananias' and Sapphira's Deaths**
vv. 1-6	Ananias dies when he lies to Holy Spirit.
vv. 7-1	Sapphira also lies to Holy Spirit and dies.
vv. 12-16	People are healed by hands of apostles from sickness and unclean spirits.
vv. 17-26	Angel of the Lord releases apostles from prison where Sadducees had them.
vv. 27-32	Apostles testify to Sadducees this Jesus whom they killed is Savior and Lord.
vv. 33-39	Gamaliel defends apostles, telling Sadducees these men may be of God.
vv. 40-42	Apostles were beaten by Jews but continued preaching Jesus as the Christ.

Chapter 6	**Seven Deacons Are Chosen from Among Disciples.**
vv. 1-6	Seven Greek Jews chosen as deacons; apostles prayed and laid hands on them.
v. 7	Disciples multiplied with many priests who converted to Christianity.
vv. 8-15	Jews conspired against Stephen because of his testimony of Jesus.
Chapter 7	**Stephen Is Stoned to Death**.
vv. 1-8	Stephen preaches about Abraham and covenant of circumcision.
vv. 9-16	Stephen tells of Jacob and Joseph's 11 brothers moving to Egypt in famine.
vv. 17-22	Moses adopted by Pharaoh's daughter, reared in wisdom and culture of Egypt.
vv. 23-29	Moses fled Egypt after killing Egyptian; lived in Midian, married with 2 sons.
vv. 30-34	At burning bush, God calls Moses to go to Egypt to deliver Hebrews.
vv. 35-43	Stephen preaches Israelites forsook the God of Moses and went after idols.
vv. 44-50	Stephen preaches that God does not dwell in temples made with hands.
vv. 51-53	Stephen now exhorts that his hearers are murderers of Jesus.
vv. 54-60	Jewish rulers stone Stephen as Jesus stands in heaven to receive His first martyr.
Chapter 8	**Philip and Ethiopian Eunuch**
vv. 1-3	Saul of Tarsus begins to persecute believers.
vv. 4-8	Philip goes down to Samaria and signs follow his ministry.
vv. 9-13	Simon former magician, believes and baptized in Name of the Lord Jesus.
vv. 14-24	John and Peter go to Samaria and lay hands on converts to receive Holy Spirit.

v. 25	Peter and John preach in Samaritan villages enroute back to Jerusalem.
vv. 26-40	Philip instructs Ethiopian Eunuch and then baptizes him in water.

Chapter 9 — Conversion of Saul

vv. 1-9	Jesus appears to Saul on road to Damascus; Saul goes blind due to bright light.
vv. 10-19	Ananias is sent by Christ to Saul who regains his sight and is baptized.
vv. 20-22	Saul preaches that Jesus is the Christ!
vv. 23-25	When Jews plotted to kill Saul, believers helped him to escape over wall.
vv. 26-30	Jews plot to kill Saul in Jerusalem; disciples send him to Caesarea and Tarsus.
v. 31	Church has rest for a while and multiplies.
vv. 32-35	Peter heals Aeneas which causes many in Lydda and Sharon to turn to the Lord.
vv. 36-43	Peter raises Tabitha from death; many in Joppa turn to the Lord.

Chapter 10 — Conversion of Cornelius; First Gentile

vv. 1-8	Angel of God tells Cornelius to get Peter at Simon the tanner's house in Joppa.
vv. 9-16	Peter sees vision of animals and reptiles; argues with God of unclean things.
vv. 17-23(a)	Three men request Peter to come to Cornelius in Caesarea and share with them.
vv. 23(b)-29	Peter tells Cornelius God said Gentiles are not to be considered unclean.
vv. 30-33	Cornelius tells Peter they are ready to hear what God commanded Peter to say.
vv. 34-43	Peter says God is not partial; whoever believes in Jesus is forgiven of sins.
vv. 44-48	Peter sees Holy Spirit poured out on Gentiles as they begin to speak in tongues.

Chapter 11	**Peter's Defense; Antioch; Agabus**
vv. 1-18	Peter explained what God revealed; Jews accepted Gentiles' conversion, valid.
vv. 19-26	Barnabas brings Saul from Tarsus to Antioch where many being converted.
vv. 27-30	Agabus prophesies famine; Barnabas and Saul take aid to Judea c. 46 A.D.
Chapter 12	**Peter's Release and Herod's Death**
vv. 1-5	Church prays for imprisoned Peter; James, brother of John, already slain.
vv. 6-11	Peter is rescued from prison by an angel of the Lord.
vv. 12-17	Peter reports to home of John Mark telling them of God delivering him.
vv. 18-19	Herod kills guards; Peter goes from Judea to Caesarea.
vv. 20-23	Herod exalts himself as god; angel strikes him; he dies about 44 A.D.
vv. 24-25	Barnabas and Paul take John Mark with them as far as Perga.
Chapter 13	**Paul and Barnabas' First Missionary Journey**
vv. 1-3	Prophets laid hands on Saul and Barnabas after Holy Spirit called them.
vv. 4-12	Saul called Paul testifies to proconsul of Cypress and withstands Elymas.
vv. 13-16(a)	Mark leaves Perga; Paul and Barnabas go to Antioch; speak in synagogue.
vv. 16(b)-25	Paul shares history of Israel up to coming of Jesus.
vv. 26-41	Paul teaches about Jesus, One Who forgives sins, what the law could not do.
vv. 43-43	People beg Paul to return the next Sabbath.
vv. 44-47	Paul is rejected by Jews and turns to Gentiles with God's message of eternal life.
vv. 48-52	Jews stir up persecution against Paul and Barnabas and drive them out.

Chapter 14	**Iconium, Lystra and Derbe**
vv. 1-7	People of Iconium tried to stone apostles, who fled to Lystra and Derbe.
vv. 8-18	Apostles resist Lycaonians worshipping them after a cripple was healed.
vv. 19-23	Paul is stoned; disciples pray; God raises him; Paul appoints church elders.
vv. 24-28	They returned to Antioch and reported all that had taken place in Asia Minor.
Chapter 15	**Council at Jerusalem and Second Missionary Journey**
vv. 1-5	Paul debates circumcisers who believe Gentiles must keep law for salvation.
vv. 6-11	Peter declares Gentiles are saved as Jews, through the grace of Lord Jesus.
vv. 12-21	James relates God's plan to save Gentiles without excessive O.T. laws.
vv. 22-29	James sends Judas, Silas and apostles to Antioch to tell decision of council.
vv. 30-35	Judas and Silas return to Jerusalem; Paul and Barnabas remain, teaching.
vv. 36-44	Barnabas takes Mark to Cyprus; Paul recruits Silas and goes to Syria and Cilicia.
Chapter 16	**Paul and Silas Jailed and Released at Philippi**
vv. 1-5	Timothy, a disciple, joins Paul at Lystra and is circumcised by Paul.
vv. 6-10	Holy Spirit forbids Paul and Silas to preach in Asia; opens door in Macedonia.
vv. 11-15	Lydia, converted and baptized, constrains Paul and Silas to stay at her house.
vv. 16-18	Annoyed by spirit of divination in slave girl, Paul commands evil spirit to leave.
vv. 19-24	Slave girl's owners cause Paul and Silas beaten and placed securely in prison.

vv. 25-34	As Paul and Silas were praising God, an earthquake set the prisoners free.
vv. 35-40	Paul demands apology and escort from prison since he is a Roman citizen.

Chapter 17 — From Thessalonica to Athens

vv. 1-9	Paul and Silas preach Jesus for 3 Sabbaths in synagogue at Thessalonica.
vv. 10-15	Paul, Silas and Timothy teach Jews in Berea but Paul has to leave for Athens.
vv. 16-21	Paul, awaiting Silas and Timothy, argues Jesus' resurrection with Athenians.
vv. 22-31	Paul presents God as their unknown god and Jesus as judge of the world.
vv. 32-34	Dionysius, the Areopagite, and Damaris, a woman, become believers with Paul.

Chapter 18 — Founding of Church in Corinth

vv. 1-4	Paul makes tents with Aguila and Priscilla in Corinth.
vv. 5-11	Paul is in Corinth 18 months, teaching God's word and making disciples.
vv. 12-17	Jews try to get Paul indicted before tribunal. Gallio will have no part in this.
vv. 18-21	Paul goes to Ephesus along with Priscilla and Aquila.
vv. 22-23	Paul goes to Antioch through Galatia and Phrygia strengthening churches.
vv. 24-28	Apollos, taught by Aquila and Priscilla. He goes to Achaia to help believers.

Chapter 19 — Paul's Ministry in Ephesus

vv. 1-7	Paul baptizes 12 believers in Name of Jesus; they receive Holy Spirit baptism.
vv. 8-10	Paul spends 2 years in Ephesus making disciples.
vv. 11-20	Paul heals sick and casts out demons. People burn expensive magic books.
vv. 21-22	Paul sends Timothy and Erastus to Macedonia while he stays longer in Asia.

vv. 23-27	Demetrius warns silversmiths Paul's preaching will put them out of business.
vv. 28-41	Demetrius stirs up people but officials calm people for fear of Rome. |//

Chapter 20 — Paul Goes to Greece and Returns to Palestine.

vv. 1-6	Paul leaves Greece learning plot by Jews to kill him. Spends 7 days in Troas.
vv. 7-12	Paul preaches; Eutychus falls from 3rd floor. Paul prays, restoring boy's life.
vv. 13-16	Paul travels by foot and boat to Miletus.
vv. 17-35	Paul, in Miletus, meets elders to admonish faithfulness of church in Ephesus.
vv. 36-38	Paul weeps with fellow elders since it will be our last time together on earth.

Chapter 21 — Paul Returns and Assaulted in Jerusalem.

vv. 1-6	Paul is told by disciples in Tyre not to go to Jerusalem.
vv. 7-14	Paul, at Philip's home, warned by prophet Agabus, not to go to Jerusalem.
vv. 15-16	Paul lodges in Jerusalem with an early disciple, Mnason of Cyprus.
vv. 17-26	Paul obeys elders in Jerusalem and purifies himself before entering Temple.
vv. 27-36	Jews tried to kill Paul by beatings. Romans placed Paul in army barracks.
vv. 37-40	Paul is permitted to speak to Jews in the Hebrew language.

Chapter 22 — Paul's Defense before People in Jerusalem

vv. 1-2	Paul addresses the crowd in Hebrew.
vv. 3-5	Paul recounts his earlier days when he persecuted Christians to their deaths.
vv. 6-11	Paul rebuked by Jesus and blinded by brightness of His resurrected body.
vv. 12-16	Ananias prays for Paul; sight restored; baptized and his sins washed away.

vv. 17-21	Paul, in a vision, commanded to leave Jerusalem and preach to Gentiles.
vv. 22-29	Paul told Roman soldiers he was a Roman citizen; they did not scourge him.
v. 30	Next day Paul is brought unbound to meet with Jewish council.
Chapter 23	**Jews Plot to Kill Paul**.
vv. 1-5	Paul answers sharply when struck on mouth by orders of High Priest Ananias.
vv. 6-10	When quarreling concerning Paul's beliefs, soldiers return him to safety.
v. 11	Next night Lord tells Paul he will testify not only in Jerusalem but also in Rome.
vv. 12-15	Forty fanatical Jews plot to kill Paul.
vv. 16-22	Paul's nephew tells chief captain of Jews' plot to assassinate Paul.
vv. 23-25	Paul leaves about 9:30 p.m. escorted by 470 Roman soldiers enroute to Caesarea.
vv. 26-30	Claudius Lysias writes to Governor Felix about Paul and Jews at Jerusalem.
vv. 31-35	Soldiers take Paul to Antipatris; 70 horsemen take him to Felix in Caesarea.
Chapter 24	**Paul before Governor Felix in Caesarea**
vv. 1-8	Priest Ananias' spokesman, Tertullus accuses Paul before governor in Caesarea.
v. 9	Jews with Ananias and Tertullus affirm accusation of Paul as troublemaker.
vv. 10-21	Paul explains before Felix as a believer in Messiah, he had done nothing wrong.
vv. 22-23	Felix puts Paul in safety until tribune Lysias comes to Caesarea from Jerusalem.
vv. 24-27	Felix and Drusilla hear Paul tell of his faith for 2 years until Festus arrives.

Chapter 25	**Paul Appeals to Emperor Caesar of Rome.**
vv. 1-5	Festus agrees for Jerusalem Jews to go to Caesarea to hear Paul's defense.
vv. 6-12	Paul appeals to Caesar since Jews at Jerusalem planned to kill Paul.
vv. 13-22	Governor Festus explains to Agrippa charges Jews brought against Paul.
vv. 23-27	Festus announces before dignitaries, Paul's case to King Agrippa and Bernice.
Chapter 26	**Paul's Defense before Agrippa II**
v. 1	King Agrippa tells Paul to go ahead and speak.
vv. 2-3	Paul gives Agrippa II his defense; Agrippa knows religious customs of Jews.
vv. 4-8	Paul explains Jewish background and expounds that God raises dead.
vv. 9-11	Paul explains he previously persecuted Christians because of faith in Jesus.
vv. 12-18	Paul tells of Jesus' appearing and commissioning to preach salvation to Gentiles.
vv. 19-23	Paul explains obedience to Jesus' heavenly calling and why Jews tried to kill him.
vv. 24-29	Festus accuses Paul of being mad as he is witnessing fervently to Agrippa.
vv. 30-31	Rulers agreed Paul could be set free if not appealing to Caesar in Rome.
Chapter 27	**Paul's Voyage to Malta and Rome**
vv. 1-8	Paul details voyage and kindness offered at Sidon by Roman officer Julius.
vv. 9-12	Paul advises centurion to anchor ship and spend winter at Fair Havens in Crete.
vv. 13-20	Ship never reached Phenice; stopped at Clauda; they lost hope during storm.

vv. 21-26	Paul tells men their lives will be saved though ship would be lost.
vv. 27-32	Centurion removed 4 small boats sailors wanted to use to escape doomed ship.
vv. 33-38	Paul eats on 14th day and 275 men eat before casting cargo of wheat into sea.
vv. 39-44	Ship hit shoal and broke apart. Soldiers, sailors and prisoners all swam to land.
Chapter 28	**Paul Arrives and Preaches at Rome, Italy.**
vv. 1-6	Paul bitten by viper and doesn't die, natives of Malta believe him to be a god.
vv. 7-10	Paul healed Publius' father; people came for healing; gifts given from Malta.
vv. 11-16	Ship went from Malta to Syracuse, Rhegium to Puteoli; and by land to Rome.
vv. 17-22	Paul meets with Jewish leaders at Rome to discuss faith in Jesus Christ.
vv. 23-29	Jewish leaders cannot accept Jesus as Savior; Paul turns to Gentiles.
vv. 30-31	Paul spends 2 years preaching kingdom of God unhindered in Rome.

ROMANS

Chapter 1	**Salutation, Thanksgiving and Judgment on Sin**
vv. 1-6	Paul identifies himself and people to whom he is writing as belonging to Jesus.
v. 7	Paul greets those in Rome as God's saints.
vv. 8-15	Paul states he longs to visit Christians in Rome so they encourage each other.
vv. 16-17	God's righteousness is from Him, not man's achievement, but man's faith in God.
vv. 18-23	God's wrath on unregenerate knowing Him as Creator but reject Him as Savior.
vv. 24-25	God gave ungodly to do what was in their wicked minds and thoughts.
vv. 26-27	Sexually impure receive in their bodies the due penalty for their sins.
vv. 28-32	Ungodly people not only do evil acts but approve of those who practice them.
Chapter 2	**Gentiles and Jews are Under Same Judgment**
vv. 1-11	God shows no partiality to Jew or Gentile in judging their good and evil.
vv. 12-16	Rule of judgment: law of Moses for Jew; law of conscience for Gentile.
vv. 17-24	Many Jews, possessing God's written law, fall short of common morality.
vv. 25-29	A true Jew is one inwardly; circumcision is of heart; spiritual not literal.

Chapter 3	**Everyone Stands Guilty Before God.**
vv. 1-8	Jews entrusted in preserving Old Testament was great advantage spiritually.
vv. 9-18	Both Jews and Gentiles are under power of sin.
vv. 19-20	No one justified by works of law, since through law comes knowledge of sin.
vv. 21-26	Redemption means "buying back" which Jesus did for mankind at Calvary's cross.
vv. 27-31	Since God is One, He will deal with Jews and Gentiles on same grounds.
Chapter 4	**Abraham, Justified by Faith**
vv. 1-8	God's blessings are to ones in faith accepting gift of forgiveness (Ps. 32:1-2).
vv. 9-12	Abraham justified before circumcision; therefore, not works but faith in God.
vv. 13-15	To those of faith in Christ belong benefits promised to Abraham.
vv. 16-25	Abraham believed God by obeying Him and doing what he was told.
Chapter 5	**Sin and Condemnation of First Man**
vv. 1-5	We have peace when we rely upon God's grace, i.e., reconciliation with Him.
vv. 6-11	Christ at death bore sins; He reconciled us to God; by His life we're saved.
vv. 12-14	Sin and death for all men followed upon Adam's disobedience.
vv. 15-17	Those receiving grace and gift of righteousness reign in life by Jesus Christ.
vv. 18-21	Life and acquittal from death came for all acting upon obedience to Christ.
Chapter 6	**Dying and Rising with Christ**
vv. 1-4	This death through baptism is a death to sin and this new life is life in God.

vv. 5-11	We must reckon ourselves dead to sin and alive to God in Christ Jesus.
vv. 12-14	Sin can no longer rule over us since we are not under law but under God's grace.
vv. 15-19	A sinner is sin's slave; when one becomes God's slave, he no longer is sin's slave.
vv. 20-23	Sanctification's end is eternal life; it is process of being entirely devoted to God.

Chapter 7 — Law of God and Sin

vv. 1-3	One dead to sin is not bound to sin; woman not bound to her deceased husband.
vv. 4-6	Verses 1-2 refer to Roman "civil law"; vv. 4-6 refer to God's laws.
vv. 7-12	Law is holy and good; it makes man conscious of sin and incites him to sin.
vv. 13-20	Sin is an evil force that enters a person's life and brings him into slavery of sin.
vv. 21-25	We serve the law of God with our mind but we serve the law of sin with our flesh.

Chapter 8 — Life in God's Holy Spirit

vv. 1-8	Condemnation equals doom; life in Spirit equals freedom to live as Christ lives.
vv. 9-11	If Spirit of God Who raised Jesus from dead is in us, we have life in bodies.
vv. 12-17	Spirit prompts us to cry "Abba Father" witnesses with our spirits we are His.
vv. 18-25	Firstfruits of Spirit are installments of full sonship we are yet to receive.
vv. 26-27	The Spirit intercedes for believers according to the will of God.
vv. 28-30	His purpose is we will be conformed to image of Jesus as fellow heirs of Christ.
vv. 31-39	Nothing can separate us from love of God in Christ Jesus our Lord.

Chapter 9	**Paul's Sorrow for Jews**
vv. 1-5	Israel got sonship, glory of His presence, covenants, law and worship.
vv. 6-13	God's promises were made to those whom He chose.
vv. 14-18	God has right to have mercy upon whomever He chooses!
vv. 19-26	God's promises include many Jews and many Gentiles.
vv. 27-29	God's promises never included all Israelites.
vv. 30-33	Righteousness comes not by law but by faith.
Chapter 10	**Jews and Gentiles are called.**
vv. 1-4	Christ is end of the law; everyone who has faith is justified.
vv. 5-13	Faith and confession in Christ are essential for justification and salvation.
vv. 14-17	Faith comes from hearing God's word preached.
vv. 18-21	Israel refused as a nation to hear and understand gospel of Jesus Christ.
Chapter 11	**Israel's Rejection Is Not Final.**
vv. 1-6	God has remnant of Israelites by grace, not works, He keeps for Himself.
vv. 7-10	God has hardened hearts of Jews so Gentiles might receive gospel.
vv. 11-12	Jews' trespasses mean spiritual riches for world.
vv. 13-15	Salvation of Gentiles is to make Jews jealous so they will be saved.
v. 16	Root stands for O.T. patriarchs, through whom Israel was consecrated.
vv. 17-24	If Gentiles go into unbelief, they'll be cut off; if Jews believe, they'll be saved.
vv. 25-32	God will one day restore Israel to Himself due to promises to Israel's forefathers.
vv. 33-36	Because of God's great mercy, Israel will be saved.
Chapter 12	**Duties of Christian Believer**
vv. 1-2	We present ourselves as living sacrifices in contrast to animal sacrifices.

vv. 3-8	We have gifts from Creator to use for needs in the body of Christ.
vv. 9-13	Love should underscore all we are and all we do.
vv. 14-21	By loving our enemies we overcome evil with good.
Chapter 13	**Christian's Civic Duty**
vv. 1-7	Christians know God ordained governments to rule; we support rulers.
vv. 8-10	By loving one's neighbor, one obeys basic commandments of God's law.
vv. 11-14	We are to always be in Spirit of Christ since His return is approaching!
Chapter 14	**We are not to Judge Fellow Believers.**
vv. 1-4	We do not judge others by what they eat or don't eat; meat vs. vegetables.
vv. 5-9	Don't argue over foods or days of worship; they all belong to the Lord.
vv. 10-12	We all will be judged by our Judge, Jesus Christ.
vv. 13-23	We aren't to destroy faith of others by what they eat, drink, or holy days.
Chapter 15	**Strong Should Bear with Weak.**
vv. 1-6	Weak and strong in faith are to both glorify Jesus in their actions and deeds.
vv. 7-13	God promised a Messiah to Jews and mercy to Gentiles.
vv. 14-21	Paul writes Romans he ministers to Gentiles; not building on other's foundations.
vv. 22-29	Paul, after taking relief funds to Jerusalem, wants to visit Rome enroute to Spain.
vv. 30-33	Paul anticipates trouble in Jerusalem and asks Roman believers to pray for him.
Chapter 16	**Paul's Personal Greetings to Believers**
vv. 1-2	Paul commends Phoebe to Roman believers because of her helpfulness.

vv. 3-16	Paul sends greetings, asking believers to get to know his friends in Rome.
vv. 17-20	Paul tells believers don't get involved with teachers who cause difficulties.
vv. 21-24	Believers with Paul also greet Christians in Rome.
vv. 25-27	Paul ends letter to Romans by encouragement and an exaltation of his Lord.

1 CORINTHIANS

Chapter 1	**Salutation, Thanksgiving, and Dissensions in Corinthian Church**
vv. 1-3	Paul and Sosthenes (Acts 18:17) greet Corinthians in letter at Ephesus.
vv. 4-9	Paul thanks God for believers; encourages them to use their spiritual gifts.
vv. 10-17	Paul rebukes church for divisions; no one baptized in his name only Jesus' name.
vv. 18-25	Paul preaches only Jesus Christ, not his own personal wisdom or philosophy.
vv. 26-31	We cannot boast of ourselves but can only boast of our Lord Jesus Christ.
Chapter 2	**Unspiritual Cannot Judge Spiritual.**
vv. 1-5	Faith of believers is not in man's wisdom but in power of God.
vv. 6-13	Only Spirit of God in believer can know God's thoughts!
vv. 14-16	Christians receive spiritual gifts; judged by God, not unbelievers.
Chapter 3	**Christ Is Church's One Foundation.**
vv. 1-4	Choosing one leader over another shows they are still baby Christians.
vv. 5-9	God uses ministers and their labors; God is to be glorified, not servants.
vv. 10-15	What done in Christ's Name, tried by Holy Spirit. What not burned, is rewarded.
vv. 16-17	As God's temple we are to honor one another as we honor God.

vv. 18-23	All church leaders belong to us since we all belong to God.
Chapter 4	**Paul Is More Than Teacher; He Is Father to Them.**
vv. 1-5	We are not to judge; God will judge when the Lord returns to earth.
vv. 6-7	All we have comes from a gift; we are not to boast in ourselves.
vv. 8-13	Apostles, Paul and Apollos, persecuted by pagans in bringing Christ to Corinth.
vv. 14-21	Paul admonishes he is more than guide or teacher; he is their spiritual father.
Chapter 5	**Immorality and Church Discipline**
vv. 1-2	Christian living with stepmother to be removed from church fellowship.
vv. 3-5	Man to be outside church's protection until he repents and is restored.
vv. 6-8	Believer's life is festival of communion, without evil and wrongdoing.
vv. 9-13	No fellowship with immoral believers; they are disfellowshipped.
Chapter 6	**Christians Settle Differences in the Church.**
vv. 1-6	Christians not to go to civil law; but before wise believers in the church.
vv. 7-8	We should suffer wrong before going to court and being judged by unbelievers.
vv. 9-11	Immoral and ungodly will not inherit kingdom of God.
vv. 12-20	If a man commits sexual sins, he sins against himself which is God's holy temple.
Chapter 7	**Directions about Marriages**
vv. 1-7	Couples must consider other's physical needs in marriage relationship.
vv. 8-9	If singles and widows cannot exercise self-control, it is better for them to marry.

vv. 10-11	Those who separate to remain single or be reconciled again as married couple.
vv. 12-16	If unbeliever chooses to live with believer children are sanctified; not unclean.
vv. 17-24	We remain in status which God assigned us when we come to know Christ.
vv. 25-31	Man does well to give daughter in marriage; better if he refrains due to world.
vv. 32-35	Married is concerned about spouse; single, about holiness unto the Lord.
vv. 36-38	Married is good; single is better since one can devote more to serving Christ.
vv. 39-40	Wife is bound to husband until he dies; later, she can marry another believer.
Chapter 8	**Food Sacrificed to Idols**
vv. 1-3	Knowledge makes us feel superior; love prefers others before ourselves.
vv. 4-6	Idols are not real; we serve the only, real God.
vv. 7-13	We consider believers, eating in a place they may consider "pagan".
Chapter 9	**Paul's Rights as an Apostle**
vv. 1-2	Corinthian church and Paul's vision of Christ prove to others his apostleship.
vv. 3-7	Anyone who plants a garden has a right to eat fruit of his labor.
vv. 8-12(a)	Person who shares spiritually has right to receive materially.
vv. 12(b)-14	Those who proclaim gospel should receive their living from gospel.
vv. 15-18	Our reward is to preach gospel free of charge.
vv. 19-23	Paul became all things to all men to win some to Christ.
vv. 24-27	Self-discipline is necessary not to wound weaker consciences of new believers.

Chapter 10	**Exhortation to Godly Living**
vv. 1-5	Baptism and Lord's Supper are no guarantee of spirituality and overcoming.
vv. 6-13	O. T. shows idolaters living immorally destroyed by destroyer.
vv. 14-22	Paul warns believers not to participate in pagan rites (due to demons).
vv. 23-30	Everything on earth belongs to God; not eat anything wounding brother.
vv. 31-33	Only do what brings glory to God and benefits His church.
Chapter 11	**Lord's Supper**
v. 1	Follow Paul as He follows Christ!
vv. 2-16	Paul exhorts men pray without head covering; women pray with covering.
vv. 17-22	Lord's Supper connected with love feast; poor were often excluded.
vv. 23-26	Communion is a living sermon of the Lord's death until He returns.
vv. 27-32	We are to partake of the Lord's Supper in a spirit of holiness.
vv. 33-34	When taking His Supper, be considerate of all church participants.
Chapter 12	**Concerning Spiritual Gifts**
vv. 1-3	When one is moved on by Holy Spirit, he cannot curse but bless Jesus as Lord.
vv. 4-11	Godhead and nine gifts of Spirit are mentioned in these verses.
vv. 12-13	Jews and Gentiles are all baptized into one body of Christ.
vv. 14-26	Since all parts complete the body, all parts are necessary.
vv. 27-31	Office gifts are important but we are to seek best gift, viz. God's love.
Chapter 13	**Way of God's Agape (Love)**
vv. 1-3	Agape (God's love manifested in Christ) is means more than spiritual gifts.

vv. 4-7	Paul describes some characteristics of God's agape (love).
vv. 8-13	Love comes from God; faith and hope, our response to what He has done for us.
Chapter 14	**Speaking in "Spirit" Language**
vv. 1-5	Making love our goal, we are to desire fervently gifts of Holy Spirit.
vv. 6-12	Speaking in tongues in assembly is good, if interpreted to edify church.
vv. 13-19	Unknown tongues have no church value unless interpreted for good of people.
vv. 20-25	Unknown tongue confuses unbelievers unless God gives understanding.
vv. 26-33(a)	God, not author of confusion; prophesy or speak in tongues one-by-one.
vv. 33(b)-36	Women should ask husbands what was taught when they are at home.
vv. 37-40	Prophesying and speaking in tongues should be done decently and orderly.
Chapter 15	**Resurrection of and Through Christ**
vv. 1-2	Paul exhorts Corinthian believers to hold fast their beliefs of gospel.
vv. 3-11	Paul proclaims apostleship; Jesus appeared to other apostles and himself.
vv. 12-19	If dead not raised, Christ was not raised and we are still in our sins.
vv. 20-28	Demonic powers, including death, will be put under Christ's feet.
vv. 29-34	If dead in Christ not raised, Paul suffered for sake of gospel in vain.
vv. 35-41	Paul tells believers resurrected bodies won't be same as earthly bodies.
vv. 42-50	Resurrected body will not be perishable but imperishable, eternal body.

vv. 51-57	Those living will be changed from perishable to imperishable bodies.
v. 58	Therefore, keep abounding in God's work!
Chapter 16	**Concluding Messages and Benediction**
vv. 1-4	Lay up contributions ahead so they will be ready when Paul arrives.
vv. 5-9	Paul wants time with Corinthians but will be in Ephesus till Pentecost.
vv. 10-11	Be kind to Timothy when he arrives.
v. 12	Apollos will come when he has opportunity.
vv. 13-14	Be strong and labor in love!
vv. 15-18	Be gracious to Stephanas, Fortunatus and Achaicus honoring them.
vv. 19-20	Aguila and Prisca along with churches of Asia send hearty greetings!
vv. 21-24	Those not loving Christ, cursed; those loving Him, blessed. Amen!

2 CORINTHIANS

Chapter 1	**Salutation and Thanksgiving**
vv. 1-2	Paul sends grace and peace from Christ to saints in Corinth and Achaia.
vv. 3-7	Paul explains as saints share in Paul's sufferings, they will share in his comfort.
vv. 8-11	Paul explains he had to lean on God's grace when he despaired of life in Asia.
vv. 12-14	Paul a righteous model wants believers to be proud of him as he is of them.
vv. 15-22	Paul assures believers his plans are from God and he is not double-minded.
vv. 23-24	Paul wants them to stand firmly in their faith to Christ.
Chapter 2	**Paul's Concern for Church**
vv. 1-4	Paul delayed his visit for all of them to have recovered from his last letter.
vv. 5-11	Paul wants restoration for man who had been living with his step-mother.
vv. 12-13	Not locating Titus at Troas, Paul went on to Macedonia.
vv. 14-17	Gospel is "sweet aroma" to those accepting Christ as their eternal Savior.
Chapter 3	**Ministers of New Covenant**
vv. 1-3	Corinthian believers were a letter of Paul's recommendation to be read by all men.
vv. 4-6	Written covenant produces despair but the Spirit gives life.
vv. 7-13	Law's splendor has faded, but splendor of New Covenant will never fade.

vv. 12-18	Spirit of the Lord needs no veil to hide a fading splendor since it never fades.
Chapter 4	**Paul's Sincerity and Faithfulness**
vv. 1-6	Paul, unlike pretending apostles, tried to preach a clear gospel of Jesus Christ.
vv. 7-12	Paul shares fact his sufferings are for these Corinthian believers' faith in Christ.
vv. 13-15	God, who raised Jesus from death, will also raise us into Christ's presence.
vv. 16-18	Paul considers his afflictions as a "momentary suffering."
Chapter 5	**Ministry of Reconciliation**
vv. 1-5	Since believers live in bodies there is a "degree of separation" from Jesus.
vv. 6-10	We shall all be judged one day according to what we have done in our bodies.
vv. 11-15	We are to live for Jesus, who died and was raised to eternal life.
vv. 16-21	Christ was made "sin" but not a "sinner" in reconciling us back to God our Father.
Chapter 6	**Work Involved in Paul's Ministry.**
vv. 1-10	Suffering Paul endured in his ministry to others in bringing them to Christ.
vv. 11-13	Paul frankly tells Corinthian believers they are continually in his heart.
vv. 14-18	Paul tells believers not to marry unbelievers nor be involved relationally.
Chapter 7	**Comfort in Affliction**
v. 1	We are to cleanse ourselves from every defilement of body and spirit.
vv. 2-4	Paul is overjoyed at restoration of good relations with Corinthian believers.
vv. 5-12	Paul rejoices at people's repentance leading to salvation and spiritual comfort.

vv. 13-16	Paul rejoices that people received Titus and Titus saw their faithfulness to Paul.
Chapter 8	**Exhortation to Help Poor in Jerusalem**
vv. 1-7	Paul praises Macedonians for contributing to famine-stricken Judeans.
vv. 8-15	Paul exhorts Corinthians to give to needs of Jerusalem believers.
vv. 16-24	Paul sends Titus and 2 others to Corinth to collect funds for Jerusalem.
Chapter 9	**Blessed Duty of Giving Financially**
vv. 1-5	Paul sends 3 men to arrange collection for believers in Jerusalem.
vv. 6-15	God will bless generous givers with more resources and righteousness.
Chapter 10	**Paul Defends Himself against Critics.**
vv. 1-6	Disobedient ones will be disciplined when church returns its loyalty to Paul.
vv. 7-12	Paul answers critics by writing he is same when present as in his letters.
vv. 13-18	Paul writes he reached Corinthians; now he desires to reach others.
Chapter 11	**Paul Justifies Himself.**
vv. 1-6	Paul may not be gifted speaker but is skilled in knowledge of gospel ministry.
vv. 7-11	Paul never burdened Corinthians financially due to others helping him.
vv. 12-15	"False apostles" claim they work as Paul does but they do not.
vv. 16-21(a)	Paul boasts he has never taken advantage of Corinthians.
vv. 21(b)-29	Paul boasts of afflictions and Jewish ancestry as well as his superior labors.
vv. 30-33	Paul recounts King Aretas tried to seize him; brethren helped him escape.

Chapter 12	**Paul's Strength in Weakness**
vv. 1-10	Paul's thorn was demons using Jews to oppose him in establishing churches.
vv. 11-13	Paul, is dead to himself, but not inferior to the "superlative apostles."
vv. 14-18	Paul, Titus and others with them never took advantage of Corinthians.
vv. 19-21	Paul thinks visit may be difficult; brethren not repented of immorality.
Chapter 13	**Conclusion and Benediction**
vv. 1-4	Paul explains this 3rd visit will be one of confrontation with his critics.
vv. 5-10	Paul writes he wants believers to be ready spiritually for his upcoming visit.
vv. 11-13	Paul asks them to mend their ways and live at peace with each other.
v. 14	He concludes with benediction of grace and love and Spirit's fellowship.

GALATIANS

Chapter 1	**Paul's Apostleship and Galatian Apostasy**
vv. 1-2	Paul states his apostleship comes from Jesus Christ and God not from man.
vv. 3-5	Paul blesses Galatians with God's grace and peace and Jesus' life for man.
vv. 6-9	Paul says stay with only true gospel of grace; not false gospel of circumcision.
v. 10	A servant of Christ cannot please men and be a servant of Christ.
vv. 11-17	Paul, as a Jew tried to destroy church; now as apostle he fights legalism.
vv. 18-24	Paul identified himself with Apostles Peter and James after his 3 years in Arabia.
Chapter 2	**Paul's Apostleship Recognized in Jerusalem.**
vv. 1-10	Paul, Barnabas and Titus approved by James, Peter and John for Gentile work.
vv. 11-21	Paul rebukes 2 apostles withdrawing from Gentiles when legalistic Jews arrived.
Chapter 3	**We Are Saved by Faith not Works (Circumcision).**
vv. 1-5	Does God work miracles among Galatians by law or by hearing with faith?
vv. 6-9	Peoples of faith in Christ are true sons of Abraham.
vv. 10-14	Because of faith in Christ, blessings of Abraham fall on Jews and Gentiles.
vv. 15-18	God gave inheritance to Abraham, not by law, but by promise.

vv. 19-20	Mosaic law could not make us righteous, it revealed our sins.
vv. 21-22	Law of Moses is not against promise of God.
vv. 23-29	Law given by God as guardian for us until faith came by Jesus Christ.
Chapter 4	**Bondage under Law and Freedom in Christ**
vv. 1-7	Pre-existent Christ became human to save us from bondage under law.
vv. 8-11	Paul reproves Galatians for adopting religious "special days" of Judaizers.
vv. 12-20	Paul implores Galatian as a father, to continue receiving truths he taught them.
vv. 21-31	Hagar (slave) and Sarah (free) show faith in God's promise of His inheritance.
Chapter 5	**Nature of Christian Liberty**
v. 1	Stand free in Christ and do not return to law of slavery.
vv. 2-12	Circumcised or not means nothing without faith which works through love.
vv. 13-15	Christians, though free from law, must not abuse liberty.
vv. 16-24	Christians are to walk in Spirit and not fulfill desires of flesh.
vv. 25-26	Walking in Spirit enables us to be compatible with other believers.
Chapter 6	**Challenge to Always do Good**
vv. 1-5	We are to help others in spirit of humility and gentleness.
v. 6	We are to help financially those who teach us God's spiritual word.
vv. 7-10	We are to help all men, especially God's people.
vv. 11-16	We are to glory in cross Jesus, not in circumcision or uncircumcision.
v. 17	Paul bears on his body marks that came on him for preaching God's grace.
v. 18	Paul ends letter by pronouncing God's grace upon his Galatian brethren.

EPHESIANS

Chapter 1	**Thanksgiving and Prayer for Wisdom**
vv. 1-2	Paul, an apostle of Christ, salutes faithful with God's grace and peace.
vv. 3-10	God's will is bringing Jew and Gentile to Himself through blood of Jesus.
vv. 11-14	We were sealed with Holy Spirit, until complete possession of inheritance.
vv. 15-23	God raised Jesus Christ, Head of Church, to sit at His right hand to rule.
Chapter 2	**Christ's Benefits for Jews and Gentiles**
vv. 1-10	God, because of our faith in Jesus, has raised us with Christ to do good works.
vv. 11-22	Jews and Gentiles, by salvation, are reconciled to God into body of Christ.
Chapter 3	**Christ's Unsearchable Riches**
vv. 1-6	God revealed to Apostle Paul that Gentiles have equal rights in Christ's body.
vv. 7-13	Paul was made a minister to Gentiles to preach unsearchable riches of Christ.
vv. 14-19	Paul prays Gentiles to be strengthened, know Christ's love, and filled with God.
vv. 20-21	Doxology celebrates God's generosity and glory in Christ and church.
Chapter 4	**An Appeal for Unity of Spirit**
vv. 1-16	Apostles, prophets, evangelists, pastors and teachers called to equip church.

vv. 17-24	Not pagan Gentiles but renewed in minds and clothed in God's righteousness.
vv. 25-32	We are to live righteously and to be kind and forgiving of one another.
Chapter 5	**Righteousness in Christian Homes**
vv. 1-2	Walk in love as Christ did when He sacrificed Himself for us.
vv. 3-14	Shun works of darkness and live for all to see God's light in His people.
vv. 15-20	We redeem time by being filled with God's Spirit and praising His Name.
vv. 21-33	Wife is to reverence her husband and husband is to love his wife.
Chapter 6	**God's Armor and Believer's Warfare**
vv. 1-4	Children are to honor parents and fathers are to carefully instruct children.
vv. 5-9	Servants serve your employers; and overseers, respect your servants (employees).
vv. 10-20	Always be in Spirit and ready to pray for others, not letting Satan affect us.
vv. 21-22	Tychicus is sent by Paul to let brethren know how prisoners are faring.
vv. 23-24	Paul closes his prison epistle with benediction of blessing, love, grace and peace.

PHILIPPIANS

Chapter 1	**Paul's Letter from Prison to Church Leaders**
vv. 1-2	Paul, greets bishops and deacons of church at Philippi, Macedonia.
vv. 3-11	Paul thanks Philippians for helping him; he encourages them to be Godly.
vv. 12-14	Paul is grateful guard has heard gospel during his imprisonment.
vv. 15-18	Paul rejoices Christ is preached whether in rivalry or in truth.
vv. 19-26	Paul does not care if martyred or if alive; alive is better for followers.
vv. 27-30	Paul encourages Philippians to be brave, even at cost of conflict and suffering.
Chapter 2	**Christ's Example of Humility and Obedience**
vv. 1-11	Jesus humbled Himself on cross; God exalted Jesus for people to accept Him.
vv. 12-13	Do your best; God is enabling you to work out your salvation.
vv. 14-18	Paul exhorts them to hold word of life in a crooked and perverse generation.
vv. 19-24	Paul promises to send Timothy to Philippi to encourage believers soon.
vv. 25-30	Paul hopes to send Epaphroditus to Philippi after recovery from sickness.
Chapter 3	**Confession and Exhortation**
v. 1	It is good to write the same things over again.

vv. 2-11	Paul counts all his righteousness as refuse compared to knowing Christ.
vv. 12-16	Righteousness is God's gift; we are to live as close to Christ as we possibly can.
vv. 17-21	We follow mature believers, not earthly-minded ones. Our reward is in heaven.
Chapter 4	**Instructions for Christian Maturity**
v. 1	Stand firmly in the beloved Lord Jesus.
vv. 2-3	Help Euodias and Syntyche be in harmony as they labor with Clement and Paul.
vv. 4-7	Release all anxieties to the Lord; He will restore peace as we thankfully pray.
vv. 8-9	Paul says to look for best people and to imitate them in the Christian faith.
vv. 10-13	Paul does everything in Christ; he is strengthened in good and hard times.
vv. 14-20	Paul praises Macedonians for financially partnering with him in the gospel.
vv. 21-22	Paul greets Macedonians along with his captors, those of Caesar's household.
v. 23	Concluding benediction is Christ's grace on Macedonians at Philippi.

COLOSSIANS

Chapter 1	**Supremacy of Jesus Christ**
v. 1	Paul presents himself as an apostle of Christ.
v. 2	He blesses brethren at Colossae with grace and peace.
vv. 3-8	Paul praises Colossians for hearing about spiritual growth through Epaphras.
vv. 9-14	Paul tells them to increase in God's knowledge; be grateful for redemption.
vv. 15-20	Christ Who is "everything" to believers is the visible fullness of God.
vv. 21-23	Paul exhorts believers; reconciled by Jesus' crucifixion; continue in faith.
vv. 24-29	Paul wants Gentiles to know God's mystery; Christ in them with maturity.
Chapter 2	**Warnings against False Teachers**
vv. 1-5	Paul tells believers, who don't know him; he is with them in prayer and spirit.
vv. 6-7	You received Christ so stay close to Him as you were previously taught.
vv. 8-15	God dwells in Christ Jesus Who defeated and disarmed all evil powers.
vv. 16-19	Be connected to Head of Body; depart from circumcising, legalistic Judaizers.
vv. 20-23	These ritualistic observances do not promote real Christianity, so avoid them.
Chapter 3	**New Life in Christ and Duties**
vv. 1-4	Being raised with Christ, we need to set our minds on things above.

vv. 5-11	Since we are all same in Christ, put off evil nature of your former life.
vv. 12-17	Put on love and be thankful as you let word of God richly dwell in your hearts.
vv. 18-25	Paul exhorts Christ-likeness in families, and all other relationships.
Chapter 4	**Concluding, Personal Greetings**
v. 1	Employers are to treat employees as they would want Christ to treat them.
vv. 2-4	Paul asks for prayer while in prison so he will clearly present message of Christ.
vv. 5-6	Conduct life that you may know how to graciously answer "outsiders" of the faith.
vv. 7-9	Paul sends Tychicus and Onesimus to tell Colossians k how he is doing in prison.
vv. 10-14	Paul sends greetings from Aristarchus, Mark, Justus, Epaphras, Luke, Demas.
vv. 15-17	Paul requests greetings to Laodicea, Nymphas' house church and Archippus.
v. 18	Paul closes by asking them to pray for him in prison.

1 THESSALONIANS

Chapter 1	**Salutation and Thanksgiving**
v. 1	Paul, Silas and Timothy salute the Thessalonians.
vv. 2-10	Paul expresses gratitude to believers who have turned from idols to Living God.
Chapter 2	**Paul's Life and Labor at Thessalonica**
vv. 1-8	Paul defends his concern and care for believers as an apostle of Jesus Christ.
vv. 9-12	Paul's conduct, while laboring among Thessalonians, was as father for children.
vv. 13-16	Paul states strongly how believers suffered for Name of Jesus by opposition.
vv. 17-20	Satan hindered Paul from Thessalonica; believers are hope, joy and crown.
Chapter 3	**Paul's Love for Thessalonians**
vv. 1-5	Paul sent Timothy to Thessalonica to see how they do during persecution.
vv. 6-10	Paul prayed night and day that he might be able to see these saints again.
vv. 11-13	Paul exhorts believers to increase in love for each other and be holy.
Chapter 4	**Pleas for Sexual Purity**
vv. 1-8	A man is to have wife in sexual purity; God judges all sexual uncleanness.
vv. 9-12	Paul exhorts saints to holiness; be good witness to outsiders of Jesus' church.

vv. 13-18	Christian dead will rise; those who are alive at Christ's return will rise.
Chapter 5	**Concluding Exhortations to Godly Living**
vv. 1-11	Christ's returns unexpectedly; keep on warriors' armor; always stand ready.
vv. 12-22	Respect spiritual leaders; do good to others; rejoice in Spirit; avoid evil.
vv. 23-24	Benediction upon their total corporate spirit, soul and body.
v. 25	Paul requests their prayers.
v. 26	Greet each other with a holy kiss.
v. 27	A command for this letter to be read to all.
v. 28	A final benediction upon the believers.

2 THESSALONIANS

Chapter 1	**Encouragement during Persecutions**
v. 1	Paul, Silas and Timothy greet Thessalonians.
v. 2	Paul salutes church with grace and peace.
vv. 3-4	Paul praises believers' faith and love amidst persecutions and afflictions.
vv. 5-12	God will avenge saints from enemies; suffering helps entrance into kingdom.
Chapter 2	**Day of the Lord**
vv. 1-12	After Jesus destroys lawless one, He returns and believers will meet Him.
vv. 13-15	God chose you to be saved through sanctification by Spirit and truth.
vv. 16-17	Paul exhorts believers to be blessed and established in every work and word.
Chapter 3	**Final Appeals, Rebukes and Prayers**
vv. 1-5	Paul prays believers to be delivered from wicked men and be steadfast in Christ.
vv. 6-13	Paul commands Thessalonians not to associate with idlers and busybodies.
vv. 14-15	Have nothing to do with brothers not working nor obeying this letter.
v. 16	Peace is invoked upon these believers.
vv. 17-18	Paul specifies this is his letter signed with his name and handwriting.

1 TIMOTHY

Chapter 1	**Paul's Defense of the Truth**
v. 1	Paul states his apostleship at the beginning of this letter.
v. 2	Paul salutes Timothy as his true son in the faith.
vv. 3-7	Paul exhorts Timothy to charge people at Ephesus to teach faith and God's love.
vv. 8-11	Law is good for ungodly and immoral people.
vv. 12-17	Paul thanks Jesus for enabling him to be in the Lord's service.
vv. 18-20	Paul gives Hymeneus and Alexander to Satan to repent and be restored.
Chapter 2	**Ordinances Regarding Worship**
vv. 1-7	God, by giving Jesus, desires that all mankind be saved!
vv. 8-15	Pray in spirit of holiness; women lead quiet lives; have no authority over men.
Chapter 3	**Problems in Church Administration**
vv. 1-7	If a man desires office of bishop he must rule his family and be respected.
vv. 8-13	Deacons and wives must rule well their families and live Godly lives.
vv. 14-16	Paul exhorts believers to act proper; Christ is mystery of our understanding.
Chapter 4	**Watch Out for False Teaching!**
vv. 1-5	Marriage is good; food is good if consecrated by word of God and prayer.
vv. 6-10	We are to hold fast good doctrine; we are to shun Godless and silly myths.

vv. 11-16	Continue public reading of scripture; boldly use gifts given with prophecy.
Chapter 5	**Pastoral Care for Widows and Elders**
vv. 1-2	Exhortation on treatment of church family in honor, respect and purity.
vv. 3-8	Anyone who does not care for his aged family members has denied the faith.
vv. 9-16	Church to help widows over 60 who have been faithful to help others.
vv. 17-22	Support preachers and teachers; respect elders ; slow in ordaining ministers.
v. 23	Timothy, use a little wine for your stomach ailments.
vv. 24-25	Some sins and good deeds are conspicuous; others are hidden from men.
Chapter 6	**Final Exhortation to Keep the Faith**
vv. 1-2	Servants to work well for employers, more so if employers are believers.
vv. 3-10	Beware of lust for money; it is opposed to Godliness; it's a temptation.
vv. 11-16	We are to be as Jesus Christ when He made His confession before Pontius Pilate.
vv. 17-19	Exhort wealthy to use riches as an honor to Christ and His kingdom.
vv. 20-21	Finally, Timothy, guard what has been entrusted to you and avoid Gnosticism.

2 TIMOTHY

Chapter 1	**Thanksgiving and Exhortation to Show Courage**
v. 1	Paul's declaration of his apostleship.
v. 2	A letter written to Paul's spiritual son, Timothy.
vv. 3-7	Paul reminds Timothy of his faith and gift that came to him by Paul's own hands.
vv. 8-14	Paul tells Timothy about his suffering; Timothy, do not be ashamed of Christ.
vv. 15-18	Paul denounces Phygellus and Hermogenes; praises Onesiphorus for faithfulness.
Chapter 2	**Exhortations to Singleness and Steadfastness**
vv. 1-7	Entrust what you have learned to faithful men who in turn will teach others.
vv. 8-13	We shall live and reign with Christ if we are faithful and never deny Him.
vv. 14-19	Present yourself to God as one approved, not like Hymeneus and Philetus.
vv. 20-26	Do not get entangled in quarrels; correct gently so they might repent.
Chapter 3	**Avoid Evil Men and Study Scriptures**.
vv. 1-9	In last days, men will try to persuade the weak to follow false teachings.
vv. 10-17	Paul tells Timothy to remember his learning and to stay in the Scriptures.
Chapter 4	**Exhortations to Fight Good Fight of Faith**
vv. 1-5	Paul exhorts Timothy to do work of an evangelist, fulfilling his ministry.

vv. 6-8	Paul's end has come and he knows there is crown of righteousness awaiting him.
vv. 9-18	Paul names people who have deserted him and those who have been faithful.
vv. 19-21	Paul's friends in Rome send greetings to Timothy whom Paul desires to visit.
v. 22	Paul blesses Timothy's spirit and sends grace to his son in the ministry.

TITUS

Chapter 1	**Appoint Good Elders in Every Town.**
vv. 1-3	Apostle Paul, has been entrusted to further faith and truth of God's elect.
v. 4	Written to Titus, Paul's son in the common faith.
vv. 5-16	Paul tells Titus to appoint family men as elders; beware of circumcision party.
Chapter 2	**Exhortations to Families and Servants**
vv. 1-10	Advice on relationships, families and servants; how to behave one to another.
vv. 11-14	Exhortation to live Godly in this world as we await return of our Lord Jesus!
v. 15	Speak with authority and do not let anyone disregard you.
Chapter 3	**Instructions to Avoid Certain Problems**
vv. 1-7	Remind people to be gracious; be grateful for Christ and the Holy Spirit.
vv. 8-11	Avoid foolish controversies; have nothing to do with a factious person.
vv. 12-14	Come to Rhome before winter; help ministers financially as Zenas and Apollos.
v. 15	Those in Rome greet you; greet those who love us, also.

PHILEMON

Chapter 1	**Exhortation for Philemon to Receive Onesimus**
vv. 1-2	Paul and Timothy write to Philemon, Apphia and Archippus and house church.
v. 3	Paul's salutation of grace and peace.
vv. 4-7	Paul rejoices in Philemon's love and comfort of saints who meet in his house.
vv. 8-14	Paul encourages Philemon to receive Onesimus, a born again brother in Christ.
vv. 15-20	Paul asks Philemon to aid him by receiving Onesimus as servant and brother.
vv. 21-22	Paul hopes soon to be set free from prison in Rome and to visit Philemon.
vv. 23-24	Epaphras, Mark, Aristarchus, Demas and Luke send greetings to Philemon.
v. 25	Paul concludes by blessing Philemon with Christ's grace upon his spirit.

HEBREWS

Chapter 1	**Christ Jesus is Superior to Angels**
vv. 1-4	After cleansing sins, Jesus sat down at right hand of God, superior to angels.
vv. 5-14	Angels, ministering spirits to serve; Jesus Christ, God's Son, our Savior
Chapter 2	**Jesus Sanctifies and Delivers from Satan and Death**.
vv. 1-4	Jesus' superiority claimed by angels, apostles, miracles and Holy Spirit's gifts.
vv. 5-9	Jesus, lower than angels in sufferings; now He is exalted above angels.
vv. 10-13	Jesus sanctifies followers by making them completely mature as Himself.
vv. 14-18	Jesus, tempted to escape the cross, helps us in fear of death and grave.
Chapter 3	**Christ, Superior to Moses, Has a Rest for Believers**.
vv. 1-6	Christ, the Son is superior to Moses, the servant.
vv. 7-19	We are to hear and obey Christ that we may enter into His rest!
Chapter 4	**God Promises Us Rest through Our High Priest.**
vv. 1-10	By faithful obedience we enter into God's rest, ceasing from our labors.
vv. 11-13	Readers are exhorted to diligence; God's Word discerns all intentions of man.
vv. 14-16	Jesus overcame all temptations; He offers mercy for sins and grace for needs.

Chapter 5	**Suffering is Necessary for Christian Maturity.**
vv. 1-4	High Priest sacrifices for his and sins of people, viz., "unwitting offenses."
vv. 5-6	God appointed Christ as "High Priest" forever after order of Melchizedek.
vv. 7-10	Jesus learned obedience in suffering and became source of eternal salvation.
vv. 11-14	Writer to immature, scattered Hebrews exhorts them to become mature.
Chapter 6	**Leaving Rudiments and Advancing in Christ**
vv. 1-8	Writer names elemental teachings; readers must advance in truths.
vv. 9-12	Writer exhorts recipients to serve one another, inheriting God's promises.
vv. 13-20	God's promises and oaths are unchangeable, securing our inheritance.
Chapter 7	**Comparing Melchizedek and Levitical Priesthood**
vv. 1-3	Melchizedek, priest-king, greater than Abraham; he resembles Jesus.
vv. 4-10	Levitical priests paid tithes through Abraham to the greater, Melchizedek.
vv. 11-14	Levitical priesthood is temporary; One similar to Melchizedek is eternal.
vv. 15-19	Jesus, unlike Levitical priesthood, appointed by God as High Priest forever!
vv. 20-22	Jesus' covenant better than Levites'; He was appointed by God.
vv. 23-25	Jesus, the only permanent Priest, who lives to make intercession for mankind.
vv. 26-28	Levites sacrificed for sinners; Jesus sacrificed Himself once for all.

Chapter 8	**Heavenly Sanctuary and New Covenant**
vv. 1-7	Jesus, ministering in heavenly sanctuary, has better tabernacle than Moses.
vv. 8-13	God's covenant, better than first covenant, promises all men will know God.
Chapter 9	**Levitical Ministry and Christ's Ministry**
vv. 1-5	Earthly sanctuary had a tent and covered Holy Place and Holy of Holies.
vv. 6-10	Levitical sacrifices can't produce inward purity; Christ's new covenant can.
vv. 11-14	Only blood of Christ can purify minds from dead works to serve living God.
vv. 15-22	Christ's death redeemed Old Covenant people and inaugurated New Covenant.
vv. 23-28	Christ died for sins and will come again to save those awaiting His appearing.
Chapter 10	**Exhortations to Follow Christ**
vv. 1-4	Old Covenant sacrifices of animals year-after-year can't perfect sinners.
vv. 5-10	Jesus came to do covenant of God by offering His body to sanctify us forever.
vv. 11-18	Christ offered single sacrifice for all time there is no longer any offering for sin.
vv. 19-25	Exhortation to faith, hope, love and good works, awaiting Jesus' return.
vv. 26-31	Sinners who spurn Jesus' blood and grace will fall under God's judgment.
vv. 32-39	We who have been persecuted and wrongly treated must never shrink back.
Chapter 11	**Examples of Heroic Faith**
vv. 1-3	By faith we know God's Word created everything out of the unseen.

vv. 4-7	By faith Abel, Enoch and Noah pleased God, by righteous gifts and building ark.
vv. 8-12	By faith, Abraham and Sarah obeyed God and had a son, Isaac, in old age.
vv. 13-16	These all died in faith believing God for a heavenly home in years to come.
vv. 17-22	Abraham received Isaac from being sacrificed; God tested his obedience.
vv. 23-28	Moses accepted sufferings than deny God's reward of delivering Israelites.
vv. 29-31	Israelites crossed Red Sea; walls of Jericho fell; Rahab was delivered by faith.
vv. 32-38	Gideon, Barak, Samson, Jephthah, David, Samuel, all heroes of faith in God.
vv. 39-40	These all died awaiting promise of God which was a better life to come.
Chapter 12	**Mount Sinai Contrasted with Mount Zion**
vv. 1-2	Let us, as Jesus and witnesses, run faithfully and lay aside what hinders us.
vv. 3-11	Discipline from God trains us and yields peaceful fruit of righteousness.
vv. 12-17	Be holy as Jesus, not bitter as Esau, despising his birthright when hungry.
vv. 18-24	We come to Mount Zion where God dwells, with Jesus and many others.
vv. 25-29	God will shake all that can be shaken so what remains will be only His kingdom.
Chapter 13	**Concluding Exhortations**
vv. 1-6	Love brethren; entertain strangers; pray for prisoners; encourage ill-treated.
vv. 7-16	Imitate leaders, especially Jesus; praise God; do good and share with poor.
v. 17	Obey and submit to your spiritual leaders.

vv. 18-19	Author requests prayer for restoration from prison to the Body of Christ.
vv. 20-21	Benediction from God and Lord Jesus for peace on recipients of this letter.
vv. 22-25	Postscript: Timothy is released from prison; greetings from scattered Jews.

JAMES
Jesus' half-brother

Chapter 1	**Blessings of Trials and True Religion**
v. 1	Apostle James, servant of God to 12 tribes scattered throughout world.
vv. 2-4	Rejoice when you go through trials that produce steadfastness.
vv. 5-8	Ask for wisdom in faith without doubting.
vv. 9-11	Rich will fade away in midst of pursuits; poor will be exalted.
vv. 12-15	God does not tempt men; blessed is he who endures temptations.
vv. 16-18	God gives good gifts to those He brings forth as His children.
vv. 19-21	Be quick to hear; slow to anger; stay clean and humbly receive God's word.
vv. 22-25	A man who is not just a hearer but a doer of Word shall be blessed.
vv. 26-27	Man who controls tongue and helps widows and orphans has real Christianity.
Chapter 2	**Respecting Poor and Faith with Works**
vv. 1-7	Do not disregard poor nor favor rich.
vv. 8-13	Showing partiality to rich over poor is sin.
vv. 14-17	Mouthing that one has faith is not same as producing works with one's faith.
vv. 18-26	Faith without works is similar to a body without spirit.

Chapter 3	**Speech and Wisdom**
vv. 1-5	If a person makes no mistakes in his speaking, he is a perfect or mature man.
vv. 6-12	It is ungodly to bless God and to curse fellow man with our speaking.
vv. 13-18	True wisdom is from God.
Chapter 4	**Contrast between Worldliness and Godliness**
vv. 1-10	We cannot love world and God, too.
vv. 11-12	We are not to be judges but law keepers.
vv. 13-17	He who knows to do right but refuses, commits sin.
Chapter 5	**Godly Receive from God.**
vv. 1-6	Rich who oppress laborers are judged for fraud.
vv. 7-11	Be patient; Jesus will reward His own.
v. 12	Be simple in your speech.
vv. 13-18	Fervent prayer and praise are effective.
vv. 19-20	Truth overcomes and delivers the soul.

1 PETER

Chapter 1	**Exhortation to Godliness**
vv. 1-2	Peter greets Gentiles and Jewish believers, scattered due to persecution.
vv. 3-9	Even though you do not see Jesus, you believe in Him and love Him.
vv. 10-12	Prophets and angels sought to know what God was doing to save people.
vv. 13-21	God planned our salvation before the foundation of world: therefore, be holy!
vv. 22-25	Word of God that resides within us abides forever.
Chapter 2	**Christ our Cornerstone**
vv. 1-3	Put aside insincerity, hunger for sincere nourishment of God's Word!
vv. 4-8	To those who accept Christ, He is precious; those who reject Christ, fall.
vv. 9-10	These Gentile believers who were no people are now God's people.
vv. 11-12	Maintain good deeds so others may glorify God when He reveals Himself to them.
vv. 13-17	Live as believers who honor those in authority.
vv. 18-25	We were healed (transformed) by Christ's death on cross when we turned to Him.
Chapter 3	**Obligations of All Believers**
vv. 1-6	Unbelieving husband may be converted by example of wife's behavior.

v. 7	Husbands live considerately with wives so your prayers will not be hindered.
vv. 8-12	We receive Lord's blessings when we bless those who would mistreat us.
vv. 13-22	Suffering as believer corresponds to Jesus' suffering to bring people to God.
Chapter 4	**Exhortations to Glorify God in Persecution**
vv. 1-6	Jesus completed His sufferings; we will be matured in sufferings, also.
vv. 7-11	We must use our gifts from God to bless His people.
vv. 12-19	As we endure persecutions, let us honor Him Who gave His life for us.
Chapter 5	**Final Exhortations to Elders in Asia Minor**
vv. 1-5	Elders treat God's people with humble care.
vv. 6-11	Be humble towards God but strong towards Satan.
vv. 12-14	Silas writes for Peter in Rome (Babylon) to Gentiles in persecution.

2 PETER

Chapter 1	**Exhortation to Holiness**
vv. 1-2	Salutation and blessing from Peter, an apostle and servant.
vv. 3-11	Seven Christian virtues listed confirming call and election into God's kingdom.
vv. 12-15	Peter's execution to be in Rome; he is exhorting believers to stand in truth.
vv. 16-21	Peter, referring to Jesus' transfiguration, exhorts people to believe in Jesus.
Chapter 2	**Denunciation of False Teachers**
vv. 1-3	As in former times, so will heretics arise to pervert God's Word.
vv. 4-10	God is faithful to keep unrighteous punished until judgment day.
vv. 11-16	Peter recounts fates of past God-haters of Old Testament.
vv. 17-22	Believer who returns to sinful ways becomes worse than at the first.
Chapter 3	**Day of Judgment Will Come.**
vv. 1-7	World was destroyed by water due to sin; it will be destroyed again by fire.
vv. 8-10	God wants us to repent due to His love; judgment will come suddenly by fire.
vv. 11-13	After destruction by fire, God will renew and transform His universe again.
vv. 14-18	Peter gives credit to Paul's writings and exhorts believers to refute false teachings.

1 JOHN

Chapter 1	**Walking in Light Versus Darkness**
vv. 1-4	Apostles knew Jesus to be God in flesh, refuting Gnostics' false teachings.
vv. 5-10	If we walk with God, who is Light, we will not be deceived by any sinfulness.
Chapter 2	**Brotherly Love and Anti-Christ Gnostics**
vv. 1-6	John writes believers will abide in Christ; if we sin, Jesus helps us overcome.
vv. 7-11	Loving fellow believers is commandment new to those who obey it.
vv. 12-14	John encourages children, fathers, and youth in relationships as overcomers.
vv. 15-17	Worldliness will pass but love of God abides forever: love God, not world.
vv. 18-25	Anti-Christ spirit denies Jesus is the Christ; believer has eternal life.
vv. 26-27	Anointing of Jesus confirms that He is the Christ.
vv. 28-29	Righteous will not be ashamed when Jesus returns.
Chapter 3	**Loving God, Jesus and Fellow Believers**
vv. 1-3	We shall be like Jesus Christ when He returns for us.
vv. 4-10	Believers born of God do not consciously sin; they abide in Christ.
vv. 11-18	God's love abides in those who sacrifice in word and deed for their brethren.
vv. 19-24	God blesses those who love His Son and the brethren, also.

Chapter 4	**God Is Love (Agape).**	
vv. 1-6	Every spirit confessing Jesus came in flesh is of God; spirit of world denies it.	
vv. 7-12	God loves us by giving Jesus; we are to love one another as He loves us.	
vv. 13-21	God is love; whoever does not love his brother does not abide in God.	
Chapter 5	**Christian's Blessed Assurance**	
vv. 1-5	We overcome world by believing Jesus is the Son of God.	
vv. 6-12	Spirit's witness is to water (Jesus' baptism); to blood (Jesus' death on cross).	
vv. 13-17	Sin unto death, mortal sin, is not an act but practice of disobedience to God.	
v. 18	Abiding in Christ keeps us free from sinning.	
v. 19	We in Christ are not in evil one's power as is the defenseless world.	
vv. 20-21	Jesus did come in human form as opposed to false view of Gnostics.	

2 JOHN

Chapter 1	**Love Brethren but Shun Gnostics**
vv. 1-2	Elect lady and children could refer to a real person, Sister Cyria.
v. 3	John proclaims a benediction over the fellowship.
vv. 4-11	John exhorts people to watch for Gnostics who deny Jesus' coming in flesh.
v. 12	John desires to fellowship with these believers face-to-face.
v. 13	The sister church at Ephesus greets this fellowship.

3 JOHN

Chapter 1	**Letter of Praise and Denunciation**
v. 1	John writes this letter to an individual named Gaius.
vv. 2-4	John congratulates Gaius for following truth.
vv. 5-8	Gaius is hospitable to travelers; ministers accept nothing from unbelievers.
vv. 9-10	John rebukes Diotrephes' refusing authority and putting believers out of church.
vv. 11-12	Demetrius, bearer of letter verifies John's claims of good versus evil.
vv. 13-14	John hopes to be able soon to talk face-to-face with these believers.
v. 15	Benediction along with a greeting from fellow Christians.

JUDE
Half-brother of Jesus

Chapter 1	**Warnings against False Teachers in Church**
v. 1	Jude, half-brother of Jesus and brother of James
v. 2	Benediction of mercy, peace and love
vv. 3-4	Contend for faith; some are perverting grace of God into worldliness.
vv. 5-7	Jude reminds believers of penalty of God's judgment on those who turn back.
vv. 8-13	Heretics in church, corrupting fellowship with false teachings and immoral living.
vv. 14-16	Jude quotes Enoch about evil people, malcontents, boasters, flatterers, etc.
vv. 17-23	Jude, says God is Father, Lord Jesus Christ and Holy Spirit, warns of heretics.
vv. 24-25	Jude closes with Jesus' protection, glory, majesty, dominion and authority.

REVELATION

Chapter 1	**John, Jesus, Seven Angels and Seven Churches**
vv. 1-3	God sent angel to John about the revealing of Jesus Christ and coming events.
vv. 4-5(a)	John, after receiving revelation, writes to seven 7 churches in Asia Minor.
vv. 5(b)-7	Jesus, who freed us from sins, is coming again with His saints.
v. 8	The Lord God, The Almighty, Is the Alpha and Omega!
vv. 9-11	John, heard Christ say "Write what you see and send it to 7 churches."
vv. 12-16	John describes Jesus in all of His majesty and glory amid 7 churches.
vv. 17-20	Jesus tells John 7 stars are 7 angels; 7 lampstands are 7 churches of Asia.
Chapter 2	**Churches at Ephesus, Smyrna, Pergamos and Thyatira**
v. 1	To church at Ephesus Jesus, holds 7 angels and walks among 7 churches.
vv. 2-7	Jesus rebukes Ephesians' leaving 1st love. He exhorts them to overcome.
v. 8	To the church in Smyrna, Jesus is He who died and was resurrected.
vv. 9-11	Believers exhorted to be faithful; receive crown; not be hurt by 2nd death.
v. 12	Pergamos, center of idolatrous worship, to be judged by Words of Jesus Christ.
vv. 13-17	Jesus blesses, rebukes, exhorts overcomers to receive names on white stones.

v. 18	To church at Thyatira, from Jesus, who has eyes of fire and feet of bronze.
vv. 19-29	Jesus commends, rebukes, exhorts overcomers, rule with Him, Morning Star.
Chapter 3	**Churches at Sardis, Philadelphia and Laodicea**
v. 1	To Sardis' church from Jesus, who has God's fullness and angels.
vv. 2-6	Jesus rebukes but promises overcomers white garments and eternal life.
v. 7	To Philadelphia church, from Jesus, Who has authority to open and shut doors.
vv. 8-13	Jesus tells overcomers in Temple with new names of God, Jerusalem and Jesus.
v. 14	To church in Laodicea, Jesus says He is Amen, True Witness and Beginning.
vv. 15-22	Jesus rebukes complacency; He tells overcomers to sit with Him on throne.
Chapter 4	**Vision of God on His Throne**
vv. 1-6(a)	John, sees God's glory as jewels, 12 O.T. atriarchs and 12 N. T. apostles.
vv. 6(b)-11	Four cherubim, as lion, an ox, a human and an eagle, worship with 24 elders.
Chapter 5	**Sealed Scroll and Lion and Lamb**
vv. 1-4	John weeps; no one in heaven or earth worthy to open scroll with seven seals.
vv. 5-10	Jesus, Lion, comes as Lamb, opening scroll as cherubim and elders worship.
vv. 11-14	Heaven's hosts, with ones on and under earth, worship Jesus, Lamb of God.
Chapter 6	**First Six Seals Are Opened.**
vv. 1-2	Conquering Rider with bow on white horse is Christ (Rev. 19:11).
vv. 3-4	Red horse's rider is permitted to cause war and bloodshed.

vv. 5-6	Rider of black horse represents famine which follows war.
vv. 7-8	Rider of pale horse is Death; Hades, and Death kill 1/4 of earth's population.
vv. 9-11	Believers, died during war cry to God Who gives them white robes and rest.
vv. 12-17	Earthquake is upheaval; people of all classes seek to escape God's judgment.
Chapter 7	**Interlude Between the Sixth and Seventh Seals**
vv. 1-8	God tells 4 angels not to harm till 144,000 Israelites are marked for safety.
vv. 9-12	After marking 144,000 Jews, all nations and all angels worship Almighty God.
vv. 13-17	Multitude of great tribulation, clothed in white robes, are protected by Jesus.
Chapter 8	**Jesus Opens Seventh Seal; Angels Blow Trumpets.**
vv. 1-5	Jesus opens 7th seal; 7 angels given 7 trumpets; saints pray; earth quakes.
v. 6	The 7 angels are preparing to blow their trumpets.
v. 7	When 1st angel blew trumpet, hail, fire & blood burned 1/3 of earth and trees.
vv. 8-9	When 2nd angel blew 1/3 sea is bloody causing 1/3 fish and ships destroyed.
vv. 10-11	The 3rd trumpet involves catastrophe contaminating drinking waters.
v. 12	With 4th trumpet, 1/3 of sun, moon and stars cause darkness.
v. 13	Eagle warns of impending judgment as last 3 trumpets prepare to sound.
Chapter 9	**Fifth and Sixth Angels and Demonic Locusts**
vv. 1-6	Satan falls and given key releasing fallen angels to torture those unsealed.
vv. 7-11	Fallen winged angels led by angel in charge of pit whose name is Destroyer.
v. 12	After this 1st woe comes 2 more.

vv. 13-19	Sixth angel releases 4 angels and 200,000,000 troops destroy 1/3 of mankind.
vv. 20-21	Killing 1/3 of mankind did not cause world to repent of its evil deeds.
Chapter 10	**Angel and Little Scroll**
vv. 1-7	John hears angel with little scroll say not to write this message but to seal it.
vv. 8-11	John eats word; it becomes bitter due to God's judgments which are coming.
Chapter 11	**Temple Measured and Two Witnesses**
vv. 1-2	John told to measure temple; outside court to be trampled on for 3 1/2 years.
vv. 3-4	These witnesses represent Word and Spirit; sackcloth is message of repentance.
vv. 5-6	God's 2 witnesses have power to stop rain and smite the earth with plagues.
vv. 7-8	After they finish testifying, the beast will kill them in Jerusalem.
vv. 9-10	Nations against Israel rejoice 3 ½ days gazing upon slain tormentors.
vv. 11-12	God receives prophets, Moses and Elijah as they ascend to heaven in cloud.
v. 13	That hour great earthquake destroys 1/10 of Jerusalem and kills 7,000 people.
v. 14	This ends the 2nd woe and the 3rd is to come.
v. 15	The 7th angel trumpets message, "kingdom of world is Lord's kingdom."
vv. 16-18	The 24 elders worship God's rewarding dead and destroying evildoers of earth.
v. 19	God's sanctuary opened with lightning, voices, thunder, earthquake, hail.
Chapter 12	**Woman, Satan, Man-child, Michael and Lamb's Blood**
vv. 1-2	Woman represents Old Testament and New Testament, Israel.

vv. 3-4	Dragon is Satan with 1/3 fallen angels; he seeks to destroy Messiah at birth.
vv. 5-6	Jesus is born; caught up to heaven; and, Israel is persecuted for long time.
vv. 7-9	Michael and his angels oust Satan and his angels to the earth.
vv. 10-12	Satan and angels conquered by blood of Lamb and testimony of believers.
vv. 13-16	Satan fights Israel; eagle (U.S.A.?) protects Israel and nations from Satan.
v. 17	Satan is furious and wages war on those who obey God's commandments.
Chapter 13	**Beast from Sea and Beast from Earth**
vv. 1-4	Beast (worldly gov't) is Roman empire and Satan, persecuting Christians.
vv. 5-10	First beast, fighting God with world military power, is the Anti-Christ.
vv. 11-18	Second beast, (religious), forces gov't worship and people to take mark of beast.
Chapter 14	**Interlude: Visions of Final Judgment**
vv. 1-5	These 144,000 follow Jesus; first fruits from believers who are in harvest.
vv. 6-7	Angel cries to fear and honor Creator; hour of judgment is at hand.
v. 8	Second angel says immoral economy of mankind has been dissolved.
vv. 9-12	Third angel, "Mark brings God's wrath in presence of Jesus and angels."
v. 13	Heavenly voice assures martyrs in the Lord they are the truly blessed ones.
vv. 14-16	Fourth angel, one like Son of man, says it is time to reap; harvest is ready.
vv. 17-20F	Fifth angel with sickle, told by 6th angel, cast people in winepress of wrath.

Chapter 15	**Preparation for Seven Vials of Wrath**
v. 1	John sees 7 angels preparing 7 plagues of God's wrath for last judgment.
vv. 2-4	Victorious martyrs in heaven sing with harps the song of Moses and the Lamb.
vv. 5-8	One of four creatures gives 7 angels 7 bowls of God's wrath to be poured on earth.
Chapter 16	**Angels Pour Seven Bowls of Wrath.**
v. 1	Temple voice orders 7 angels to pour upon earth 7 bowls of God's wrath.
v. 2	First angel pours bowl on earth; sores come on those bearing mark of beast.
v. 3	Second angel pours bowl in the sea and everything in sea dies.
vv. 4-7	Third angel pours bowl in rivers; fountains of water become blood.
vv. 8-9	Fourth angel bowl on sun, scorching pours men with fire.
vv. 10-11	Fifth angel pours bowl of God's wrath on beast, causing darkness to kingdom.
vv. 12-16	Sixth angel pours bowl on Euphrates, preparing invasion of eastern kings.
vv. 17-21	Seventh angel pours bowl in air; hailstones fall; earthquake destroys earth.
Chapter 17	**Fall of Babylon**
vv. 1-6	One angel shows John sins of Rome and ruler who killed many Christians.
vv. 7-14	Beast ruling 7 kings with 10 other kings, fight and defeated by Jesus Christ.
vv. 15-18	Harlot (Rome), rules commercial world, destroyed by beast and 10 lesser kings.
Chapter 18	**Dirge over Fallen City**
vv. 1-3	Angel cries Babylon (Rome ?) is fallen due to her corruption.

vv. 4-8	Voice from heaven begs believers to leave city; her destruction is coming.
vv. 9-10	In one hour Babylon's (Rome's) judgment will come.
vv. 11-20	Commercial community will weep as God judges Rome in one hour's time.
vv. 21-24	Angel gives symbolic action representing destruction of this once great city.
Chapter 19	**Return of Christ in Glory**
vv. 1-3	Multitudes praise God for judging harlot (Rome's wickedness) for her sins.
v. 4	The 24 elders and the 4 living creatures worship God.
v. 5	Voice from throne commands everyone to praise God.
vv. 6-8	Formal presentation of Bridegroom (Christ) to His bride is now ready.
vv. 9-10	Angel forbids worship of himself; Blessed are those invited to marriage supper.
vv. 11-16	Heaven opened, showing Jesus and victorious armies over all of His enemies.
vv. 17-18	Angel calls birds of prey to eat flesh of horses and men defeated in battle.
vv. 19-21	Jesus defeats enemies; beast and false prophet are cast into lake of fire.
Chapter 20	**Satan Bound, Loosed and Defeated**
vv. 1-3	Angel hurls Satan into bottomless pit; seals pit to contain him for 1000 years.
v. 4	Martyrs who resisted beast live and rule with Christ during these 1000 years.
vv. 5-6	Other believers will not take part in first resurrection, only the overcomers.
vv. 7-8	Satan loosed from pit, gathers people to war against Israelites and Christians.
vv. 9-10	God defeats enemies; Satan cast into lake of fire with beast and false prophet.

v. 11	God is seated upon His great white throne of judgment.
vv. 12-15	Dead judged by God; Death and Hades cast into lake of fire, the 2nd death.

Chapter 21 — New Heaven, New Earth and New Jerusalem

v. 1	John sees a new heaven and a new earth.
vv. 2-4	In new Jerusalem God dwells with His people and continually cares for them.
vv. 5-8	God makes everything new; He casts unbelievers into lake of fire, 2nd death.
vv. 9-14	One angel reveals Bride of Jesus, new Jerusalem, coming to new earth.
vv. 15-21	Angel measures new Jerusalem; explains brilliance, 12 foundations, 12 gates.
vv. 22-27	No Temple in new Jerusalem; God /Jesus is light in Holy City (Bride).

Chapter 22 — River, Tree of Life and Epilogue

vv. 1-5	Tree of life, on each side of river, gives healing to nations in Holy City (Bride).
vv. 6-7	Angel says Jesus Christ is soon coming; blessed, obeying words of Revelation.
vv. 8-9	John is told not to worship the angel but only to worship God.
vv. 10-11	Do not seal Book; it is for all people to read; end is too near for change.
vv. 12-13	Christ is returning to reward each person for what he has done in this life.
vv. 14-15	Blessed are righteous; cursed are unrighteous who cannot enter Holy City, Bride.
v. 16	Jesus, Morning Star, has sent His angel to testify to churches.
v. 17	Holy Spirit and Bride invite thirsty for God to drink water of Life without cost.

vv. 18-19	Adding to Revelation brings plagues; deleting Revelation, loses tree of life.
v. 20	Jesus says "Surely I am coming soon!"
v. 21	John says, "The grace of the Lord Jesus be with all the Saints. Amen!"

BOOKS COMPARED WITH THE KING JAMES VERSION

The Revised Standard Version, "The New Oxford Annotated Bible with the Apocrypha," 1962.

The Authorized Standard Version, "The Criswell Study Bible," 1979.

The Authorized Standard Version, "The Companion Bible," 1964.

The Amplified New Testament, 1958.

The Wycliffe Bible Commentary, 1962.

Evangelical Commentary on The Bible, 1989.

The New International Commentary on the New Testament, 1977.

Webster's New Dictionary, 1994.

www.ingramcontent.com/pod-product-compliance
Lightning Source LLC
Chambersburg PA
CBHW071950070526
44583CB00015B/1140